THE UPPER ROOM DISCIPLINES

1985

THE UPPER ROOM

DISCIPLINES

1985

Coordinating Editor
Tom Page

Edited by
Mary Ruth Coffman
Barnita Hayes
Charla Honea
Jan McNish
Tom Page
Mary Lou Redding
Judy Smith
Pamela Watkins

The Upper Room Disciplines 1985

ISBN 0-8358-0477-1

Cover photo taken at James White's Fort, Knoxville, Tennessee, by Charles L. Tucker.

CONTENTS

FOREWORD

Shoulder my yoke and learn from me, for I am gentle and humble in heart, and you will find rest for your souls. (Matt. 11:29-30, TJB)

The deepest cry of the human spirit is the cry for God. As Christians, we believe that this cry for God has been profoundly answered in Jesus Christ. That is why at Christmastime we celebrate with joy the remarkable good news that God is with us. The Savior's birth reminds us that we are not alone.

In our day, there seems to be another cry of the human spirit. It is heard from every continent and from every country. It is uttered in every language and rises from every culture. It flows out of every social group and every race on the face of the earth. It is a cry found on the lips of the very young and very old. It is the cry for peace.

It is not a new cry. It has been a part of humankind's longing from generation to generation. However, it may be that the threat of nuclear annihilation is pressing upon humankind with such force that there is an almost universal cry for peace. There is a new awareness that no person and no country can escape the horror of a nuclear exchange. We know more clearly than ever the futility of seeking to solve the world's problems with larger and larger war machines. The very thought of such a war is preposterous.

Is there an alternative? Can peace come to our troubled world? Can we know peace deep within our troubled lives? Both seem so impossible. You and I know our own brokenness, our own incompleteness. In our honest moments we must ask, Can this life of mine be made new?

Even more impossible it seems is the healing of our broken and fractured world. Can it ever be put back together again so that harmony, justice, mercy, and peace will prevail? Can the world be made whole and new again?

11

The truth out of which we may fashion a response to these deep and penetrating questions is found in Jesus Christ: "Learn from me, for I am gentle and humble in heart, and you will find rest for your souls."

We offer the *1985 Disciplines* with the prayer that every individual reader will be led in the personal journey of transformation and wholeness and in the social journey of peacemaking. The scripture readings and the thoughtful reflections by each writer are intended to point us to Jesus Christ, from whom we may learn how to live as whole persons in a broken world and how to function as peacemakers in a troubled world.

Rueben P. Job

Rueben P. Job

World Editor

Editor's note: With this edition of Disciplines *we will be using the New Common Lectionary as the basis for the weekly meditations. This new lectionary has been jointly prepared by all the major denominations in North America that support the use of a lectionary. We hope readers will find the New Common Lectionary helpful and will secure the complete lectionary, cycles A, B, and C. The full listings for calendar year 1985 are at the back of this book.*

PROMISES TO KEEP

January 1-6, 1985   **Dudley Condron†**
Tuesday, January 1   Read Isaiah 60:1-6.

I've had the same doctor for twenty years. Strange, the effect his words have on the way I feel. He chooses what he says carefully, knowing they can open the way to my recovery, or make me fearful and resistant.

Isaiah-of-the-Exile had some of my doctor in his soul. He knew how to help keep faith alive in the hearts of a defeated people. Read Isaiah 59 again; a graphic description of the wretched plight of Israel in Babylon. Gone was the nation; gone, too, their beloved fellowship. Gone were their leaders, the priests and kings, and their business, homes, and family members as well. All described in Isaiah 59.

Then come those grand opening words of Isaiah 60: "Arise, shine; for your light has come, and the glory of the Lord has risen upon you." He was wishing his people a "happy new year."

What Isaiah said was not rooted in fantasy. God, Isaiah believed, had promises to keep. He made a powerful call to Israel to move with courage into the future prepared for them by God.

Ours are dark times also. Can we believe God has a future for us? Some look at our troubled times and conclude it is the end of the world. Isaiah provides a refreshingly hopeful view of the faith required to move us into the new year.

Prayer: *O Lord, enable us to rise and shine; to join that growing number of people who are pushing back the darkness, through Christ, the Lord. Amen.*

---

†Director of the Division of Education for Mission, the Board of Missions of the Cumberland Presbyterian Church, Memphis, Tennessee.

Wednesday, January 2   Read Psalm 72.

There have always been those who have been able to *imagine* a world better than the one we happen to have. It takes more than a vivid imagination to change reality. Psalm 72 is a prayer for the nation's leader. Scholars now tell us that the poem was not originally intended to be about the coming Messiah. Nevertheless, Jesus fits the pattern.

"He delivers the needy when he calls, the poor and him who has no helper. He has pity on the weak and the needy. . . . And precious is their blood in his sight" (vs. 12-14). The enemies of Jesus would accuse him of many things. They never once said he didn't care about people. "When he saw the multitude," said Matthew, "he was moved with compassion on them, because they fainted, and were scattered abroad, as sheep having no shepherd" (Matt. 9:36, KJV). Jesus was one who cared.

The blessed communities envisioned in Isaiah 60 and Psalm 72 are not going to happen without *us*. Granted, we are saved by grace, through faith. It is faith that cares for people. Psalm 72 challenges those who lead the nation to be attentive to the poor and weak, to practice righteousness and justice, and to rule favorably toward peace.

Communities do not go to wrack and ruin when people care for one another. Out there in the dark, near-distance, is a piteous, ill-clad multitude of hungry people. Such psalms as this one should serve to heighten our sense of responsibility for those with whom we share the earth.

Prayer: *Dear God, show us how we can reach out in love, not only to those we know and care about, but to people we don't know—even to those we see as our enemies. Amen.*

Thursday, January 3   Read Matthew 2:1-8.

Cunning and cruel, Herod had been made "king of the Jews" in 40 B.C. by Rome. When the "wise men from the East" reported the nature of their search to Herod, he encouraged them to find the child that he might worship him also.

The story of Epiphany is set against the stark background of monstrous evil in the highest places. It is no marginal theme in scripture. When it deals with human nature, the Bible is not sentimental. When we speak of a community better than that which we have, the problem of human sin must always be dealt with.

The Bible simply asserts that Herod's evil intention will not defeat God's eternal purpose. At the center of all human existence a sovereign God is at work. God has a covenant to keep.

It would be easier to affirm that there is a God who keeps watch over his promises if we did not know that scores of innocent children were to die in Bethlehem because of Herod's fear (v. 16). We need to remind ourselves as we begin a new year that the world is not the way God made it, and it is not God's fault.

Surprisingly, Herod had the support of the people; many of whom called him "Great." Just so do we tend to overlook the weaknesses of our leaders if they serve our personal or national interests. In his memoirs, Albert Speer explained the failure of the German people to challenge Hitler's excesses. "We chose not to know," said Speer.

Prayer: *Father, send us back to Bethlehem where, in humility and faith, we can recover a proper perspective of how you enter our world and rule. Amen.*

Friday, January 4   Read Matthew 2:8-12.

Since childhood we have known that the "wise men from the East" were foreigners. Do we understand Matthew's meaning? This Messiah, he is saying, is going to be everyone's Savior!

Jesus' birth is presented as the fulfillment of Isaiah 60. "And nations shall come to your light, and kings to the brightness of your rising" (v. 3). Our differences as we draw near to Christ need not disappear. They simply no longer really matter. It is a good way to begin writing a Gospel.

Yet that idea grew very slowly in the early Christian community. Too many in the church wanted to believe that they enjoyed a unique, privileged position with God. It was not easy to give up the traditions that had kept Gentiles at arm's length.

Who are the "gentiles" in our own communities? Whom do we try to exclude or make conform to our ways of thinking and acting? The Magi were astrologers. They were the secular scientists of the day and quite outside the traditional, Jewish notions of what it meant to be "men of faith."

The scientific community today fares poorly at the hands of the church. It is our tendency to judge their faith that puts distance between us. The story of the Wise Men might serve to remind us that there are many roads that lead to Christ. What God can choose to do among us will always be far greater and more mysterious than we can imagine.

Prayer: *Father, we thank you for the universal scope of your divine intention. Help us to celebrate your concern for the whole world. Amen.*

Saturday, January 5　　　　　　　　Read Ephesians 3:1-6.

It has been twenty centuries since Paul wrote that it took a revelation to show him "how the Gentiles are fellow heirs . . . of the promise in Christ Jesus through the gospel." The notion excited Paul. For those of us whose favorite Bible verse has been John 3:16 since our childhood, it is the one thing we have always known about God. "God so loved the world. . . ."

It took Christ to show us how much the whole human community is loved by God. The mystery Paul speaks of in our text has to do with how God wanted, from the beginning, for all of us to be co-heirs, co-members of the same body, sharers of the promise.

Had Paul been one of the twelve disciples, such an idea might not have been so mysterious. Jesus ministered to Jew and Gentile without discrimination. Perhaps Peter had told Paul how Jesus had spent an afternoon talking to a Samaritan woman who was half-pagan, half-Jewish at a well (see John 4:5-30).

Yet, even Peter needed a vision to clear his thinking about the new community God had in mind. In talking to Cornelius about the vision which had come to him on the rooftop of the house of Simon-the-Tanner, Peter said, "Truly I perceive that God shows no partiality" (Acts 10:34). What's so mysterious about that? Nothing, if Jesus comes into our hearts.

Prayer: *Help us, O Lord, to be more grateful for the liberating freedom we have found in Christ to love all humankind. Amen.*

17

Sunday, January 6 (Epiphany)
Read Ephesians 3:7-13.

These verses describe Paul's move into an evangelistic lifestyle. "Of this gospel," he wrote, "I was made a minister according to the gift of God's grace which was given me." Never again would Paul be preoccupied with simply maintaining his life as part of a religious institution.

The rest of Paul's life was spent preaching good news to the Gentiles, calling his message "the unsearchable riches of Christ."

What is the great danger we face in the church? Is it not an all-too-human tendency to see the church as somehow existing to serve us? The preaching, singing, fellowship—do we not tend to focus on these as our main reason for being a part of that particular congregation? Or, we can go from there a step further and come to expect God to serve *us*, rather than the other way around. There is always the danger that our life in the church will too narrowly define our reason for being in it. We are in the church *to minister*.

We derive help from the church by being in it, of course— and we do have legitimate needs. But the help we derive is to enable us to help others. "By the gift of God's grace," Paul said, "I was made a minister." So are we all. It is by God's grace we get life. By God's grace we receive gifts. By God's grace we discover a mission, a ministry. That task, as was Paul's, is "to preach . . . the unsearchable riches of Christ, and to make all men see what is the plan of the mystery hidden for ages. . . ."

Prayer: *Holy God, teach us how to proclaim the whole gospel, to the whole person, in the whole world. Amen.*

GOD'S CREATIVE WORD

January 7-13, 1985   **Natalie Barber†**
Monday, January 7   Read Gen. 1:1-5;
                               John 1:1-3.

The human race has attempted to explain the mystery of Creation through the ages. Today, such scientific explanations as the "big bang" theory are accepted by many.

At one time I also wondered if God created the universe or if God even existed. As a biology major in college, I was fascinated by the structure of all life forms. Each type of animal and plant adapted to its environment in such a marvelous way that its species could survive generation after generation. These studies made clear to me that I could not explain the existence of such a complex universe without a Creator. "In the beginning God. . . ."

According to the Bible, God's word spoke the cosmos into being. God gave the command, "Let there be . . . ," and everything came about in its time and order: the firmament, the earth, light, and life.

However, God also has revealed to us that there is more to Creation than the act of a God who spoke the universe into being and then stood off to let it swirl through space on its own. Our God cares for all of Creation. God's voice speaks forth in love.

Prayer: *Thank you, God, that we are part of the wonder that is Creation. May we hear your voice in all things and know that it is the voice of love. Amen.*

---

†Former United Methodist missionary; mission interpreter; author (*Dr. and Mrs. Fix-It*, Friendship Press, 1970), Albuquerque, New Mexico.

Tuesday, January 8   Read Psalm 29;
                                          Psalm 19:1-4.

In the beginning God's creative word spoke in power and majesty, declaring God's glory. Throughout time the forces of nature have continued to obey the same word.

We, too, as the psalmist, yearn to express our reverence before the majesty of Creation. The composer Franz Joseph Haydn felt this as he was composing his oratorio, "The Creation." He said, "I felt myself so penetrated with religious feeling that before I sat down to the pianoforte I prayed to God with earnestness that He would enable me to praise him worthily."* The well-known anthem from Psalm 19 was one of the majestic hymns Haydn wrote for this oratorio.

A young hiker I know had reached the top of a 13,000-foot peak in the Rockies when suddenly he was flung off his feet. He came to his senses a few minutes later some distance away from where he had been standing. He will vouch for the awesome force of this unannounced bolt of lightning. Natural phenomena all around us tell of the powerful results of God's creative word.

We might not be psalmists, composers, or hikers, but when we experience the grandeur of God's world, we stand in awe, knowing that God's voice has spoken. Our whole being longs to cry out in praise and thanksgiving.

Prayer: *Almighty God, may I see your power and your glory in everything around me, and may I praise you for it. "For thine is the kingdom, and the power, and the glory, for ever." Amen.*

---

*Ewen, David, *Great Composers 1300-1900* (New York: H. W. Wilson Co., 1966), p. 185.

Wednesday, January 9   Read Gen. 1:14-18;
                                                         John 1:4-5.

In the beginning God spoke light into being. God created the stars and our sun and moon making them so that they would give off light.

Can you imagine the earth without the light of the sun? It probably would be much like the planet Pluto: dark, piercingly cold, and certainly lifeless. The sun appears only as a bright star there.

Light dispels darkness. Even a tiny beam can penetrate the most intense night. During World War II practice blackouts were a familiar occurrence in the United States. Civilians were instructed not to use a flashlight or candle while curtains were open, because even this small amount of light could be spotted from the sky.

Light makes things clear. When we want to scrutinize any object, we take it to the window or a bright light.

Light makes it possible for life to exist. For almost all types of plant life, sunlight is necessary for photosynthesis. Animal life is dependent upon plants which provide both food and oxygen.

In our own lives, when we are bathed in God's light the darkness of despair disappears, solutions to problems become clearer, and living closer to our full potential becomes a possibility. Christ is the key to God's light in our lives. "Again Jesus spoke to them, saying, 'I am the light of the world; he who follows me will not walk in darkness, but will have the light of life' " (John 8:12).

Prayer: *O God, creator of light, help me to walk in your light, to be guided by your light within me, and to be a light to others. Amen.*

21

Thursday, January 10   Read 1 Peter 1:23-25;
1 John 5:4-12.

In the beginning God's word created life and the human race. God recreates us now through Jesus Christ: "The Word became flesh and dwelt among us" (John 1:14). Christ is God's creative word giving us a new birth, and a rich and eternal life.

Back in the days when almost all movies were filmed in black and white, I saw one that was different from any other. I'll never forget the impression it made on me, because the last few scenes were filmed in color. What a difference this made in the dramatic effect of the story! Suddenly, action that had taken place in black and white leapt out in brilliant colors!

We can live our lives without Christ, but it is not God's will for us to do so. God's will is redemption through Christ. Therefore, life without Christ is often a gray form of existence. On the other hand, life with Christ at the center is transformed into bright new colors, and two dimensions become three.

Jesus said, "I came that they may have life, and have it abundantly" (John 10:10). Through Christ we learn the meaning of all aspects of wholeness: physical, mental, and spiritual. This abundant life is God's good news for us and the world. God cares that much for us.

Prayer: *Dear Lord, I want to be recreated in Christ. May I live life in all its fullness in Christ. Amen.*

Friday, January 11   Read Mark 1:4-11;
                                           Acts 19:1-7.

In order for God's re-creating word to work change in our lives, repentance and cleansing are necessary. John's water baptism symbolizes repentance followed by washing away debris of the old life: the sins, attitudes, and habits that keep us from abundant life in Christ. Even though water baptism takes place only once, the symbolism of this cleansing is there in our hearts each time we repent and accept God's forgiveness.

Paul speaks of another baptism that creates even greater potential for change—the baptism of the Holy Spirit given in the name of Jesus. This is an outpouring of God's Spirit upon those who follow Christ, a baptism of faith and power given to help us grow in obedience and love. Peace, joy, and love plus other fruits and gifts can be bestowed by the Spirit as we grow toward Christian maturity.

The Spirit is given to glorify God and help the church to grow. "But you shall receive power when the Holy Spirit has come upon you; and you shall be my witnesses in Jerusalem and in all Judea and Samaria and to the end of the earth" (Acts 1:8).

We are Christ's church. With the Spirit's help we can grow in Christian love and understanding and the church through us can become a more effective expression of God's word in the world.

Suggestion for meditation: *Am I allowing the Holy Spirit to work within me? In what ways do I feel I am being changed?*

Saturday, January 12
Read 1 Kings 19:9-12;
John 14:16-17, 25-26.

The Holy Spirit within us, although a quiet voice, can be as powerful and earthshaking as any wind, earthquake, or fire. This recreating voice transforms lives and cultures. It remakes history, as we have seen during the days of the Acts of the Apostles and through the centuries since then.

The Holy Spirit is always available to us. The Spirit can be compared to electrical power. We can't see electricity, but it is a potent force in modern civilization. However, if we don't plug our electrical appliances and machinery into it, they will remain lifeless and useless. In the same way, if we don't plug into the Holy Spirit within us, we might be able to run on our own steam, but this will be a faint source of power compared to what God is willing to give.

The Holy Spirit speaks to us as a counselor and a guide, bringing to mind words from the Bible, helping us make decisions, reprimanding us when necessary, and encouraging us.

The connection to this power is by means of prayer, a two-way communication between ourselves and God. We communicate with God as we are willing to listen and obey in trust. Through practice we can learn to be sensitive to this guide and counselor within us.

Suggestion for meditation: *Am I learning to listen to the voice of the Holy Spirit, letting the Spirit guide me in my daily life? What insights do I feel I have received recently?*

Sunday, January 13   Read 1 John 4:13-21;
                                              1 Cor. 13:12-13.

God spoke out in love and all things came into being. Could this command be the "big bang" that reverberated to the edge of the universe and continues in creation and re-creation today?

The one single theme throughout the Bible is how much God loves us all. And so, when the human race strayed, God's word made a way for redemption. "God so loved the world that he gave his only Son" (John 3:16).

As we think back over our own lifetimes, can we doubt God's love for us? We can ask ourselves, "How many times have I heard God speak in love to me? Through a friend when I needed one? Through family when I was hurting? Through forgiveness when I erred? Through guidance?" Each of us, I believe, can count the ways we have experienced God's love for us. Or maybe the ways are too many to be counted.

The love of God is too great to keep to ourselves. We have to share it. As God gave Jesus, we are to give ourselves. This is the culmination of God's re-creating word in us. As we reach toward God in love and obedience, God pours love through us helping us to touch others.

God's creative word is love, and that love is ours forever. Is this the meaning of creation that we seek?

Prayer: *Thank you, Lord, for this chance to live so that I can know your love, and by knowing it, share it with others. Amen.*

SEEING AND BELIEVING

January 14-20, 1985   **Peggy Way†**
Monday, January 14   Read Psalm 63:1-4.

Let us value our search for God in our own places. In the Hebrew-Christian view of the world the "ordinary time" of the seeker is the tenting place of Yahweh. The psalmist addresses God in a human place, a wilderness, and with human images of thirsting, fainting, and being without the nurturing waters of life. Our own places are such places where God has chosen to dwell, and out of them is lifted up the psalmist's voice—and our own! This valuation of "ordinary time" is enhanced in the Incarnation, God choosing to be embodied in a historical human, living in a particular time and place. Such images allow us to take our own places, experiences, and day-by-day lives with full seriousness.

This week's scripture passages allow us to explore a variety of ways in which we might become better "seers" in our own places. Our faith's view of the world is a perspective on everyday situations. It offers a surprise view among the competing bombardments of everyday life in which we too frequently become jaded, and from which we often seek to escape. We may view another place as "more exciting," as closer to being "God's place."

This week's passages also offer a perspective on how we might become agents of revelation to others. Even as we seek, we may help others "see" that same God whom the psalmist beholds.

Prayer: *May I be like the psalmist in my own place, O God, however dry and weary, beholding even here your steadfast love. As we tent together, help me to remember and expect. Amen.*

---

†Associate Professor of Pastoral Theology, Vanderbilt Divinity School, Nashville, Tennessee.

Tuesday, January 15   Read 1 Samuel 3:1-9.

Focus upon Eli for a moment, and make Samuel a subordinate character. These are dry times; and there is no frequent vision. Eli's vision is dim. His sons have been disappointments, and his house is in deep trouble with the Lord. In modern terms, we might refer to Eli as among the needy, both personally and because of unfulfilled priesthood.

The boy Samuel, who is ministering under him, could easily be a threat, with his youthful sight and energy. Yet Eli is gentle to the naive one who is yet unacquainted with the Lord. Three times the boy runs to Eli, yet Eli neither ridicules nor becomes testy when disturbed in what we might imagine as an old person's resting time. What Eli *does* do, although blind, is to "see" what is actually going on! Rather than experiencing jealousy or continuing to live out of old failure or despair, he helps the boy to see. Eli invites Samuel to the freshness of his own religious experience and instructs him in the basic ways of recognizing and responding to God.

Surely Eli serves as an "agent of revelation." He helps Samuel see what is occurring within him. Eli does not get in the way or tell Samuel what God wants. He doesn't let his own needs and disappointments create cynicism or bitterness in Samuel. In his own place, at sunset, resting his weary eyes and body, Eli serves as midwife to Samuel's religious experience. Eli is strong enough to let go, to invite, and to be the agent of one who would follow and be greater.

Prayer: *In my own place, O God, help me to see freshness in another even when my eyes grow dim. Make my wisdom available to others, that they might see their possibilities anew. Free me to be your agent for revelation as you reach out to others. Amen.*

Wednesday, January 16   Read 1 Samuel 3:1-9.

Focus your attention upon Samuel. Our ordinary times are full of dramas. Eli and Samuel were each resting in his own place. Not much was going on! Yet one was to be an agent of revelation, and the other was puzzled at hearing a strange voice.

In our own places many voices call our name. It is no wonder that we are often puzzled as to which one to answer. We may run here and there, unsettled, unfulfilled, sometimes torn asunder. One does not have to be a young Samuel to have difficulty in discerning God's voice.

In our own places we may need to seek after one who listens with us and for us, a soul friend, one more experienced than we are in perceiving Who is addressing us. Without such a person, it may be helpful sometimes just to *wait*, not to run hither and yon, not to assume that we know and have already heard or seen perceptively. We may need an Eli to say: Wait! Something more is going on here. Or we may need to learn to pause and ask ourselves: What does this mean? Who is calling?

Samuel was in need of and ready to respond to a wise interpreter of new possibilities. As we come to value our own places, and see the dramas going on in which we are included, we may find ourselves seeing new possibilities for our spiritual growth and our ministries. This may happen even at dusk—even within our own places. What dramas are occurring around you? In what drama of call and revelation might you even today be involved?

Prayer: *O God, may I not become routinized to the dramas occurring in my own place. May I be able to see freshly, both for myself and as a willing agent for another. And may I be forever open to the voice of another or the Other who says, Wait! Listen! See! Amen.*

Thursday, January 17   Read Psalm 63:1-8.

This psalm in its entirety allows for both dryness and feast. The Psalms allow for a panoply of human experiences—rage, despair, weariness, as well as feast, sustenance, joy.

In this psalm the one who praises does not have to go to a mountaintop or descend into a valley of despair. Lying in bed, *in one's own place*, there can be active memories of the God who has been known, even if God's absence has recently been felt. And expectation comes to new life with such memories: Because "thou hast been my help," surely you are now, and will forever be.

In ordinary time it is well to prepare for times of dryness and weakness of the spirit. It is astonishing how often such times take us by surprise, almost as if there should come some guarantee that such moments are not intrinsic in the Hebrew-Christian pilgrimage. When we forget that dry times will come again, we sometimes also forget those other ordinary times when we were not faint, weak, downhearted, but actually experienced rising up on wings like eagles! Such forgetting makes the dryness seem to be the only reality, untempered by the real gifts that have been received and can expect to be received again. For the ones who sing God's song can expect some verses of dryness even when hungering to sing the chorus of joy and hope! To have it any other way would not be the ways of ordinary time, in the midst of history, where we are finite and not in control. And yet through memory and expectation, the finitude of dryness and weakness can be transformed into singing for joy if we rest in the shadow of God's wings.

Prayer: *O God, in the dry times of my own finite places, may my memory of other times and expectation of future times ease my weakness. May I know that even my finitude is your gift as it opens me to being upheld by your right hand. Amen.*

Friday, January 18   Read 1 Corinthians 6:12-20.

In Hebrew-Christian perspective, as ordinary time is hallowed through God's presence, so, too, is the human body. For it was as flesh that Jesus came among us. We do not need to pretend either that we do not have bodies, or that they are negative encumbrances. Some Christians relate to their bodies as "the heavy bear that goes with me," as a modern poem states.* And indeed we allow our bodies to encumber us with their fat or addictions or excessive demands. Another error is to see people as only bodies, rather than as the dwelling place of a kindred spirit. Thus we may not "see" the person within the "imperfect" or "disabled" body.

It should not surprise us that so much attention is paid to bodies, for they are, after all, our most personal living places. This passage may help us to view them as valued places, to be nurtured and cared for. But at the same time they are only dwelling places of valued persons, and the body is not to be identified with the spirit of personhood. This passage offers new invitations to "see" bodies. The one who views his or her body as burden is invited to view it as gift to be cared for. The one who views body as gift meant only for self pleasure is invited to view it as gift to be valued with others in mind. And those who turn away from bodies that appear to be misused, or aging, disabled, or misshapen, are invited to view the spiritual quality of the person who resides within.

We are creatures created by God. We belong to God, even as we share the world with many others. Our bodies are our embodied spirits, powers, and structures for mission.

Prayer: *Thank you for this embodied place in which I dwell, dear God. Through it may I better serve both you and your other creatures who share existence with me. Amen.*

---

*Delmore Schwartz, "The Heavy Bear That Goes with Me."

Saturday, January 19   Read John 1:35-39.

The Hebrew-Christian way of seeing is filled with surprises. Routinized views are broken open, and established patterns are shattered and come together again in new ways. Eli's vision was failing, but he saw. The psalmist's place was dry, yet a feast was possible. The heavy bear of the body is the embodiment of the human spirit which belongs to God.

A freshness of vision is one of the great promises of scripture. That which we think of as ordinary (meaning routine or dull) is transformed into ordinary (meaning hallowed) as we see in new ways. A routinized, dull, and boring office place can be reenergized when viewed as God's finite folk seeking to embody a Hebrew-Christian way of living in the world. A person viewed in new ways may open up for both of us new possibilities, on the other side of stereotypes or taken-for-granteds.

It may be that some of our despair or disappointments in ordinary time come about because we have let go the capacity to see freshly. As Samuel needed an Eli to be able to discern God's voice, se we may need a John who says: "Behold!" Sometimes we have let go this capacity in our own places, and see only out of somebody else's places—the social scientist's, the psychologist's, the academician's. Yet it is in the middle of history that Eli says, "Listen!" and John says, "Behold!" And it is to each of us in our own places that the invitation is offered by Jesus himself: "Come and see." The disciples seek the place where Jesus is staying, and it is a part of and within their own place, their own religious history. Two of the disciples saw, and went, and stayed, and out of their particular history came a power that affects ours.

Prayer: *Change and decay—and boredom and banality—all around I see. Free me to behold your presence and power and invitation in their very midst, O God. Amen.*

Sunday, January 20   Read John 1:40-42.

In history we live in continual tension between naming ourselves and being named by others. Liberation movements are about self-naming. One person or a group of persons refuse any longer to live out of the ways in which they have been seen and named by others. Yet even as they resist those imposed names, in Hebrew-Christian perspective they still seek to be named by God.

In history we are also continually about the naming of God. As humans, we try to name God out of our own images or needs, which is quite natural since that is who we are and what we have to work with. The problem is that our namings are always inadequate, and God powerfully slips out of the categories that are imposed and thunders (or whispers), "I am who I am!" (see Exod. 3:13-15)

We, too, seek to slip out of categories or namings that are imposed upon us and to shout, No, that is not who I am! A part of the kind of seeing that is the gift of the Hebrew-Christian perspective is to see beyond and through all categories. Other persons, and even social or historical situations, cry out just as we do for participatory naming. In history, a primary way of seeing is not through concept or abstraction but through allowing concrete persons and particular situations to disclose their own realities.

And yet naming goes with seeing. Andrew sees and names: "We have found the Messiah!" And Jesus sees and names Simon: "You shall be called Cephas." This drama of naming speaks eloquently of the power of seeing and of naming—and of its delicacies—that we both see and name truthfully and with the other person's participation.

Prayer: *Keep us alert to the ways in which we seek to name others, O God, while remaining always open to your invitation to us to live out of our Hebrew-Christian naming. In Jesus' name. Amen.*

UNDIVIDED DEVOTION TO THE LORD

January 21-27, 1985   **Mark W. Gustafson†**
Monday, January 21   Read 1 Corinthians 7:25-35.

For the apostle Paul the time was short and the end of the world near. He was anxious to get Christians to focus their hearts and minds on God and doing God's will. The work of the church was "to secure your undivided devotion to the Lord."

Given the constant threat of a thermonuclear holocaust, we can identify with Paul and his sense of urgency about world conditions and the church. Survival into the next century is questionable and will depend on bold action from present-day Christians to promote peace and love of life. Our boldness will grow as we discipline ourselves to greater allegiance to God. Our work within the church seeks to promote increased faith through the practice of worship, study, and mission. And we hope this will build desire for more creative ways to live with all peoples. God is our hope and our strength. "I know the plans I have for you, says the Lord, plans for welfare and not for evil, to give you a future and a hope. Then you will call upon me and come and pray to me, and I will hear you" (Jer. 29:11-12).

Prayer: *God, our strength and hope, give us a vision of peace and justice for all people. Strengthen our efforts to serve your kingdom here on earth through our single-minded devotion to you. Amen.*

---

†Minister, Winchester, Massachusetts.

Tuesday, January 22   Read Jonah 3:1-5, 10.

Undivided devotion to God means willingness to repent.

Repentance happened rather dramatically in the Book of Jonah. The message of the prophet to his Hebrew audience was clear: Look how quickly those who do not know God respond to the word; you are called to such willing devotion to Yahweh.

In the story, Jonah completed only one-third of his preaching job before the people of Nineveh responded in a positive manner. Those pagan people quickly acted with ritual repentance through the putting on of sackcloth, sitting in ashes, and fasting. The Hebrew notion that God would demonstrate anger and judgment through defeat in war was strong in Jonah's preaching. Whether the people of Nineveh acted out of fear of destruction or religious fervor we do not know. We do know they readily responded to Jonah's preaching and changed their ways.

You and I are called by God's only Son, Jesus, to change our ways in order to enter the kingdom. We are called to free ourselves from the darkness of hatred, anger, and bitterness and to dwell in the city of the Lord who is the light of our lives and faith. God draws us near in blessedness. God, our light, sent Jesus as light to all peoples, even those who are ignorant of the Creator. When we listen, ponder the word, and act, seeking and finding forgiveness, God is willing to turn away from anger and receive us.

Prayer: *O God, comfort the fear in our stubborn hearts. Give us the strength to change and turn to you in trust and willing obedience. Amen.*

Wednesday, January 23   Read Matthew 6:25-33.

Undivided devotion to God means dropping our worship of fear.

For years, the prophets of Israel preached against the worship of other gods. They called on Israel to return to worship and praise the one true God.

Jesus challenged his followers to worship only the true God. He knew that people often turn to other gods to avoid taking responsibility for themselves and others. Some folks turn to the god of fear and make it first in their lives. Fear can become an excuse for not boldly living the Christian life.

Fear is natural and useful to help us, for example, keep away from dangerous places like the edge of a cliff. But when it is used as a block to serving God and living fully, then we do a disservice to ourselves and God. Jesus said, "Seek first [God's] kingdom and his righteousness, and all these shall be yours as well." God will provide for our every need. "Trust in him at all times, O people; pour out your heart before him," said the psalmist (Ps. 62:8). When we treat God like a trusted friend to whom we can tell all, our devotion to God will increase. This puts our fears in healthy perspective. We will feel more in touch with God and more willing to respond to God's direction.

Prayer: *O God, teach me to trust you in all things. Help me to focus myself on you, making you first in my life. Forgive my unfaithful ways, and turn me back to you. Guide and protect me that I may be a willing servant in your service. Amen.*

Thursday, January 24 Read Luke 12:13-21.

Undivided devotion to God means keeping wealth in proper perspective.

There are many distractions along the road of faith for the modern-day Christian. Effort is required for us to remain focused on nurturing and building our relationship with God. We dare not waste our efforts in distractions such as acquiring material wealth. All of us need material goods and money for living. But we need to be careful not to be distracted from the task of first importance—giving ourselves in love and service to others. The mistake made by the rich man in the parable is that he was concerned only with acquiring more goods. He did not share himself and his property with others. When his soul was required of him, he was poor.

Jesus' parable carries a message for wealthy people today: the ultimate priority should be richness toward God. We need to heed the wisdom of the psalmist, "If riches increase, set not your heart on them" (Ps. 62:10). Wealth should serve us so we can give more of ourselves to others. Undivided devotion to God then means trusting God, keeping focused on doing God's will and work. Singleminded devotion is knowing that what we possess is temporarily ours. On the other hand, treasures of our work for the Lord last for a lifetime and beyond.

Prayer: *Lord God, sometimes our perspective gets hazy, and we grow lazy and fat on the riches of our land. Redirect our ways and help us focus our attention and energy on faithful service to you and those in need. Make us rich with your grace. Amen.*

Friday, January 25   Read Matthew 6:5-13.

Undivided devotion to God means practicing the discipline of prayer.

In teaching the disciples, Jesus said a startling thing, "And when you pray." He did not say *if* or anything similar but "*when* you pray." The assumption is strong that all his followers will practice the discipline of prayer for the upbuilding of faith. Jesus was simply giving lessons in the best manner of prayer. Prayer was central to the ministry and mission of Jesus. He repeatedly set aside time for prayer by withdrawing from the crowds and sometimes from his disciples. Before making crucial decisions, Jesus withdrew to pray. The most profound example of prayer before a decision was in the garden before his trial and crucifixion.

For us, prayer can be no less significant to our ministry and mission. The discipline of daily prayer keeps us open to the leading of the Holy Spirit. Regular prayer is a source of power and strength to live according to the ways of God. Prayer keeps us aligned with eternal purposes and helps us treat others in more loving and understanding ways. Through daily prayer we grow in the strength of our Christian convictions and feel the power of God's presence. Each morning, trust in God can be renewed and deepened with prayer. At the end of the day, thanksgiving to God for all our blessings can be shared through prayer.

Devotional exercise: *Study the "how to" in Jesus' lesson prayer in the above scripture. Take time each day to read prayers and reflections on prayer by modern writers of your choice. Read also writers such as Augustine, Thomas à Kempis, and Brother Lawrence.*

37

Saturday, January 26   Read Mark 1:14-20.

Undivided devotion to God means obedience to God's call.

"Immediately they . . . followed him." I am continually amazed that men like Simon and Andrew dropped everything and followed Jesus. James and John also left their work and father and joined Jesus in his ministry. In all likelihood they had known Jesus prior to this incident and responded to the influence of his personality and the call of God.

God calls you and me. In ways small and large we are challenged to respond to that call to ministry. Through our prayer life, conscience, feelings, and convictions God calls for an immediate, obedient response. God would have us live with an attitude of willing obedience.

Living with such willingness may mean risking the offering of material aid to someone in need. Obedience to God's call could challenge us to risk confronting others with our feelings and convictions. We may feel called to take an unpopular stand in our community for an important issue or share our love with an unlovely person. In all these ways we can respond positively to the word of God for us. Our willingness to follow God is a sign of our turning away from destructive behavior to constructive work for the kingdom of God. That willing attitude and obedience renews and strengthens our faith.

Prayer: *Lord God, obedience to your will is a tough row to hoe. Sometimes I get scared and resist doing your work, never knowing how much more you will demand of me. God, make me bold in my response to your leading. Fill my heart with longing to give myself in service to you. Amen.*

Sunday, January 27   Read Psalm 62.

Undivided devotion to God means putting our trust in God.

The theme of Psalm 62 is trust and confidence in the Lord. Trusting the Lord is what our faith is all about and is central to our religious life. Trust in God is essential to us who would pattern our lives after the example of the Christ. Through this trust we find the source and power of our salvation. God is power, and that power is for us. Each day as we discipline ourselves to worship God, we will gain the strength to love God and other people. Our inner life will find new reserves of energy and willpower useful in coping with the stresses and pressures of living.

Every morning, before our daily activities start, we can take time to "pour out [our] heart." The discipline of morning scripture reading and prayer is a source of strength for living each day. Through prayer, we open ourselves to God's renewing strength. When we take the risk of sharing all our feelings, pressing needs, failings, and joys, we feel more acceptable to ourselves and God.

Then, each evening, we pray to God in a spirit of thanksgiving for all that was experienced throughout the day. Thanking God for all things lifts us above our daily circumstances and truly makes us victors in the midst of strife.

Prayer: *Thank you, God, for joys and troubles. Open me with your Holy Spirit that I may more deeply feel the joys of life. Help me to learn from my troubles how to more faithfully serve you. Guide me in your wisdom. Amen.*

RESPONDING TO THE LORD

January 28–February 3, 1985 **Mary Frances Owens†**
Monday, January 28 Read Deut. 18:15-20.

This week's meditations focus on how God expects us to respond to various situations. Today's Bible reading comes from a series of laws that relate to the function of worship leaders. It concerns the question, How shall I respond to the revealed will of God?

God reveals the divine will through human channels, and our scripture passage relates to the role of prophets in this revelation process. Moses, and others like him, became instruments of God's purpose. They served as mediators between God and humankind, transmitters of God's message, and authoritative spokespersons for the Lord. Prediction of the future was not their main function.

The Lord instructed worshipers to heed the words of authentic prophets as coming directly from the Lord. To assure righteous leadership, the Lord commanded the penalty of death for any spokesperson who deliberately misled the people.

The primary teaching in these verses is that God expects us to respond with obedience to the divine will. However, this scripture also puts heavy responsibility on those persons who reveal God's message. God holds all spokespersons accountable for right use of their privilege. These words carry a timely reminder for preachers and other religious leaders of today.

Prayer: *Lord, help us to respond to thy revealed will with obedience and righteous service. Amen.*

---

†Free-lance writer, Louisville, Kentucky.

Tuesday, January 29   Read Psalm 111:1-4.

How should I respond to the great works of the Lord? Psalm 111 contains a lesson on our need to offer God grateful praise.

Psalm 111 is an acrostic hymn of praise, each line beginning with a successive letter of the Hebrew alphabet. In verse 1 the psalmist summoned worshipers to praise the Lord. The psalmist did not call upon them to do anything that he did not intend to do. The leadership example of the psalmist brings to mind the importance of setting the right leadership example today. Grateful praise to God should come from leaders and laity alike—and not in a mechanical way, but with whole-hearted devotion.

Verses 2-4 outline a broad view of why worshipers should offer praise and thanksgiving to God. God's people saw firsthand the evidence of God's greatness. Their Lord was not a passive being who merely existed, but an active God who made things happen. God's works constantly bore witness of the majestic, righteous, gracious, and merciful nature of the Lord they worshiped. Such greatness elicited their adoration.

Knowing our thoughts anyway, does the Lord really care whether we express our grateful praise? The psalmist evidently thought so. The Psalter contains 150 psalms; an overwhelming theme throughout the writings of the Psalms is the offering of praise to God—whether directly or indirectly.

Grateful praise is an appropriate response to the great works of God. It reveals our remembrance of, and thankfulness for, what the Lord has done.

Prayer: *We offer our praise and thanksgiving, Lord, for thy marvelous works. Help us never to forget your greatness. Amen.*

Wednesday, January 30   Read Psalm 111:5-10.

How should I respond to the compassion and redemptive grace of God? Psalm 111:5-10 recommends reverential awe.

The first four verses of this psalm focus on audible praise as a fitting response to God's works. Even more basic than words of praise, however, was the reverential awe that motivated the praise.

Verses 5-8 outline in more detail what the psalmist had said earlier. These verses list some reasons why the psalmist had called God's works "great."

First, the Lord had provided daily sustenance for the people. In verse 5 the psalmist likely had in mind God's miraculous provisions in the wilderness. However, God's gracious concern continued to be evident throughout Israel's history.

Second, the Lord's greatness was demonstrated when Canaan was given to Israel as a heritage. Conquest of the promised land could not have come without God's help. Israel had only been a straggly band of tribes with very little unity. The Lord had fought for Israel time and time again.

Third, the Lord had executed justice and trustworthiness both in actions and in commandments. The Lord had established righteous rule over the people.

In brief, the psalmist summoned the worshipers to respond to God's compassion and deliverance with reverential awe. "Fear of the Lord" was and is the starting point of spiritual wisdom. Casual or irreverent attitudes toward God have no place in the lives of worshipers.

Prayer: *Compassionate and gracious Lord, help us respond to thy greatness with reverential worship. Amen.*

Thursday, January 31   Read 1 Cor. 8:1-3.

How should I respond to the possession of knowledge? First Corinthians 8:1-3 deals with this sensitive issue.

Apparently the church at Corinth had asked Paul concerning the eating of food offered to idols (a matter we will examine more specifically on Saturday). Before Paul answered their inquiry, he wanted to lay some groundwork. He recognized a principle that the church people needed to understand before they could resolve the "food offered to idols" issue.

The principle involved the relationship between knowledge and love. Paul tactfully assumed that his inquirers did possess knowledge. Nevertheless, he knew that even a good gift like knowledge had its drawbacks. Paul wanted these Christians to see knowledge in its proper perspective.

Paul put the difference between these two gifts in focus. " 'Knowledge' puffs up, but love builds up." We might say that knowledge builds up the mind, whereas love builds up the spirit. A wise person will agree with Paul: "If any one imagines that he knows something, he does not yet know as he ought to know." Knowledge, whether imagined or known in the mind, is something other than love in the heart. The more vital issue is not how much we know, but how strong our desire is to build up God's spirit in us through our love of God. God knows us by the love we have for him.

The proper responses to the gift of knowledge are humility and a love that values God and other persons above selfish personal interests.

Prayer: *Lord, teach us to value the gift of knowledge enough to use it responsibly and in a spirit of sensitive love. Amen.*

Friday, February 1   Read 1 Cor. 8:4-6.

How should I respond to the uniqueness of the true God in a society filled with false gods? This question has real pertinence for modern Christians who must struggle to keep from making false gods out of secular pursuits. We could hardly dismiss financial and vocational success as irrelevant in our era of economic insecurity. Nevertheless, neither should we make success our god.

In First Corinthians 8:4-6, Paul was laying a background for his answer to the question of eating food offered to idols. He circumvented the main issue briefly in order to clarify his stand on the existence of idols.

Because of his Jewish background, Paul had strong convictions about the uniqueness of God. The Shema clearly stated: "The Lord our God is one Lord" (Deut. 6:4, KJV). Paul conceded that numerous idols existed. He pointed out, however, that their existence had no spiritual validity. He affirmed, "There is one God, the Father, from whom are all things . . . and one Lord, Jesus Christ."

Some Christians of today live in areas that still have literal idol worship. For most of us, however, Paul's words apply best as a reminder to keep our priorities straight. Such false gods as wealth and prestige exist, but they are fickle, transient, and without spiritual value. Only the Lord can fill humankind's deepest needs.

The proper response to a knowledge of God's oneness is wholehearted devotion to God. Secular goals must be subordinate to worship of the one true God.

Prayer: *Loving God, grant us wisdom to respond to thee with wholehearted devotion. Amen.*

Saturday, February 2   Read 1 Cor. 8:7-13.

How should I respond to Christian freedom? Paul answered this question in today's Bible reading.

A group of the Corinthian Christians considered themselves more intellectually enlightened than the others. They argued that since idols meant nothing to them, they could eat food offered to idols in good conscience. Meat left over from pagan sacrificial offerings was the highest quality meat available at marketplaces. Why should not the knowledgeable Christians show their freedom by eating the meat?

Paul replied, in effect: Christians must use their freedom responsibly. Exercising freedom when it becomes a stumbling block to others is not a responsible use of it!

Paul reminded these intellectually enlightened persons that from a spiritual standpoint food had no value. The problem was that if weaker Christians saw more knowledgeable ones eating food that had been offered to idols, they might stumble because of it. The question needing evaluation was: Which is more important—the right to exercise personal freedom, or the duty to prevent the destruction of a brother or sister for whom Christ died? Paul personally testified that he would rather go without meat than make his brother or sister stumble.

Love must supersede personal liberty in every area of life. The proper response to Christian freedom involves concern not only for our own consciences, but also for the consciences of others. Love should be the deciding factor in matters of right and liberty.

Prayer: *Gracious Lord, help us to exercise our freedom in a spirit of Christian love. Amen.*

Sunday, February 3   Read Mark 1:21-28.

How should I respond to the Lord's authority? This response takes precedence over all else in life.

The incident narrated in Mark 1:21-28 occurred at the beginning of Jesus' ministry. Jesus and his disciples had walked to Capernaum, and he began to teach in the synagogue there.

The other worshipers listened with astonishment as Jesus taught. They were amazed that he was not like the scribes who merely parroted what they had learned. Jesus spoke with personal authority.

A man with an unclean spirit (demon possessed) had entered the synagogue. Demon possession was considered ritually unclean because it prevented the victim from proper worship of God. The demon within the man recognized the authority of Jesus and felt threatened. He cried out, "Have you come to destroy us?" Jesus silenced him and performed an exorcism.

The worshipers reacted again with astonishment. Jesus had revealed his authority not only in teaching but also in exorcising the demon. Jesus' fame spread throughout Galilee.

These acts of authority were a fitting start to Jesus' earthly ministry. They became an earnest for the authority he would continue to exert over the power of evil. Today the transformed lives of men and women bear witness to what happens when persons seriously recognize the authority of the Lord.

This week's meditations on responding to the Lord end on this positive note. Faith and obedience are the righteous responses God expects of us.

Prayer: *Help us, Lord, to submit to thy authority in faith and loving obedience. Amen.*

THE CHRISTIAN WITNESS

February 4-10, 1985   **Fran Greenway†**
Monday, February 4   Read Job 7:1-7.

Humanity's need for the Christian witness is brought to mind as Job holds forth on life's woes. What a difference Jesus has made in our own lives!

Diagnosing Job's ailment is purely academic and is not our purpose here. It is important, though, that we recognize his predicament as one of genuine suffering, both physical and emotional. This enables us to sympathize, if not identify, as he complains.

Strictly from a human standpoint, life is filled with drudgery and weariness (vs. 1-2). It is a drag: meaningless days of nothingness punctuated by nights of restlessness (vs. 3-4). Job's affliction intensified, if not generated, this pessimistic outlook by adding bodily pain, stench, and ugliness (v. 5).

Job had hardly finished asking God to snuff out his life, releasing him from the misery of it (6:8-9), when he grumbled of the brevity of his existence (7:6). Life was generally considered desirable, hence the mourning of the swift passage of it. Job lamented, "My days pass by without hope . . . my happiness has already ended" (vs. 6-7, TEV).

The Christian witness, the good news of Jesus Christ, offers hope in the midst of despair, joy even in sorrow, fulfillment in seemingly purposeless circumstances.

Suggestion for prayer: *Pray that we may know God's Son in the personal way that gives hope both in this life and in the life to come.*

---

†Missionary doctor, Baptist Medical Centre, Nalerigu via Gambaga, Ghana, West Africa.

Tuesday, February 5   Read Psalm 147:1-11.

Response to the Christian witness produces certain predictable qualities: rejoicing, gratitude, reverence, hope. Jesus Christ brings meaning and exhilaration to life.

Scholars divide Psalm 147 into 3 sections, the first two of which are in verses 1-11. The first section praises God for rebuilding Jerusalem. Israel, returning from Babylonian captivity, is referred to as outcasts, the brokenhearted, the downtrodden. Verses 1-6 describe these exiles as being gathered by a gracious God who restores them to their own land. God binds their wounds, heals and lifts them up. So knowledgeable and powerful is God that God counts and even names the stars in creation. God is a God of detail. Tenderly supportive of these children, God crushes their oppressors.

Verses 7-11 are a song of thanksgiving to God, the sustainer of creation. God produces clouds, which in turn provide rain, thus causing grass to grow. In such orderly fashion God sustains all living things.

God delights in all the creatures of the world and is truly pleased by their structure and prowess. But God's ultimate pleasure is not in things physical. God doesn't place priority on the rippling muscles of a sleek horse or on the stamina and swiftness of an athlete's legs. God's greatest enjoyment is in those who trust, love, and have hope in their Creator. God supremely delights in those who thus respond because in doing so they manifest spiritual strength.

Prayer: *Creator God, we praise you and thank you, submitting ourselves totally to you to become the creatures you have designed us to be. In Christ's name. Amen.*

Wednesday, February 6   Read 1 Cor. 9:16-18.

A certain compulsion makes the Christian witness an inescapable duty. The apostle Paul experienced this over-whelming necessity to proclaim the Good News. He did not choose to preach; he was chosen. He absolutely could not avoid it. He had either to preach or be extremely miserable. Therefore, he deserved no credit for preaching and could not boast of it.

If the idea had been born of him and he had volunteered his services, he would deserve and could expect to be paid. There is precedent for that in scripture, though the exact nature of the wages is unclear. Perhaps Paul refers to financial support in First Corinthians 9:14. Some feel that the wages are satisfaction derived from the very doing of the job. John 4:36 suggests that our witness brings a spiritual reward.

But Paul had not volunteered; he obeyed an irresistible command. God had commissioned him; therefore, he preached the gospel for the pure joy of it and for the privilege of that trust. Verse 18 indicates that Paul's ability to earn his living other than by preaching was meaningful to him.

We can identify with Paul in his sense of a call to preach the gospel. Many of us are engaged in full-time salaried Christian vocations. Some of us are bivocational in an effort to perform that same task. Still others have secular callings. Nonetheless, all of us as Christians are obligated to share the good news of Jesus Christ. According to God's plan, the compulsion needs to be equally strong and the commitment equally necessary among all of us.

Prayer: *We thank you, God, that you call us as individuals to specific places of service. We ask that we each have the assurance of being in your perfect will as we witness to your love and grace. Amen.*

Thursday, February 7   Read 1 Cor. 9:19-23.

A sensible strategy of Christian witness puts us alongside the unsaved person we desire to win. Paul's method, identifying with those he purposed to lead to Jesus, is a vital process in our own ministry today.

In Christ, Paul had true freedom. Yet, because of his keen sense of Christian responsibility, he voluntarily made himself subject to others in order to be a usable vessel in their midst. He acknowledged partnership with God in winning the lost (v. 19).

Paul demonstrated remarkable adaptability without compromise of Christian principles. Examples of accommodation to the Jews are Paul's circumcision of Timothy (Acts 16:3) and purification of himself in the temple (Acts 21:26). Whether verse 20*b* is a restatement to provide a smoother transition to verse 21 or refers to the Gentiles who followed Jewish customs is inconsequential to the basic teaching: Paul always sought common ground with his associates to provide rapport as a vehicle for the gospel. Not lawless, though appearing so to the Gentiles, Paul maintained constant awareness of belonging to Christ. His flexibility and amiability in no way sacrificed Christian principles.

Paul accommodated himself to the weak by respecting their conscientious scruples even though he knew they were mistaken (1 Cor. 8:13). He did it all because of the preciousness of the gospel, the blessings of which he wanted to share.

Suggestion for prayer: *Ask God to burden you for the lost, drawing you into genuine friendship and unfeigned concern through which your witness can flow. Earnestly seek guidance for ways to have meaningful relationships with those who need to know God's love.*

Friday, February 8   Read Mark 1:29-34.

For effectiveness in Christian witness, our lives must be compatible with the gospel we put forth. An extreme example of incongruous testimony is that of demons. The usual interpretation of verse 34*b* is that Jesus refused them voice because they were diametrically opposed to all for which he stood.

Preceding verses relate the instantaneous, complete healing of Simon Peter's mother-in-law. Her ability, immediately upon the departure of a high fever, to arise and serve guests was a fantastic advertisement. As soon as the Sabbath was officially over and the people were free to do so, they began carrying the sick in a steady stream to Jesus. All who were ill were brought to him. The demonized were included because of the news of the casting out of the demon in the synagogue (v. 26).

"In many cases he expelled evil spirits; but he would not allow them to say a word, for they knew perfectly well who he was" (PHILLIPS). The Greek indicates it was a continuous refusal; apparently the demons were clamoring to be heard. The assumption is that their declaration would be of the same pattern as that of verse 24. The most apt explanation for the denial is the inappropriateness of that source of testimony concerning "the Holy One of God." However, even the disciples were warned not to make Jesus' true identity known because time to do so had not yet come (Luke 9:21). Some believe it had to do with Jesus' already overpublicized ministry in Galilee and therefore was in the same vein as his admonition to the leper in verse 44.

Suggestion for prayer: *Pray that all areas and every detail of your life will magnify Christ.*

Saturday, February 9   Read Mark 1:35.

The power of the Christian witness comes from above. Jesus spent hours in prayer to his heavenly father. He set an example for us in so doing; however, the compulsion for intimate communication came from within himself, born of need.

Praying all night (Luke 6:12) and arising a great while before day to pray seem so in character for Jesus that we imagine it was always easy for him. If we believe Jesus was indeed tempted in all things as we are (Heb. 4:15), we must accept the probability that at least one time it was difficult. It is often necessary to put forth effort in order to spend time with God in prayer. Jesus did, and he expects us to do the same.

We sometimes make great to-do about meeting God in the morning in preference to other times. Scripture puts emphasis on aloneness with God (Matt. 6:6) rather than on the time of day devoted to prayer. Being constantly in an attitude of prayer (1 Thess. 5:17) helps us find time for the more intense encounters. Likewise, systematic unrushed private prayer time fosters praying without ceasing.

Jesus so interspersed prayer with ministry that we must conclude he found in it strength, courage, and direction to do God's will. During heavy periods of teaching, preaching, and healing, he felt the need to slip away to quiet places and pray (Luke 5:16). Mark 6:46 describes a withdrawal for prayer at the end of a busy day. The Gethsemane experience is a supreme example of prayer in preparation for a specific event (Matt. 26:36-46).

Suggestion for prayer: *Thank God for the delight and refreshment of prayer and for strength to accept its disciplines.*

Sunday, February 10   Read Mark 1:36-39.

Fellowship with the Lord of the Christian witness is not only readily available to us but is necessary for our effectiveness as ministers. And we are, every one of us, ministers. Every Christian is called to share Christ in that very obligatory way that permeates our whole being.

The disciples had the benefit of this nurturing closeness to our Lord. Immediately upon arising to find Jesus gone, they tracked him down with the apparent intent of returning him to Capernaum to deal with the gathering crowds. They doubtless felt pride in their Master's popularity in their own town. This perhaps led to their excited declaration that "every one is searching for you."

But Jesus purposed to move on. There is speculation about his reasons. Some say Simon's news of the demanding masses precipitated a sudden decision. More likely he came to the secluded prayer site specifically to prepare for the anticipated preaching mission. It is also possible that the prayer time itself helped Jesus to know what he must do.

Another discussion concerns the meaning of "for that is why I came out." Some contend it refers to leaving Capernaum; some are convinced it speaks of Jesus' coming into the world. Others claim the language is indefinite, leaving the interpretation up to the reader. All seem in agreement that his moving out is in keeping with his overall mission of seeking and saving the lost, as also is his emphasis on preaching.

Suggestion for prayer: *Pray for guidance to have the right priorities and for the discipline to look to Jesus for direction.*

CALLED TO GOD'S LIGHT

February 11-17, 1985   **Jeanne Gramstorff†**
Monday, February 11   Read Psalm 50:1-2;
                Psalm 104.

Hear the declaration: "God shines out from Zion, perfect in beauty" (NEB). God summons us with the divine word and with light. In Psalm 104 the psalmist pictures God, creator of the heavens and earth and ruler of all creation, wrapped in a robe of light. From the time of Genesis, light has been a central symbol of the Judeo-Christian faith. God's creatures rely upon the constancy of our Creator's light.

On a recent early morning drive, my way was obscured by dense fog. Although I travel the route very often, I could find no familiar landmarks. My body tensed as I peered into unrelieved darkness. The drive seemed even longer than usual. After some time, my car topped a small hill. For an incomparable moment, the light of the morning sun bathed the earth in dazzling, shimmering light. Immediately a pea-soup world enveloped me again. But comfort had come. I had seen the light of the heavens.

The light of God's summons constantly breaks through the fog of our everyday existence. We are called to respond to the glory of God's shining light of love that God may rejoice in all creation. The psalmist vows, "I will sing to the Lord as long as I live."

Prayer: *I welcome the light of your love, O God. May I respond with courage and faith to your call. Amen.*

---

†Writer, chairperson of children's section of Curriculum Resources Committee, United Methodist Church, Farnsworth, Texas.

54

Tuesday, February 12   Read 2 Kings 2:1-12.

Often we receive God's summons through the vision and guidance of a friend. Elisha continued to travel beside Elijah long after he was told to turn back. He hoped that through Elijah's eyes he, too, would be allowed to behold the glory of God. When other followers turned away, Elisha refused to leave his mentor. He persevered and was rewarded by seeing Elijah part the waters of the Jordan. When Elijah ascended into heaven, Elisha's path of faith was lighted by the magnificent fiery vision of chariots and horses.

Friends bring clear vision into our lives, greater insights which reveal the light of the Eternal. But in order to behold the light in its fullest glory, we must remain steadfast after others turn away. We, like Elisha, must persist when we would feel safer turning back.

The paths of lasting friendships are not always smooth and broad. Our cultural standards demand that we be totally self-reliant. We are taught to depend ultimately only on ourselves. How can we put trust in someone else when we are unable to put total reliance even upon God? We fear betrayal. We barricade against attack. Elijah counseled Elisha to turn back. Did he fear that Elisha, like other friends, was not ready to face the test of faith? Can we dare seek such an intimate friendship?

Prayer: *God, you know that I do not want to lose the little light that I have captured. I do not want to share my light because I fear my faith could not withstand the assault of another's questions. Yet my faith needs the strength of another's vision of your light. Be with me as I seek a friend. Amen.*

Wednesday, February 13   Read Mark 9:2-9.

Jesus leads his friends, Peter, James, and John, to the top of the mountain. There the dazzling light of the presence of God transfigures the Son. A voice declares, "This is my Son, my Beloved; listen to him" (NEB).

The holy light continues to bear the summons of God's presence. Moses beheld the light of God's call in the fire of the burning bush. Elijah was carried up to heaven on a whirlwind coming from the vision of chariots and horses of fiery light. Now, again, Elijah and Moses appear in the light which anoints the Son of God.

I wonder why we humans, no matter how inspired, seem often to make improper responses to wondrous happenings. I am unable to say the words which would tell my friend of the transformation of my life by his love for me. Peter could not conceive God's plan unfolding in the miraculous moment of his friend's transfiguration.

Unfortunately, we who are the church continue to make inadequate attempts to carry out God's plan. Catching a glimpse of the presence in light, we choose to stay high on the mountain, to build magnificent altars bathed in the glow of our understanding. We do not listen. Jesus, transfigured, called his disciples to return into the world bearing the light to all people.

"This is my Son, my Beloved; listen to him" (NEB). The call has been given.

Prayer: *O God, Father of our Lord Jesus, give us courage to strengthen the church as the messenger of the love of Jesus Christ. Amen.*

Thursday, February 14   Read Matthew 5:14-16;
Luke 8:16-18.

The parable reminds us that only as the light can be seen is it useful. Jesus commands that we take his light into the world that all nations may praise God. But my light is so small! It would not brighten even a tiny corner. I am sure that someone else could be a better lamp for his important message.

I visited a construction site recently. Workers were putting an acoustical ceiling in place. They were hanging the metal framework without measuring. I wondered how they knew that the frames holding the tiles were level. The answer was to be found in the work of a small machine which was mounted on the wall in one corner of the room. A very tiny ray of laser light was constantly flashing all about the room at exactly the level of the ceiling installation. The signal was easily seen by those who were shown how to look for it. When I put my hand at the level desired for the ceiling, rays of laser light crossed it in a pulsating rhythm. The framework for the ceiling tiles was placed at the level of the light, eliminating the possibility of inaccurate measurements.

A laser leveler solves many construction problems. God's creative possibilities are limited only by human understanding. As we learn more, we are led to enlarge our learning potential. We become more useful for God's purposes.

Our lights may be the size of the tiny laser leveler beam. In God's creation there are uses for tiny lasers and giant floodlights.

Prayer: *Eternal One, may the laser beam remind me to use my own small light in your world. Amen.*

Friday, February 15   Read 2 Corinthians 4:3-6.

Paul tells us that in spite of the darkness and evil of this world of unbelievers, the light of the good news of the glory of Christ is available to all who will accept it. Read the final verses of chapter 3 of this letter. Paul says, "We all reflect as in a mirror the splendour of the Lord" (NEB).

Paul realizes, however, that many persons do not choose to follow God. He cannot understand why, unless they are so blinded by the evil of the "god of this passing age" (NEB) that they cannot be drawn to the light. When the laser leveler light was demonstrated for me at the construction site, I wondered why I had been so blind to it. I had to be led to be able to see the light.

It is the privilege and the obligation of believers to proclaim Christ Jesus to the world, even to those who may choose not to believe. How can my neighbor see the glory of God's splendor when I have turned my mirror to the ground?

God's word nurtures our Christian lives. Through study we gradually add skills with which to proclaim the light of the message of Christ. Dawn is here. Are we able to behold it? Tiny rays edge above the horizon long before the sunshine bursts upon our sight. Paul admonishes us to tilt our mirrors to more truly reflect the splendor of the Lord.

Suggestion for meditation: *Today I will count the tiny rays of dawn which I have been able to see in my own life this year. I will renew my study that I may learn to be a truer reflection of the nature of God to others.*

Saturday, February 16   Read Psalm 50:3-6;
     Psalm 67.

The "day of the Lord" will come when the Creator who guides history shall ultimately judge the world, destroy evil, and bring forth a time of eternal blessings. God's loyal servants will be brought forth to share in the justice that the heavens proclaim.

Who are God's loyal servants? Perhaps they are those who accept the responsibility of bringing about justice in a world of evil and darkness. Are they the undaunted ones who carry their torches against the dark nights of slavery, the holocaust, political injustices, economic oppressions, nuclear disasters? Even when forces of evil plunge whole nations into darkness, do the lights of God's loyal servants blaze forth to transform peoples and nations?

God's judgment is justice for the world. Where are the servants who will bring that judgment? May their prophecies renew our hope, their exhortations bring new resolve!

Is it possible that I, too, am called to this mission? God's face shines upon us "that his ways may be known on earth and his saving power among all the nations" (NEB).

"Let the peoples praise thee, O God; let all peoples praise thee" (NEB).

Suggestion for meditation: *Reflect upon the injustices in your community, your city, your world today. Do we have the responsibility of bringing about the justice of God's judgment? How can you begin to bring justice in your world?*

Sunday, February 17   Read John 8:12.

To a world filled with the agony of darkness and injustice, God sent the light of Jesus Christ. The children of God would no longer be forced to wander aimlessly in the dark. Creative justice entered a bright new day. Charles Wesley's great hymn tells the story of the glory of Christ's coming.

Christ, whose glory fills the skies,
Christ, the true, the only light,
Sun of Righteousness, arise,
Triumph o'er the shades of night;
Dayspring from on high, be near;
Daystar, in my heart appear.

Dark and cheerless is the morn
Unaccompanied by thee;
Joyless is the day's return
Till thy mercy's beams I see;
Till they inward light impart,
Cheer my eyes and warm my heart.

Visit, then, this soul of mine;
Pierce the gloom of sin and grief;
Fill me, Radiancy divine;
Scatter all my unbelief;
More and more thyself display,
Shining to the perfect day.

Prayer: *Creator of light eternal, I have seen your summons. May I dare to reflect that radiant light all the days of my life. Amen.*

GOD CREATES AND SUSTAINS

February 18-24, 1985   **J. Edwin Coates†**
Monday, February 18   Read Mark 1:9-15.

My friend Al, who has remarkable spiritual acuity, tells of a dream he had.

It was quitting time on a construction job, and he was putting tools away: shovels and picks, hammers and sledges, saws and levels. But among the tools were many that were broken; many worn-out and useless tools. He tossed them into a heap outside the storage shed and put the others away for another day. Just then, the boss came.

Gathering all the bent and broken tools into his arms, the head man said, "These are my tools, my very good tools; they are precious to me, for they were broken in my service."

Then, Al said, his dream eyes of the spirit were opened, and he recognized the Master Carpenter. As he looked at the broken tools, he saw men and women—faithful souls— wearied and tired, used up, worn out, broken down in service to Christ and precious in his sight. They were tools that had been tempted and had resisted; tools that had been molded by the trials of life; tools whose time had been fulfilled; tools the Master loved and in whom he was well pleased.

Prayer: *Master workman of the race, tested and tempted as we shall never be; strengthen us in the service we are called to do, despite hardships and trials. Use us while there is use left in us. Then, in thy grace, grant us rest at last. Amen.*

---

†Pastor, The United Methodist Church, Winner, South Dakota.

Tuesday, February 19　　　　　　Read 1 Peter 3:18.

I have become a gatherer of aluminum cans. As I walk, I am constantly alert for the discarded can—out in the street, down in the gutter, cast in the brush. Some are smashed by a succession of tires, and some are twisted and torn by macho fists. Some are dirty and muddied; others are bright and sparkly, cylindrically perfect. But all are has-beens, castaways, rejects. Whether their earthly purpose had been wholesome or evil, whether they had ministered to comfort or sin, whether they had brought joy or misery—their purpose was over and they had been thrown away.

It is a redemptive act to gather these used cans and haul them for recycling. They can be turned into something useful again. And their usefulness is an immediate thing, too. Every seven cans brings a nickel to be used in ministry: cancer fund, world hunger, the church's mission.

Jesus, the good shepherd, is a collector, too—searching the valleys and hills, busy streets and dirty alleys for the lost and lonely, the used-up and empty, thrown-down and trampled-on, twisted and smashed lost human beings. They think they can't; he knows they can. With loving hands, he picks them up and recycles their usefulness.

It is sobering and wonderful to reflect that sometimes I have been like a discarded can—empty and flat. And sometimes I have been the hands of Christ—lifting, loving, restoring.

Prayer: *O God, as members of the body of Christ, make of us loving hearts, faithful feet, and capable hands. Lead us to the persons who feel troubled and empty. In Jesus' name. Amen.*

Wednesday, February 20   Read Psalm 25:1-5.

At calving time, the hours are long and the work demanding. A young rancher in my church tells of a night last spring. He had gone out at 2:00 a.m. to check the heifers in his corral. One was just starting labor, so he went back in to give nature time. He sat in a chair, picked up the Bible, and read for a bit with the silence of nighttime all about. In the quietness, he breathed the almost automatic prayer of a cowman who loves his work and is awed by the miracles of life; a prayer, if it be God's will, for an easy birth to a healthy calf.

When he went out again, it was not an easy birth. The calf couldn't come; the cow needed help. So he helped. He's good at that. He quietly drove the cow into a chute, and easily, swiftly delivered the calf—a fine, strapping calf.

But he wondered about his prayer—about God's will. Why had it not been God's will for a natural birth?

Then, he reports, "A clear impression was placed on my mind: *This is your job, your very purpose in life. If I did every task for you, there would be no reason for your being.*

He reported, "I know God was walking with me that night, helping me. But my hands and skills were needed. I have a new awareness of my task in life. If there is an idea struggling for birth, perhaps my lips are needed. If there is work to be done, perhaps my hands are needed."

Prayer: *God, be in my lips, in my hands, in my life; that I may comfort with my words, heal with my touch, bring joy with my presence. In Jesus' name. Amen.*

Thursday, February 21   Read Psalm 25:4-10.

I am moving, Lord, and I cannot bear the thought. I have invested love and care in the people and institutions of this community—in ideas and dreams, theirs and mine and ours. I have invested, and great have been the dividends. But the investment is not liquid. Investments of love—genuine and deep—and belly laughs and tears, cannot be withdrawn on call or without penalty. Only time and distance reclaim that capital, very slowly, and then not completely.

Like a child who loses a pet and vows never to have another; like the lover who loves and loses and vows never to love again—I am tempted to make no more such investments of friendship and care. The risk is too great and the loss too certain. I know there will be moves again, and loss, and pain; if not my move, then the moves of friends. Where's the wisdom; what's the profit?

My child, one does not make such investments for capital gain. In matters of life and love, of service and friendship, it is the dividends which are valued, never the conservation of capital. Joy consists not in withholding one's love and friendship fearing pain of separation. Joy comes in giving freely, plunging completely, committing fully, enjoying the benefits of the moment, the daily dividends of usefulness, faithfulness, appreciation. And the greatest dividend is that through the practice of giving up and leaving you overcome fear of the final leave-taking, when you give up everything that you might receive all.

Friday, February 22   Read Mark 1:9-11.

Tonight at the school there was an extravaganza: American Education Week. The kids put on a program, and the parents doted. Then the children returned to their rooms to proudly host their parents. The rooms were gaily decorated. Each child's desk was unnaturally clean and orderly; with a psychedelic name on top and best-papers piled up for parental inspection. Beside each desk stood a little scholar at modified attention.

The transparent faces of those third-graders revealed their emotional state—anxiety, worry, a little impatience as each awaited a special family or person. It's a great thing to be able to show one's parents something they do not know. You could see the thrill in each child's eyes as we came through the door.

But when we left there was one little boy still standing by his desk. He had cleaned the desk, assembled his proud handiwork, and lovingly designed his nameplate. He had witnessed, with near unbearable longing, the glee of his classmates and their proud parents. He could not keep his wondering eyes off the door.

Where were his folks? Were they still in his brother's room? Visiting in the hall? Out bowling? Were they prevented from attending by an emergency? Or did they consider American Education Week a ridiculous invention, not worthy of their time? I know nothing of the parent's whereabouts or intentions, only the effect upon their child.

Prayer: *Lord, make us mindful of the needs and desires of our loved ones. Show us how easily we can satisfy those needs, even as you expressed pleasure in your Son. Amen.*

Saturday, February 23　　　　　Read Genesis 9:8-12.

It's late February. Since November we have fought cold and snow. With bravery and fortitude, highway maintenance personnel have done battle with an ice age moving in from the north—as far as the highway. But there they have stopped it, chipping off the growing tentacles every day. Early calves are born and die the same day. Emotions have worn thin; machinery has broken; fences and trees are beaten down and busted. Budgets for fuel, maintenance, and snow removal have long since been exhausted and overspent. It has been a hard winter, and now we have had a week-long blizzard.

Prayer: *O God of power and love, we give you thanks for warm spots in the cold. Thanks for telephones which combat isolation and maintain contact. Thanks for radio and TV, with advance warnings and necessary bulletins. Thanks for hard-working men and women whose tractors and trucks, snowplows and switchboards bring early relief and a measure of security. And thanks for much-needed moisture and the promise it brings.*

Sustain, we pray, those with newborn calves and death in their lots. Comfort the worn-out and wearied, physically beat from lengthy hours and strenuous work, drained by tension and strain, vulnerable to fears, doubts, and intemperate acts. Relieve the sorrowing. Compensate the losses with a fuller sense of your presence. And in every time of confusion or loss, hold our hands lest we despair.

Finally, in this and all the storms of life, help us to see the green beneath the white, to center more on the life-giving ponds than the death-dealing blizzard, to remember that the winter is not forever. In the name of Christ who endured a cold, dark Calvary to know a brilliant resurrection. Amen.

Sunday, February 24   Read Genesis 9:13-17.

It was early morning following a moonless night. My car rolled on, eastward bound, hurrying to a distant meeting. In God's good time, as it has done for a dozen eons, the horizon lightened just a bit, but with a promise of light for the day. In the reflected light from the promised sun—an hour yet below the horizon—two satellites of earth came into view. One was made by human hands, a twink of light in the still-dark sky. It moved overhead, slowly, steadily on its programmed mission—bringing television to the far-flung populace, or mapping the earth, or tracking the weather.

The other was the moon, only the thinnest sliver of it, but suggesting its globular wholeness. One could not see its movement, but one knew it—faster than the other, but less perceptible to the watching eye. It made its stately circuit, moving the tides of ocean and emotion, affecting the weather, the heart, the spirit.

One was made by human beings; one was made by God. The age of one is measured in months; the other, in billions of years. One makes weather; the other reports it. And both are finite! They have their place; they have their purpose; they have their end.

But I, who see and use and benefit—I, through the grace of God, am infinite. For I am a child of God, who has established with me a covenant, revealed to me divine grace, and died for me. All this, so that I, unworthy though I be, might live forever.

Prayer: *Eternal God, you have put signs in the sky and buried truth in the heart. Help me to see the signs and hear the truth today and know that I am yours. Through Jesus Christ. Amen.*

OUTWARD SYMBOLS OF FAITH

February 25–March 3, 1985   **Sherrie Boyens Dobbs†**
Monday, February 25   Read Genesis 17:1-10.

When two parties enter into a legal agreement, they sign a contract. These signatures become the intent of the parties to honor the terms of the contract. We witness a similar kind of signing in God's covenant with Abraham. But Abraham's expression of intent did not absolve him from fulfilling the meat of the agreement. As important as circumcision was as a part of the covenant, the hard terms called for Abraham as father and teacher of generations to "live always in my presence and be perfect" (NEB).

If Abraham had stopped at circumcision, we would have indeed been lost! Outward symbols of faith are those most readily visible to the world. Our churches and temples are outward symbols of faith. Our rites and sacraments are outward symbols of faith. But it is our inner commitment to be faithful that is the meat of our religion. It was Abraham's continued faithfulness that God desired. In fact, Abraham's faithfulness was the reason he was selected as party to the covenant. Faith was the only collateral he had to offer.

God's gifts to us are based on faith—God's faith in us and our faith in God. Abraham believed that God would give him and his wife a son, though both were well past the age to conceive. God gave Abraham and Sarah the son because Abraham had been faithful. This two-way faith far surpasses outward symbols.

Prayer: *God Almighty, give us the faith to receive the gifts that only you can give. Amen.*

---

†Managing editor, *Response* magazine, New York, New York.

Tuesday, February 26   Read Genesis 17:15-19.

"Can a son be born to a man who is a hundred years old? Can Sarah bear a son when she is ninety?" (NEB) Abraham asked God this at the promise of making Sarah "mother of nations."

This is only a preview of God's resurrection power—bringing forth life from a dead womb. God asks so little of us, but is willing to give so much. All that was asked of Sarah was to change her name from Sarai. God elevated her both in name and in being, as some scholars believe her new name meant queen. Abraham, too, was commanded to change his name from Abram. Such a small symbolic act! In return Sarah was promised that "kings [should] spring from her."

When we profess our belief in God and in Jesus Christ, we also change our names. We call ourselves *Christian*. The name we wear is only a symbol attesting to our faithfulness. With our profession, we also receive new life.

Behind our name should lie a strong belief in God's word and a willingness to be used as an instrument of the faith. When our name is called, visions of deeds should appear—visions of feeding the sheep, visiting the sick, liberating the oppressed. Christians should be able to stand behind their name in all they do—in love, in forgiveness, in obedience. Our name is a symbolic commitment to God to follow the teachings of Jesus.

Prayer: *Giver of life, help us realize that we are not only life-producers, but also care-givers. We are the peacemakers. We are the pure in heart. We are the merciful. We are the meek. Rekindle our faith so that we are strengthened to stand behind our name. Amen.*

Wednesday, February 27   Read Psalm 105:1-6.

What are the terms for which we have contracted as Christians? Psalm 105:1-6 poetically spells out the terms.

One clear commitment in the psalm is to evangelism. How willing are we to use the Lord's name sincerely in our work places or at social gatherings? Does praising God publicly, outside the church, seem somehow unfashionable? The Bible verse "The wages of sin is death" (Rom. 6:23, KJV) is rarely heard anymore in this permissive society, and too many people haven't the vaguest notion of what is meant by the remainder of that verse, "but the gift of God is eternal life through Jesus Christ our Lord" (KJV).

As offspring of Abraham, we have an obligation to make the Lord's deeds known in all the world, inside the church and outside the church. But our songs and our witness are only symbols of our faith. The fervor with which we sing reflects the depth of our relationship with the Lord and the Lord's mighty works. Our witness should make others want to take up the cross and follow Christ. But the voice that sings should also be the voice that speaks for justice; the hand that passes the collection plate should also be the hand that brings food to the poor.

As Abraham was God's servant, so must his descendants be. We must make known God's power and God's laws. We must be doers of the word and preachers and teachers of the word beyond our songs and witness.

Prayer: *Hear our song, O God! You have done great things, your power is boundless, your grace is sufficient. Help us sing our song of praise so loudly and sincerely that Abraham's heart swells with pride. Amen.*

Thursday, February 28   Read Psalm 105:7-11.

In verses 9 and 10, reference is made to "the covenant made with Abraham, his oath given to Isaac, the decree by which he bound himself for Jacob" (NEB). The fact that the psalmist did not stop with Abraham but went on to list other descendants with whom the Lord had made covenants, tells us that the Lord's covenant is forever. We are one of the "thousand generations" to which God's promise extends.

What kind of outward symbol is required today to reflect our commitment? Have we used the land God has given us for the good of humanity or for our own good exclusively? Have we used the land only to build our own brand of altars?

In this time in history when there are many refugees who, like Abraham and his people before the covenant, have neither land nor homes, we are called on to be fulfillers of the covenant in a way that is more than symbolic. Churches increasingly serve as places of refuge for the uprooted. Congregations find themselves called to house the Haitians, find jobs for the Cubans, clothe the Salvadorans.

In other lands, lands that have not prospered as ours has, the church has bound physical as well as spiritual wounds. At the same time more churches were built, huts were also built. The church has been in those lands; Abraham's descendants have been in those lands, baptizing and digging wells, all for the joy of fulfilling the covenant!

Prayer: *This is my song, O God of all the nations, that people the world over will come to know of your greatness and benefit from the terms of your covenant. Amen.*

Friday, March 1   Read Romans 4:16-25.

Was Abraham chosen by God because he had obeyed the law? Romans 4:16 says, "The promise was made on the ground of faith, in order that it might be a matter of sheer grace . . . not only for those who hold by the law, but for those also who have the faith of Abraham" (NEB).

What was the nature of those with whom God chose to bargain? Should they have adhered to every commandment and every facet of scripture? The criterion was based on their "righteousness that came from faith" (Rom. 4:13, NEB).

God enters into contracts with twentieth-century servants, too. One such servant was a man of unshakable faith, a leader of a refugee people of sorts—Dr. Martin Luther King, Jr. When he went to the mountaintop, to which he referred in a speech during his last days, was it to make a covenant with the Lord? It was as if he had received a promise on the day he declared his dream of a time when the children of slaves and slaveholders would live in brotherhood and Mississippi would become a stronghold of freedom and justice.

Can such a promise come to pass in a nation of institutional racism and global corporate exploitation? King believed it would come to pass; he died for it. Today changes have taken place that those past 40 years of age thought they would never witness. What reason do we have to doubt that the full promise will be fulfilled?

Our marches and protests are but symbols of a deeper faith, a deeper commitment to bring about equality in this land and in other lands.

Prayer: *Dear God, you are known for showing yourself to the oppressed, for making them your servants—servants to their own liberation and to the liberation of others. Thank you for your "sheer grace." Amen.*

Saturday, March 2   Read Mark 8:31-32.

When persons make a commitment to follow Christ, the terms of fulfillment are not easy. Nothing in Christianity promises a life free of trials and tribulations. On the contrary. During his final days Jesus told his disciples that "the Son of Man had to undergo great sufferings, and to be rejected by the elders, chief priests, and doctors of the law; to be put to death, and to rise again three days afterwards" (NEB).

Peter was perplexed. Had not Jesus just told them he was the Messiah? If this was what was in store for the Messiah, what would be the lot of ordinary flesh?

Jesus' rebuttal was that Peter was thinking as humans think, not as God thinks. Because we have been baptized, has this symbolic act overcome our love of comfort? Just as our baptism did not necessarily elevate us in the eyes of our forebears, our family, our church, probably we will still not be praised for our Christlike deeds.

Following the "law" can earn us such disparaging labels as "Puritan," "self-righteous," "holier-than-thou." Showing grace can win us such labels as "coward," "submissive," "fool." Leaders in movements for justice, as a rule, have short lives. Is it any wonder that many "Christians" stop with the outward symbols?

In order to fulfill our commitment as Christians, we cannot be concerned with the consequences of being Christlike. Rising above such concerns is a milestone in our Christian development for which we should sing praises to the Lord.

Prayer: *Understand us, Lord, and give us strength, strength to be what we say we are. Give us courage, courage to model our lives after the Christ. All praises to the Messiah! Amen.*

73

Sunday, March 3   Read Mark 8:34-38.

"If anyone wants to come with me . . . he must forget himself, carry his cross, and follow me. For whoever wants to save his own life will lose it; but whoever loses his life for me and for the gospel will save it" (TEV).

Often Christians confuse taking up the cross with flaunting the cross. They become more self-centered than Christ-centered. The glow of our costume-jewelry crosses can blind us to the true meaning of what we are to be about. Pastors with the gift to preach find it difficult to go to a trouble-torn, poverty-stricken church. It is better if the church is able to pay upward of $30,000 and is in a city where the family can be adequately entertained and the children properly schooled.

We judge our ministry by our membership rosters. Our churches cannot be used for shelters because the hungry and weary may mess up the carpet. Only the educated can lead, lest the uneducated get too emotional on our televised worship service, and our congregation be seen as unsophisticated.

The difference between the outward symbol and the inner commitment is the difference between gaining the world and losing one's own soul. We, like Jacob, have built places of worship in response to a call from God, but many of these places have become white elephants that the members have deserted because other racial groups have taken over "their" church.

Outward symbols of faith are empty without an inner commitment to God's kingdom.

Prayer: *God Almighty, strengthen our commitment. Dedicate our hearts, our ambitions, our actions to building a world capable of fulfilling every physical and spiritual need. Amen.*

NEW LIFE AND OLD LAWS

March 4-10, 1985   **Richard W. Fisher†**
Monday, March 4   Read Exodus 20:1-17.

"God spoke, and these were his words: . . . "(TEV)

What a task! Sorting out the words of Moses from those of later editors . . . Deciding which commandments reflect a long development of social and cultic patterns . . . Concluding whether the Decalogue came first as the footing of the whole covenant enterprise, or whether it came last as the capstone of evolving civil and cultic law.

What a cacophony! Lengthy arguments developed into manuscripts and shelved . . . Liberals arguing with conservatives . . . Scholars of the twentieth century debating scholars of the nineteenth century . . . Voices babbling in German and French and Swedish and English . . . Shouts from the Third World rising to a crescendo.

Then, suddenly, silence! "God speaks, and these are God's words . . . "

How do you hear the voice of God? It is there, mixed in with the voices of Moses and tradition, distorted at times, but it is there. It is there in the arguments of scholars and the puzzlements of students. Suddenly, unexpectedly, it breaks through. And when it does, there is no mistaking it. God speaks. The will and power and wisdom of God breaks through the babble, and there is silence. There is solitude.

Prayer: *O thou life-giving Word, incarnate in human voices and human flesh, break through once more. Share your vision of our lives lived in harmony with you and with all humanity. In Jesus' name. Amen.*

---

†Superintendent, Western District, South Dakota Conference, The United Methodist Church, Rapid City, South Dakota.

Tuesday, March 5 Read Deuteronomy 6:4-15.

"I am the Lord your God, who brought you out of . . . bondage" (Exod. 20:2).

Where do the Ten Commandments begin? I remember my surprise when I discovered that Lutherans and Roman Catholics number their commandments differently than my denomination does. While not a major stumbling block to the ecumenical spirit, it did remind me that not all persons read the scripture in the same way.

There is, however, general agreement among Christians that the Ten Commandments begin with the command, "Thou shalt have no other gods." Perhaps that explains our stereotype of the Old Testament: "The Old Testament is the book of law, while the New Testament is the book of grace," we casually remark.

What a distortion! For the Jews, the first commandment is, "I am the Lord your God who brought you out of Egypt, out of the land of slavery."

The commandments are grounded in grace! Before there is law, there is liberation. Deliverance precedes obedience, and the two taken together become salvation.

The Decalogue is not some law imposed upon us to keep us from having a good time. Nor is the Decalogue a description of what we must do in order to please God. Rather, the Ten Commandments describe our best possible response to the God who created us and who liberates us from the destructive powers of life. They give clues to what our salvation entails. They become instruments of our salvation because they describe the two basic relationships of life: to God and to neighbor.

Devotional exercise: *Reflect on an experience of grace that resulted in a change in your behavior.*

Wednesday, March 6   Read Deuteronomy 8:11-18.

"You shall have no other gods before me" (Exod. 20:3).

This commandment is the hardest. If we can get this one right, the others will fall into place. The problem is we don't often get it right. We know we should, and that is somewhat important. We want to get it right, and that is even more important. But actually to put God first in our lives, in practice—that is something else!

There are so many things close at hand that keep getting our attention! They occupy so much of our time and thoughts, and, yes, money. All of them are attractive, and some of them are even important.

History, indeed, is a rather tragic narrative of the ways we allow other things to come before God. We love God; but we also love our nation and, well, the nation exerts more pressure to conform than God does, so. . . . We love God, but we also want to feel secure, and there are many ways we can insure our security, so. . . . We love God, but God defines the good life in terms of servanthood, and we want to be free of menial tasks and to fulfill ourselves, so. . . .

We develop sophisticated ways to get around this commandment, fooling ourselves and sometimes others. We try to get God to bless those activities and loves which are really most important in our lives. Somehow, if I can convince myself that God really wants me to serve Old First Church with its fifteen-room parsonage in the better part of town, then I don't have to choose between materialism and God. The first commandment is the hardest.

Prayer: *Merciful God, I need you to be first in my life, not just because you insist on it but because I know that the only way I'll ever get all the pieces to fall into place is to put first things first. Amen.*

Thursday, March 7   Read John 2:13-22.

"Remember the sabbath day, to keep it holy" (Exod. 20:8).

The Sabbath is to be kept holy, not because God needs it but because we need it. We need it to remind ourselves of the value of the sacred in life. Some things are to be treated with respect so that all things may be respected.

Perhaps that is why Jesus cleansed the Temple. It wasn't because it was wrong for religious pilgrims to purchase sacrifices. It wasn't because it was wrong to sell sacrificial animals and birds to tourists. It was wrong because somewhere along the line the sellers forgot why they were selling, forgot that their calling was to provide a service to devout worshipers.

They had begun to count the crowds. They entered each holiday season hoping the take would be the best ever. They began to dream up gimmicks to increase their sales. Almost unconsciously, they had evolved from servants into merchandisers. What had begun as a service to travellers had been perverted. The sacred was profaned.

The Sabbath, like the Temple, was intended to be kept holy, to be set apart for rest and remembrance. In the economy of the late twentieth century, it may be impossible to recapture the letter of the law, but we would do well to consider the spirit of the law. We need time for rest and reflection. We need holy space to remind ourselves of the presence of the sacred in life.

Prayer: *Holy God, you have set us apart for servanthood, and you have given us holy time and holy places for remembrance and reflection. Help us to respect what is sacred—in us and in others and in the world—for our sake and for Christ's sake. Amen.*

Friday, March 8   Read Deuteronomy 5:1-5.

The Ten Commandments are a part of our identity as the people of God. When my teenage son emerged from his cabin at church camp one Sunday morning, he was all dressed up, even wearing a shirt and tie. The other youths, still in cut-offs and jeans, began to tease him. It did not seem to bother them that they were about to go into town to worship. John took the teasing for a few minutes, then straightened his five-foot-five-inch body and said, "Listen, you guys! Wearing a shirt and tie on Sunday morning is a family tradition!"

In that moment, at least, my son remembered who he was by remembering whose he was. He expressed that identity in his behavior.

So it is with the people of God. Why do we keep God's commandments? Because we are members of God's family, and it is a tradition of that family to live according to the commandments. That obedience tells us who we are by reminding us whose we are. We are God's people. We are the people who observe the Sabbath. We are the people who honor our parents. We are the people who do not murder or commit adultery or steal or bear false witness. Why? Because it is a family tradition that began with our spiritual ancestors.

Is there pride here? There can be. Is there pretension here? There may be. But there is also a sense of identity. We know who we are by what we do. We obey or at least we seek to obey the Ten Commandments because we are the people of the God who gave them to us.

Prayer: *O God, our parent, we would keep the traditions alive because they remind us that we belong to you and because they give glimpses of the ways you would have your people relate to you and to each other. Amen.*

Saturday, March 9 Read 2 Corinthians 4:5-7.

"You shall not make for yourself a graven image" (Exod. 20:4*a*).

No images! The God who speaks through earthquake, wind, and fire does not want earthquake, wind, or fire to be substitutes for God. No event or experience is to be mistaken for the God who acts in world events and human experiences.

No images! The God of Abraham and Sarah, of Moses and Miriam, and of Jesus Christ has always been an elusive sort of God. Even the name by which God is revealed to Moses is elusive: *Yahweh,* we read; but how do we translate it?

"I am who I am."
"I shall be who I shall be."
"I bring to pass what I bring to pass."
"I shall be present the way I choose to be."

No single translation adequately captures all that the sacred name contains. As a confirmation student translated it one day, "You can't put God in a cage!"

We catch glimpses of God, but we cannot catch God. Images are stop-action photography. They tell us what has been. They express the when and what and how of our experiences of God, whether in wind and fire or in mountain vista or in word and sacrament. The Hidden One has stepped forth in a particular way and in a particular moment, and life has taken on new meaning. That is the source of images. The danger comes when any particular moment, any particular insight is held up as if it were the only true portrait of God.

A book may be the place an author encounters us, but the book is not the author! No images!

Devotional exercise: *Breathe in God's renewing and empowering Spirit. Breathe out images and theologies that have become stale.*

Sunday, March 10   Read Ro

The Ten Commandments speak of the future
sent God's vision of what life for the covenant   ... snall
become. They are promise.

So then, are the thou-shalt-nots replaced by thou-shalts?
Does the word of obligation grow faint while the word of
permission becomes louder? If this is a promise of what you
will become in God's time, is the obligation any less?

The day is coming when you and I shall be satisfied by
God, when we turn to God as the source and fulfillment of
life, when we live and move and have our being in that
relationship with God. The time will come when we stop
searching for God in places where God can't be found, when
we stop seeking substitutes for the real thing. The day is
coming when our relationships with family members and
friends and neighbors and all fellow humans will be lived in
the context of mutual love.

Therefore, because that is who we shall some day be, why
not begin living that way today? If that is who we shall be,
then even now we are free to become the people the commandments describe. We are free to become God's children in
deeds because we have become the children of God's promises. We shall continue to have moments of failure, but we
know who we are and who we are becoming! There will be
days when the promise takes on power, when we are moved
and empowered to step toward the new relationships that the
Ten Commandments hold out to us. Wholeness is restored.
Reconciliation is achieved. Shalom is realized. We are children of God, and therefore, children of the promise!

Prayer: *Lord God, help us to live today in a closer relationship with
you. Amen.*

THROUGH JUDGMENT TO JOY

March 11-17, 1985   **John A. Cairns†**
Monday, March 11   Read 2 Chronicles 36:14-23.

These final verses of Second Chronicles detail the conquest of Jerusalem and the beginning of the Babylonian exile. The writer hints at the overwhelming evidence which has built up against the Hebrew people. The prophets had warned them, and now God has judged them. That judgment is not transcendent nor supernatural; it is real and historical.

We have difficulty seeing how the hand of God could be present in the destruction of the Temple and the slaughter or exile of the Chosen People. But the "chronicler" has a larger view of God and God's justice. God's judgment is neither frivolous nor misguided. It finds its mark and establishes its result in the people's history.

Could it be that we, like many of the ancient Hebrews, complain so loudly about God's judgment that we never see the redemption? The editors of Chronicles made no such mistake. They ended their history with the announcement of the coming of God's redemption (vs. 22-23). Our Lenten reflections on God's judgment must never be without this companion note of hope and salvation.

Prayer: *(As you pray this week try to "listen" for twice as long as you "talk.") God, we own our need to be judged and our desire to be redeemed. Deal with us lovingly, we pray. Amen.*

---

†Minister of Education and Administration, First Community Church, Columbus, Ohio.

Tuesday, March 12   Read Jeremiah 6:16-21;
                                              Psalm 137:1.

Jerusalem has fallen. The healthy, productive, and fit among the people of Judah have been convoyed into Babylon. A time of exile has begun. It is an experience of death.

The psalmist describes the traditional Semitic mourning custom in the opening verse. It was the custom for people in that part of the world to do their grieving seated on the ground. The mourning the psalm describes is not only for the loss of human life but for the loss of a way of life. In the midst of competing cultures and rival religions, God's chosen people had held onto their uniqueness; but as the prophets had told them time and time again, they were hanging on to only the externals. They had maintained the requirements of Hebrew practice while ignoring the will of God of their ancestors.

To some of those exiled Hebrews of the sixth century B.C. the loss of Jerusalem could have prompted a switch to a rival god, to a deity with ample power to insure that its followers would never have to undergo such a tragedy. Yet this prophet's faith in Yahweh does not waver.

Without the threat of political or religious oppression, it is easy to focus our attention on the identifiable external traits of our religious practice. When we mourn the departure of a pastor more than our lack of faith, cultural trappings have ensnared us once again.

Prayer: *Lord, as we consider all of the externals of our Christian faith, help us to separate means from ends and bring clarity to our internal commitments. Amen.*

Wednesday, March 13   Read Psalm 137.

In his Broadway musical *Godspell,* Stephen Schwartz used a musical setting of Psalm 137 to provide the background for Christ's crucifixion. It would be no surprise to see a contemporary writer take liberties with a biblical text, but Schwartz does not. The show song follows the psalm (vs. 2-4) carefully except for one meaningful change—in verse 2, where the psalm reads " . . . we hung up our lyres," he substitutes the word *lives* for lyres.

The psalmist reports the resistance of the exiled Israelites. They refused to allow their songs of faith to become simply entertainment for their captors. As a kind of practical protest, they "hung up their lyres," resisting the attempt to trivialize their heritage and their hope.

Facing the cross, the stakes increase. It is easy to trivialize the sacrifice of Christ for each of us. To stand against that temptation requires the sacrifice of all that we are, of our very lives. When we take our faith-stand, we are required to hang our lives on that same cross, lest the story of Golgotha become trivial entertainment.

The forces and the objects of life that hold each of us captive will make constant and heavy demands upon us. We would like to be at peace with our "captors," but we cannot compromise principles and remain faithful to our calling. So we endure humiliation because we know that if we were to capitulate, we would, like the psalmist (vs. 5-6), find even greater agony.

Prayer: *Lord, help us to know the reality of your pain and sacrifice for us. Then give us courage to take our stand for you. Amen.*

Thursday, March 14   Read John 3:11-15.

In talking with Nicodemus, Jesus refers to an episode recorded in Numbers 21:1-9. It was an Exodus event. The Israelites were complaining bitterly about their wilderness surroundings, yearning to return to the familiar settings of Egypt. And God brought judgment to bear on their faithfulness and impatience. Fiery serpents invaded the camp "and they bit the people, so that many people of Israel died" (Num. 21:6).

In the midst of this judgment, God instructed Moses to make a bronze serpent and put it on a pole. Anyone who looked at that serpent after having been bitten, God declared, would live.

Now, in his nighttime conversation with a teacher of the scriptures, Jesus alludes to that historic episode in order to reveal the purpose of his life and ministry. He is the new serpent who must be lifted up so that those under judgment can live.

It takes only momentary reflection to recognize the points of similarity between our patterns and those of the ancient Israelites. We are pleased and proud to be God's people, but we want to maintain control of our lives. We criticize God, trusting only in ourselves. And God judges us harshly for our faithlessness and impatience. Still, God is merciful and has provided a means of deliverance for us. "As Moses lifted up the serpent in the wilderness, so must the Son of man be lifted up" (John 3:14). And Jesus Christ was lifted up—on the cross and in the ascension. We have only to look up and live.

Prayer: *Keep our eyes and our lives fixed on you, O Lord. Amen.*

85

Friday, March 15   Read John 3:16-21.

Passages of scripture become familiar because they contain kernels of value and importance. Yet as we hear such passages over and over again, they can lose their impact. The words become so familiar we don't really listen to them any longer. Such can easily be the case for this chapter of John.

John helps us separate judgment from condemnation. As we have reflected on God's judgment, we have seen steady reference to human disasters. Rulers are overthrown; cities are destroyed; lives are threatened or lost. It is easy to stop our reading at that point and identify God's judgment with "cruel and unusual punishment." We need to "let the other shoe drop," the shoe of mercy and redemption.

When Jesus says that he has not come to condemn the world, he is speaking to that issue. Clearly we are to be held accountable for the way we live our lives; God has expectations for our behavior. It remains true that "all have sinned and fall short of the glory of God" (Rom. 3:23), but the Incarnation is true as well. God sent the Son; the "other shoe" dropped. And the Christ comes into our midst not with a pointed finger but with open arms, making sure we know how much God loves us and is willing to forgive us.

To pretend we do not deserve to be judged is a foolhardy attempt to replace God's authority with our own. Our joy is knowing how mercifully our Lord, the Almighty, wields authority.

Prayer: *O Lord, give us the honesty to acknowledge how much we need your mercy. Bring fresh reality into John's familiar words of promise. Amen.*

Saturday, March 16   Read Ephesians 2:4-10.

To be alive—to be ALIVE! There is an exhilaration and joy that comes just in saying the words. And when our frame of reference shifts from "having a wonderful day" to sharing life in God's presence for ages and ages to come, the euphoria can be overwhelming. Our enthusiasm is dampened, however, when we note Paul's description of our necessary death.

Clearly Paul speaks not of physical death but spiritual death. Our question is, What does that mean? Those of whom he speaks obviously have a bodily life. But spiritual death is the result of alienation, feeling forsaken by God and turned over to the power of evil. To Paul's audience such a death was a dreadful experience, and to be rescued out of the midst of it was an offer of life with unlimited possibility.

In our technological culture we have defined death only in physical terms. Yet our experiences often suggest that Paul's definition was closer to the truth of our nature. The words of the prodigal's father, "My son was dead, and is alive again" (Luke 15:24), ring true. They describe not only the lives of people we know about but in many cases our own lives as well.

The celebration of life is given meaning by the reality of the living death from which we have been rescued. Only as we recognize where we have been are we able to fully celebrate this gift of God which we so glibly call *life*.

Prayer: *Dear God, in our alienation help us to see where we have taken ourselves and how foreign that is to our created nature. Deliver us from our spiritual death and restore us to life, in the name of Jesus Christ our Savior. Amen.*

Sunday, March 17   Read Ephesians 2:14-18.

The mission and the message of Jesus came to those who were far off and those who were near; those whose life journeys had carried them in many directions (most of which would be quickly labeled non-Christian) and those whose journeys were limited to brief and semi-bold junkets never out of sight of their home base.

Those of us who have wandered far afield know the ambiguity of such freedom. The essential pegs seem to be missing. There is no place to hang our hat, focus our attention, or draw our strength. We become restless hearts.

Those who have never ventured beyond their personal "sheltered walkway" also feel at a loss. It is impossible to own something you've never put to the test. Life becomes an example of the old proverb, "Nothing ventured, nothing gained."

Understanding the agonies of our self-chosen paths, God offers us peace in knowing Christ. Here the wanderer can find a home and the reluctant disciple a challenge. Here the lost can find a point of focus and the weak a new source of strength. And for each misfit, Christ promises the reconciliation we have sought but never been able to accomplish with our Creator.

Now we are made whole. Our joy is full because we have become what we are meant to be—part of the one body of Christ, those who have found their peace in the One who was dead but now lives so that we may live also!

Prayer: *We rejoice, O Lord, in the life you offer us in Jesus Christ. Disturb us; keep us restless until we find the peace that you have made ready for our homecoming. Amen.*

A New Heart and a New Covenant

March 18-24, 1985   **Bill Bates†**
Monday, March 18   Read Psalm 51:10-14.

Sometime during the argument I suddenly realized that I was wrong. By the time I came to that realization, I was also angry—very angry. My pride wouldn't let me back down, so I stomped out of the committee meeting having said what should have been left unsaid. The meeting continued without me.

Back in the church office I sat behind my desk trembling with anger. But shortly, the anger with another turned into anger with myself. The fact of the matter was that I had been wrong and had compounded the wrong by the way I had acted and by what I had said.

My notes from that morning's sermon were scattered all over the desk. The scripture text was from Psalm 51. "Create in me a clean heart, O God, and put a new and right spirit within me." If I could have sent my heart to a dry cleaner, I would have, because I was not feeling good about myself. "Cast me not away from thy presence, and take not thy Holy Spirit from me." *God* hadn't taken the Spirit away. *I* had walked away.

Clearly, God's presence was very much back in that room in the committee meeting. And the only way that I could restore a clean heart and right spirit was to swallow my foolish pride, go back, and apologize.

Prayer: *Lord God, a clean heart and steadfast spirit do not come easily for me. Uphold me with your Spirit even in my most obstinate moments. Amen.*

---

†Pastor, Zion United Methodist Church, Grand Forks, North Dakota.

Tuesday, March 19   Read Psalm 51:15-17.

Any animal bigger than a Saint Bernard makes me nervous. Nevertheless, I let my son talk me into a horseback ride in the Theodore Roosevelt National Park in western North Dakota. Take one great big horse named Boomer, add steep and narrow trails; you have all the ingredients necessary for a rather major anxiety attack.

As I climbed onto this enormous animal's back, one of the ranch hands said, "Don't worry. He's trail broke." And Boomer was a marvelously surefooted and gentle horse. I was able to enjoy the beautiful panorama as we rode because Boomer had been well trained.

The psalmist speaks of a broken spirit and a broken and contrite heart as being an acceptable sacrifice to God. God doesn't want a broken-down spirit or a broken-into-pieces spirit, but rather a spirit that has been gentled and tamed to the Presence, a spirit that does not shy away at the Touch.

As Holy Week draws near, the picture of Jesus in the garden of Gethsemane comes into focus. On his knees, he struggles with a humanness that wishes not to succumb. But finally it comes down to "not my will, but thine, be done" (Luke 22:42*b*). His was a spirit that was comfortable in the presence of God, a spirit acceptive of the Creator's will.

As long as my spirit craves to do its own thing, it will never be attentive to God's will. Unrepentant, I will not be wild and free roaming the wide open plains. Rather, unrepentant, I will be wild and alone—and separated from God.

Prayer: *(Reread Psalm 51:15-17.) Lord, shape me and use me today. Amen.*

Wednesday, March 20   Read Jeremiah 31:31-32.

While my son was small, we had a rule that we held hands when we crossed streets on our walks or when we got out of the car in the Sears parking lot. Often, I would have to remind him to wait for me; but occasionally, he remembered the rule and sought my hand and hurried us on our way.

One day, I'm not exactly sure when and I'm not sure who decided; but one day, he no longer needed to be taken by the hand and led in safe paths. We had come to recognize that that particular rule, that covenant, was no longer an essential part of our relationship. We made a new covenant; he conscientiously looks both ways in crossing streets, and he doesn't jump and run from the car. But he doesn't need any hand to keep the covenant.

God had an old covenant with the children of Israel in which God took them by the hand and led them by the law. If they would but keep the terms of the covenant, they would be guided in paths of righteousness. However, the children of Israel kept turning loose of God's hand and running off in the traffic. So God told Jeremiah to announce that a new covenant was in the works. Even Jeremiah didn't know the lengths to which God would go to pay the price of the new covenant. No longer a guiding hand of law to lead them, God would live out a covenant of grace to show them the way.

I like to think it was because of parental example that my son is careful to look both ways at street crossings, and that sometimes he *chooses* to hold my hand and walk with me.

Prayer: *Thank you, Lord, for the care and guidance you continue to give us when we don't choose to hold your hand. Amen.*

Thursday, March 21   Read Jeremiah 31:33-34.

"What's it say?" she demanded to know thrusting the heart-shaped locket in my face. Opening it, I saw the Lord's Prayer written in tiny print.

Annie was three, almost four, and although she couldn't read, she knew the words in the golden locket must be significant. So I read them. "I know that! We say it in church." She insisted that we read it again, and she repeated each phrase after me. Ten minutes later she was back, and we read it again.

The next Sunday in church Annie could pray most of the Lord's Prayer along with the congregation. She had learned the words because they had become important to her.

What a marvelous image Jeremiah chose to announce God's new covenant! A covenant written upon our hearts. God had long covenanted with people, but at a distance. It had been Moses and God on Mt. Sinai and the people down below. The prophet was alone and intimate with God and then went forth to proclaim God's word to the people. The priest in the Holy of Holies alone with God interceded on behalf of the people, but the people weren't there.

But now God says, "I'll no longer cut my covenant in stone. Rather, I'll write it on each human heart. They will know me as their God, and I will know them as my people, each and every one" (AP).

Even before we can read it ourselves, others read the message of God's love on our hearts; and covenantal water is sprinkled on our heads. God's new covenant came in the flesh, incarnate, in Christ Jesus. It remains incarnate, as promised, written on our hearts.

Prayer: *I am yours, God, and you are mine. Amen.*

Friday, March 22   Read John 12:20-26.

The temptation is to skip past those curious Greeks who wanted to meet Jesus and get on to his important message. And yet, their quest for Jesus seems to be the triggering event for the glorifying of Christ. Time and again Jesus had said, "The hour has not yet come" (John 2:4; 7:6, 30; 8:20). But now he says, "The hour has come for the Son of man to be glorified."

Was it that now Jesus could see that his handful of followers would not remain a tiny Jewish sect? Could he see past a few Greeks to untold millions of Gentiles who would seek him in the future?

"We wish to see Jesus," they said. Is that not even now the beginning point of faith? And because we start at that point, does he not still say, "Now the hour has come."

In the scripture passage, at first it seems that Jesus is not answering the request. Gradually, an awareness grows that here is how to conduct our quest for the Savior.

He says that when we are ready to die to ourselves like the single seed in the fertile soil, which dies and becomes fruitful, then we will see him. When we begin to love life in his kingdom more than we love a self-centered, self-serving existence, then we will see him. When we willingly follow and serve him, we will see him and be honored by our Creator.

We dare not ignore those Greek seekers because they are you and I.

Prayer: *We wish to see you, Jesus. Amen.*

Saturday, March 23   Read John 12:27-33.

A half hour earlier it had seemed like an adventure as we sat in the canoe 25 feet below the verticle granite wall. So we had climbed back around through the dense Minnesota forest and worked our way to the sheer drop-off. We were going to jump like cliff divers into the deep, green water below . . . far below . . . very far below. We both looked down, and then with queasy stomachs and jelly legs, we looked at each other.

With all the fear and trembling of his humanity Jesus looked over the edge and said, "Now my heart is troubled" (TEV). He knew why he had come to this point in his life. He knew what God was calling him to do. And in his humanness he knew the cost, the suffering that would be his.

I have to believe that even at this point he could have stepped back and said, "No!" To deny that he had a choice is to deny his humanity. To have submitted without inner turmoil would have denied the cost of God's grace.

"But this is why I came," he said, "for this very hour of suffering" (AP). Jesus accepted the cost because he knew there was a reason to pay the price, a new covenant of grace to be confirmed.

"When I am lifted up from the earth, I will draw everyone to me" (TEV).

My friend and I climbed down the rocks and tamely jumped into the water from a safer height. But I thank God that Jesus did not climb down. High and lifted up, he still draws me to his side.

Prayer: *Lord Jesus, I am eternally indebted to you for choosing to save my life at the cost of yours. Amen.*

Sunday, March 24   Read Hebrews 5:7-10.

In algebra, a formula tells you how to put together a set of symbols to express a mathematical truth. In baking, a recipe tells you how to combine certain ingredients to make a cake. In construction, a blueprint tells you how to put the materials together to erect a building.

The writer of Hebrews wants to be sure we have the formula that expresses God's new covenant, the recipe for the glorification of Christ, the blueprint for our salvation.

Jesus came in the flesh, human in every sense of the word. Because he was human, he did not seek death. It was only through prayers and tears that he was able to submit to God's will. God heard him and taught him obedience through his suffering. It was in his total submission to the divine will that Jesus was glorified and made perfect. And only then could he become the means of our salvation, the sufficient sacrifice, the expression of God's grace.

Having successfully become the victim of our sins, Christ was made the high priest, Melchizedek, the King of Righteousness.

The formula is completed when I recognize how I fit into the equation. God became human *for me*; Jesus submitted to the cross *for me*, was made perfect *for me*, offers God's grace *for me*.

I have done nothing to deserve such a covenant. I am simply the grateful recipient of the peace and strength that comes from God.

Prayer: *Knowing what you have done and are doing for me, may I live confidently in your grace, loving God. Amen.*

March 25-31, 1985
Monday, March 25

Carol Foltz†
Read Mark 10:32-34;
Psalm 31:9-16.

We can only imagine what it was like for Jesus to be going to Jerusalem this time. He knew that this would be his last trip to Jerusalem with his friends. No one else seemed to realize it. The disciples could not grasp what Jesus was trying to tell them when he said that he would suffer many things and be rejected by the leaders of his people, and that he would die. For them it was just another year, another Passover. Jesus knew he was going to die.

How could he go, knowing that what was awaiting him was total rejection and misunderstanding? Even his closest friends could not be with him on this part of his journey. He was alone.

One reality kept Jesus going toward Jerusalem. He knew that even though no other person would be with him, and even though he would be rejected by the religious leaders, and even though he would die a repulsive death, God was with him. His Father was his advocate. Jesus could even face the cross knowing that God was his deliverer.

Suggestion for meditation: *Meditate on Jesus' trip to Jerusalem. He was with his friends, but they did not understand the awesome task he had. He was going for a joyous celebration, but during this celebration he would be crucified. His only source of strength was God, and Jesus knew that God would provide. Has God ever given you a task that people who are close to you have not understood? When you are alone, who is your source of support?*

†Director of Christian Education and Youth Ministries, Board of Christian Education and Evangelism, Moravian Church in America, South, Winston-Salem, North Carolina.

Tuesday, March 26   Read Mark 10:35-45;
                                Psalm 31:9-16.

James and John had a very important request to ask of Jesus. They wanted to sit beside him in his glory; to have the places of honor reserved for the king's most trusted friends and advisors, the ones who did what the king needed to have done. James and John wanted to know if they were the closest to Jesus.

Jesus clarified their relationship to him, but he did not answer their questions about seating. He said, "Can you drink the cup I drink or be baptized with the baptism I am baptized with?" (NIV) Jesus was telling them that in order for them to be the ones he could depend on, they would have to travel a road very much like his. This road was not a road of honor; it was a road of service. "For even the Son of Man did not come to be served, but to serve, and to give his life as a ransom for many" (NIV). Before they could sit at the banquet with him, they had work to do.

Jesus knew his call was a call to service. Our call is the same. We are called to give, not to get. Serving as Jesus did will not bring us honor from people, but it will allow us to drink from the cup Jesus drank from and to be baptized with the baptism he was baptized with.

Prayer: *Lord, give us grace to see that serving you is our call. Humble us so that we will be able to serve. Amen.*

97

Wednesday, March 27   Read Isaiah 50:4-9*a*.

God is Lord. God is Sovereign. This means that God has ultimate control over everything in the universe. Fortunately, Jesus knew this. As he faced the certainty of his crucifixion, he was not frightened by the apparent hopelessness of the situation. He knew that God was in control of everything that was happening to him.

He knew that within a few days he would be crucified, but he also knew that God would not let him stay dead. No, the ultimate issue was not that Jesus would die, but, that he would live again! Death is frightening, but resurrection is glorious. Jesus could see what God was going to do.

Wouldn't it be great if we could look at life as Jesus did— knowing what is ultimate and what is not. With this knowledge, Jesus was even able to see beyond his death. Think of how it would be to look beyond our temporary concerns, no matter how difficult they are, and to know that ultimately God is in control. We can when we know the truth. God is Sovereign.

Prayer: *God, you are Sovereign. You have control over the universe and over our lives. May we not be stifled by fear but live in freedom because we know that you are the Sovereign God. Take from us the temporary concerns of our lives that act as blinders so that we can see what is true. Help us face the circumstances of our lives with confidence that you will help us overcome. Amen.*

Thursday, March 28   Read Mark 10:46-52.

There came a time in Jesus' ministry when he deliberately made his way to Jerusalem. His task was no longer to heal and preach, but to go to Jerusalem. In the drama of this situation, one can picture Jesus making his way to Jerusalem with the weight of his task bearing him down.

Everywhere he went, crowds gathered around him asking for his help. On this particular day he was walking through Jericho accompanied by his disciples and the crowds of people. There was a blind man, Bartimaeus, who was sitting by the road as Jesus passed. He called out for Jesus to help him. Jesus heard him and told him that his faith had made him well. Jesus took the time to listen to this man even when he had the world's salvation as his task. He was not too involved in his own concerns to show this blind beggar his love.

A friend said once that she does not ask God to help her with the everyday things of life. She only goes to God with the major problems. Bartimaeus knew something that this friend has not yet learned. Jesus cares about us all the time. He stopped on the way to the cross to help the blind man. Surely, he will help us with every part of our lives.

Prayer: *Lord, help us to realize that you want to be involved with every part of our lives, not just what we think is important. Thank you for caring. Amen.*

Friday, March 29   Read John 12:1-8.

Before Jesus went to Jerusalem, he spent some time with his friends Mary, Martha, and Lazarus. They gave a dinner to honor him. During the dinner Mary took some expensive perfume and anointed Jesus' feet with it, and then she wiped his feet with her hair. When Judas protested this action, Jesus silenced him. He accepted her gift. Mary's gift reminded Jesus that a burial was awaiting him.

This action showed Mary's great love for Jesus. Could it be that Mary's gift of love helped give Jesus the courage to go on to Jerusalem? Mary offered him support at this time in his life. She probably did not understand what Jesus was talking about when he mentioned burial; but he did not need her understanding, only her love.

Mary ministered to Jesus. The secret of her ministry was that she expressed her love to Jesus, and this met a need he had. Mary was willing to risk the disapproval of the others in order to express her love for Jesus. Often we are afraid to risk and express our love for others, and in doing so we miss opportunities for ministry. There may be someone we know who is facing some serious circumstances in life and we have the opportunity to minister to that person by our love.

Prayer: *(Think of someone you love and keep this person in mind as you pray.) Lord, help me to be available to minister to my friend. Amen.*

Saturday, March 30   Read Psalm 118:19-29;
                                          Acts 4:1-12.

Words from the Old Testament continually find their way into the writings of the New Testament. In some cases words that were not written specifically as prophecy are interpreted as prophecy.

After Pentecost, when Peter was explaining about Jesus' death to the elders of the law in Jerusalem, he referred to Jesus as the "stone you builders rejected, which has become the capstone" (NIV). He borrowed this verse from the Psalms, but these words became alive for Peter when he saw them in light of Jesus' death and resurrection. He now saw Jesus as the stone the builders rejected and the one who became the capstone.

Peter had experienced both a relationship with Jesus and a filling by the Holy Spirit. With these, God's word became real and took on new meaning. He could interpret the happenings in his own life in light of the scripture.

We have that same privilege. The scripture can become as real to us and enlighten our lives today just as it did for Peter. But we must read it and then put it into our hearts in order for it to make such a difference. If we take the time to do this, God's word will flow through us and out of us and enrich our lives.

Prayer: *Dear God, bind your word to our hearts, and let your word enlighten our lives. Make us hungry for your word, and don't let us be content in not knowing it. Amen.*

March 31 (Palm Sunday)
Read Mark 11:1-11.

"Hosanna! Blessed is he who comes in the name of the Lord!"

As the people gathered for the Passover festival, they brought with them a great anticipation that the Messiah would come. This is why Jesus was greeted with the palms and the hosannas. People were ready for the Messiah. They hoped and begged that he would come soon and relieve them of the burden of Rome. Each year they greeted people with hosannas and palms in hope that this would be the year.

This was the year, but only Jesus realized it. It is possible that his disciples had some hint that Jesus was the Messiah, but they expected him to bring in his kingdom immediately. They did not expect him to die.

Jesus knew that he was the Messiah, but he also knew that humankind didn't stand a chance if he didn't go the way of the cross. So he rode the donkey into Jerusalem listening to the welcome, and he prepared himself for his death. Thankfully for us, he chose the suffering way and not the way his disciples would have chosen. Any other way but the cross would have been a shortcut. Indeed, no other way would have achieved the divine intent and purpose. Jesus knew it and chose to give us salvation.

Prayer: *Jesus, give us grace to accept your gift of salvation. Never let us take your gift lightly. Amen.*

GOD'S RESPONSE TO OUR HUMAN CONDITION

April 1-7, 1985   **Robert V. Dodd†**
Monday, April 1   Read 1 Corinthians 1:18-31.

When in the wilderness the Israelites encountered poisonous snakes which bit many of them and caused them to die, God instructed Moses to make a bronze snake and put it up on a pole. Then God promised that anyone who was bitten by a snake and looked at the symbolic image would not die from the deadly bite (Num. 21:8-9). Jesus referred to this incident and compared himself to the bronze snake when he said, "Just as Moses lifted up the snake in the desert, so the Son of Man must be lifted up, that everyone who believes in him may have eternal life" (John 3:14-15, NIV).

In Christ we find God's wisdom most fully expressed as God responds to our human condition. Our human condition means that we are both perpetrators of sin and also victims of it. But God has given us hope in Christ, so that everyone who looks to Christ may have assurance of eternal life and experience freedom from bondage to sin.

Paul suggested that the Gentiles sought to address the human condition through a system of correct thought, and the Jews sought to address it through miraculous signs of God's approval. But God's wisdom provides us with a solution that meets both needs. Take a long hard look at the Christ of Calvary and you will discover a God who is on your side.

Prayer affirmation: *Christ is my power and wisdom.*

---

†Pastor, Stanley United Methodist Church, Stanley, North Carolina.

Tuesday, April 2   Read Hebrews 4:14-16; 5:7-9.

Where would we be without our friends, those people who know all about us and truly care for us? Count yourself fortunate if you have a few such friends that you can trust with your innermost thoughts and feelings.

Sometimes we experience a sense of loneliness, thinking that nobody really cares what happens to us or fully understands us. We mistakenly believe that no one else has ever dealt with the kinds of temptations, frustrations, and disappointments which we face. No one has ever harbored the secret dreams and ambitions which we possess. But scripture reminds us that there is a friend who is closer than even a sister or brother is. Christ knows what it is like to be fully human and to experience the same kinds of frustrations and aspirations which we experience. Christ walked where we walk and yet never lost that vital connection with God.

As the great High Priest who enters the holy place on our behalf, Christ identifies with our humanity. *In Christ we find a friend who knows all about us and yet still loves us enough to die for us.* Christ sees the best that is within us as well as the worst. Jesus not only anticipated Peter's denial and the scattering of the disciples, but also made provision for their regrouping and becoming spiritually empowered to fulfill God's mission for their lives. Truly we have a friend in high places!

Prayer affirmation: *Jesus is always with me, fully understands me, and is a friend who is totally trustworthy.*

Wednesday, April 3   Read Acts 10:34-43.

For over an hour, the man poured out his grief concerning his disintegrating marriage. He and his wife had tried everything they knew to resolve their differences, but nothing seemed to work. Knowing that they were both Christians, I said to the man, "Never underestimate the power of Jesus to help and to heal you." After a few months, with their attention focused upon Jesus as their source of healing, and with much prayer and dialogue, their marriage was revitalized.

Our tendency is to want to patch things up piecemeal, applying bandages to first one sore spot and then another. But it is only as the reality of Jesus touches our lives that we are made completely whole. There are sins that need to be forgiven, harmful attitudes and destructive habits that need to be corrected, hurts that need to be healed, spiritual energies that need to be intensified or redirected, broken relationships that need to be mended, and physical illnesses that need to be cured. *But it is only in Christ that we find our ultimate source of healing and wholeness.*

Simon Peter gladly announced to a paralytic named Aeneas, "Jesus Christ heals you" (Acts 9:34, NIV), and the man was instantly healed of his infirmity. As Peter later discovered through a vision which the Lord gave him and through a Gentile named Cornelius, the Lord's blessings are for everyone without regard to race, nationality, or culture. That includes you and me because "Jesus Christ is the same yesterday and today and forever" (Heb. 13:8, NIV).

Prayer affirmation: *Jesus Christ can heal me.*

Thursday, April 4   Read Mark 14:12-26;
                                        Isaiah 52:13–53:12.

She came down the aisle wrapped in furs and sparkling with diamonds and knelt to receive Holy Communion. As I held the tray of wafers before her, I said, "Jesus loves you and died for you." The expression of shock and amazement on her face suggested that perhaps for the first time in many years she had understood the true meaning of Holy Communion. No matter how rich or famous we are, we never outgrow our need for the Savior.

We were originally created to believe, to trust, to obey, and to enjoy meaningful communion with our Creator. But sin entered our world and distorted our perceptions, so that we often see God as enemy rather than as friend. To us God is either a vindictive judge or some impersonal, disinterested, and uncaring force. Thus, we experience ambivalent feelings: We cannot fully live without God, but we are also afraid of what living with God might cost us.

In Christ we find God's love spelled out in human terms. The most precious gift that one person can give another is the gift of life. And Jesus says to each of us, "This is my body and blood which is for you!" (AP) If Jesus Christ is for us, then nothing can ultimately defeat us. There is nothing that we can do to make God love us any more or any less. But Holy Communion helps us to accept and thereby experience God's love.

Prayer affirmation: *The cross of Christ proves to me that I am loved with an everlasting love.*

April 5 (Good Friday)
Read John 19:17-30.

Who can fully explain the mystery of the Atonement? I cannot adequately explain it, but I do know that Jesus died for us physically so that we might be brought to life in Christ. We do not always accomplish what we set out to do. Our lives are filled with broken promises, shattered dreams, and unfulfilled expectations. But Jesus' declaration upon the cross, "It is finished!" was a shout of victory instead of a cry of despair and defeat.

In Christ we find one who fulfills God's mission and accomplishes what God set out to do. The One who came into the world to die for us, so that we might live forever, has fulfilled that purpose. And that is why we call the darkest day in human history Good Friday!

> O love divine, what hast thou done!
> Th'incarnate God hath died for me!
> The Father's co-eternal Son
> Bore all my sins upon the tree!
> The Son of God for me hath died:
> My Lord, my Love, is crucified.*

It is finished! Christ has fulfilled God's plan. Hallelujah!

Prayer: *Lord Jesus, I do not fully understand it, but I believe that you died upon that cross nearly two thousnad years ago so that I can live with you forever in glory. At this moment I give my life to you and thank you for what you did for me at Calvary. Amen.*

---

*Charles Wesley, "O Love Divine, What Hast Thou Done," The United Methodist *Book of Hymns*, no. 420.

Saturday, April 6   Read Isaiah 42:1-9.

Who was in control of the situation at the crucifixion? The bloodthirsty mob was in a frenzy. Pontius Pilate symbolically washed his hands of the matter. The disciples panicked and ran away. Peter denied that he even knew Jesus. The Roman soldiers were simply following orders. It seems that only the victim was in control of himself or the situation.

See how confidently and majestically Jesus goes to his death. As the prophet wrote, "He will not shout or cry out, or raise his voice in the streets. A bruised reed he will not break" (Isa. 42:2-3, NIV).

But there was something disturbing about Jesus' manner. It was almost as if he knew something that the others did not know. Jesus knew who he was and the nature and power of his authority. He once told the disciples concerning his life, "No one takes it from me, but I lay it down of my own accord" (John 10:18, NIV). Jesus could have called on a legion of angels or sneaked away in the garden like the disciples. But he freely chose the cup of suffering which God had given him. Jesus also knew the end of the story and told his followers, "The Son of Man will be handed over to men who will kill him. Three days later, however, he will rise to life" (Mark 9:31, TEV). But they did not comprehend what Jesus was saying to them.

In Christ we find a unique source of inner strength and confidence. As we grow in our knowledge of Christ, we, too, will begin to express that same poise in response to our life situation.

Prayer affirmation: *"I can do all things through Christ."* *

---
*Phil. 4:13, KJV.

108

April 7 (Easter Sunday)
Read John 20:1-18.

The powers of darkness had done their worst in a futile attempt to destroy the Author of Life. "But God raised him from the dead, freeing him from the agony of death, because it was impossible for death to keep its hold on him" (Acts 2:24, NIV). That was the central message of the early church. And even though things looked bleak on Friday and Saturday, Jesus' resurrection was as inevitable as the rising of the sun in the morning. Not only had Jesus spoken of it in advance, but the powerful love of God must triumph over death. Perhaps the resurrection should not have taken any of the disciples by surprise. After all, Jesus had tried to prepare them for it. But such an event was unprecedented in human experience.

In Christ we find the hope of glory! Our personal darkness can be turned to light and our sorrow turned to joy because Christ lives. Jesus of Nazareth had died a terrible death. But God raised Jesus up! And God will also raise us to new life so that we can live this day and forever with Christ. Jesus says to each of us, "Because I live, you also will live" (John 14:19, NIV).

It is significant that Jesus' immediate instructions to Mary of Magdala in the garden outside the tomb were for her to go and tell the others. We, too, can help spread the word that Jesus Christ is alive and undefeated by every foe.

Prayer affirmation: *The same power that raised Jesus from the dead is at work in my life, cleansing and renewing me completely— from the inside out!*

THE COMMUNITY OF THE RISEN CHRIST

April 8-14, 1985   **John D. Copenhaver†**
Monday, April 8   Read John 20:19-20.

In this passage John pictures the disciples before and after their encounter with the risen Christ. Prior to this encounter they were confused and fearful. Their confusion was not allayed in the least by Mary's report that Jesus had appeared to her. In fact, her report only added to their confusion because it seemed so preposterous. They were fearful because they knew that the authorities who had brutally crucified Jesus would not hesitate to kill them. So they were huddling behind closed doors as they tried to sort out the events of the past week.

Suddenly Jesus comes and stands among them. This person is unmistakably Jesus for he shows them his hands and his side; and yet, something has changed. The risen Christ has a body that is not limited by space or time. This is the *pneumatic* (spiritual) body which the apostle Paul declares will be the inheritance of all Christians in the eschaton (see 1 Cor. 15). Naturally, the disciples are startled and afraid. Christ calms them with the words, "Peace be with you."

The confusion and fear of the disciples are forgotten as they are filled with joy at being with Jesus again. All the questions raised by Mary's report are superfluous now that they, too, have encountered the risen Christ. Jesus Christ is risen from the dead, and the disciples are overwhelmed with a new understanding of his life and ministry.

Prayer: *Risen Lord, help us so to love you that your presence fills us with joy and frees us for joyful service. Amen.*

†United Methodist minister (Virginia Conference); Ph.D. student at Catholic University of America (Washington, D.C.), Falls Church, Virginia.

Tuesday, April 9   Read John 20:19-23.

Three changes occur during the disciples' first encounter with the risen Christ. First of all, their fear is replaced by joy as they realize that Jesus is alive. Secondly, their confusion is replaced by a sense of purpose. Thirdly, their despair is replaced by empowerment. Since the first change was discussed yesterday, let us focus on the second and third changes.

The confusion of the disciples is replaced by a sense of purpose when Jesus commissions them to continue his ministry. "As the Father sent me, so I am sending you" (TJB). Jesus' unique ministry of reconciliation and liberation is passed on to his disciples. They are no longer to be spectators, observing Jesus' ministry, but are called now to participate in that ministry. Now they are commissioned to bring good news to the poor, to proclaim liberty to captives, to open the eyes of the blind, and to set the downtrodden free. The disciples have *come of age* and have an awesome responsibility. "For those whose sins you forgive, they are forgiven; for those whose sins you retain, they are retained" (TJB). The disciples are given authority to act as Jesus' representatives in the world.

The despair of the disciples reminds us of the Philistines after their champion, Goliath, had been slain. Like the Philistines, they lose heart and make a hasty retreat. However, despair is replaced by empowerment as Jesus breathes on them and says, "Receive the Holy Spirit." This is the same Spirit that inspired and empowered the ministry of Jesus. Now the Spirit is upon the disciples to continue Jesus' reconciling and liberating ministry.

Prayer: *Thank you, God, for giving my life a purpose and for supplying the power to fulfill that purpose. Amen.*

Wednesday, April 10   Read John 20:24-29.

Thomas has received a lot of bad press because of the incident described here. He is not really that different from the other disciples. None of them had believed Mary's report. If they had, they would not have gathered in fear! What John is emphasizing here is that no one was prepared for the resurrection of Jesus.

We must also remember that this same doubting Thomas is the disciple who said, "Let us go too, [to Jerusalem] and die with him" (John 11:16, TJB). Thomas does not lack commitment or courage, but he expected the worst. However, when Jesus was crucified, Thomas was no less heartbroken because he expected it. Some scholars speculate that Thomas went off by himself to mourn and that is why he was absent when Jesus appeared to the disciples the first time.

We can learn several important lessons from Thomas. First of all, we learn that it is a mistake to withdraw from Christian fellowship during a time of sorrow. The Christian community is the place where we are most likely to encounter Christ and his healing power. Secondly, we learn that honest doubt is permissible within the Christian community. In fact, it is certainly preferable to an easy credulity which glibly affirms the mysteries of the Christian faith. Thirdly, we learn that it is the risen Christ who convinces the doubtful, not us.

Prayer: *My Lord and my God, may Thomas' example of honesty, courage, and commitment inspire these same virtues in me. Amen.*

Thursday, April 11   Read Psalm 133.

Imagine being exposed to freezing winds all day and finally coming home to sink into a warm bath. Or imagine being on a long, hot, dusty, hike without any drinking water and finally quenching your thirst from a pure mountain stream. These are both images of relief. The simple statement that a warm bath is nice or that spring water is refreshing does not convey the same power as an image.

The psalmist, when extolling the blessings of harmonious human fellowship, uses images in order to evoke a feeling. The feeling that the psalmist wants to evoke is that of well-being, *shalom*. *Shalom* is often translated "peace" but it means far more—it means well-being in all aspects of existence.

The two images that the psalmist uses are put in the form of similes. The first image, which is drawn from Israel's history, likens the blessing of harmonious human fellowship (*shalom* community) to the precious oil which was poured so lavishly upon the head of Aaron. There is no containing the blessing. it runs down over Aaron's beard to the collar of his robe.

The second image, which is drawn from Israel's geography, indicates that the blessing of *shalom* community is like the dew which falls so profusely on the mountains of Zion. The dew comes faithfully and brings freshness to all life. Not only is the blessing profuse, it lasts forever. "For there the Lord has commanded the blessing, life for evermore."

The *shalom* community which enjoys everlasting life finds its fullest expression in the community of the risen Christ.

Suggestion for prayer: *Recall your most profound experiences of Christian fellowship. Give thanks for them and for your present Christian community.*

Friday, April 12 Read Acts 4:32-35.

This description of the early Christian community has always intrigued and challenged me. Here is a company of women and men so united in heart and soul that all possessions are held in common. There is such a strong sense of responsibility for one another that no one can imagine holding on to any possession while another sister or brother is in need. This company is a true *shalom* community since it is concerned with the well-being of each person.

The decision to share their goods with one another arose out of a transforming awareness of unity in the risen Christ. There was no compulsion to share—it was a spontaneous expression of profound unity.

I do not really think the early disciples are all that different from Christians today. There are some contemporary Christian communities and religious orders that practice community of goods. They are an important and indispensable witness to the transforming power of the risen Christ. However, the vast majority of Christians, even in the New Testament church, did not adopt this practice. These Christians have sought to express Christian unity through sacrificial giving. The real tragedy is not that there are not more Christian communities practicing community of goods, but that there is so little sacrificial giving.

One reason for the rarity of sacrificial giving is that many churches have isolated and insulated themselves from the poor. Since the poor are distant and anonymous, our compassion is rarely engaged. What is needed today is a vivid awareness of our unity with the poor in our own country and around the world and the sensitivity to realize that they are our brothers and sisters.

Prayer: *O God, give me such a love for my sisters and brothers that I will seek out the poor and respond to their needs. Amen.*

Saturday, April 13   Read 1 John 1:1-7.

In the first verses of this letter, John seeks to establish his personal knowledge of the "word of life" and to witness to its physical reality. The "word of life" is, of course, Jesus Christ. John wants to establish the physical reality of Christ because some people (the Docetists) taught that Christ only "seemed" to have a material body. This teaching is refuted when John affirms that he heard, saw, and touched Jesus. The incarnation of Christ was indispensable in John's understanding of Christian faith. John proclaims this faith in order that the readers may enter into this faith and into the fellowship of the apostles, whose fellowship is with God.

In the rest of this letter, John describes the conditions for being in fellowship with the community of the risen Christ. The first condition for fellowship is walking in the light. Walking in the light means living in the awareness of God's presence. God is light. God is holy. God is love. When we live our lives in the presence of God, we are aware of God's will— we have the mind of Christ. When we avoid or neglect the presence of God, we walk in darkness. Without a knowledge of God's will, we become enslaved by selfish desires and we conform to worldly attitudes. Our foundation for moral judgment becomes as unstable as quicksand.

We must walk in the light if we intend to be part of the fellowship of the risen Christ.

Prayer: *O God, who is light, help me this day to be constantly aware of your presence and, so, to walk in the light. Amen.*

Sunday, April 14   Read 1 John 1:5–2:2.

In most Christian worship services there is a time for confession. Usually the confession comes early in the service because as we begin worship our awareness of God's holiness is heightened. We become aware of our shortcomings and our creaturehood. Only God is holy, infinite, and immortal. The confession of sin is a sort of reality therapy. It acknowledges the human condition and our own humanity.

Just as confession comes early in the worship service, it is the first condition John makes for walking in the light. To persist in the self-deceit that one has not sinned is to walk in darkness. Those who claim to have no sin have an inadequate understanding of the word. Although it may refer to specific actions, it goes far beyond this limited interpretation. A more comprehensive understanding is that sin refers to the universal human attitude of selfish independence. We make our decisions independent of the divine will because we want to make sure that our will is done. This attitude leads to all the other sins.

The good news is that God became a human being and understands human weakness. God is eager to forgive our sins if we will confess them. What we must not do is hide our sins or pretend that they are not all that bad. When we confess our sins, God forgives us and cleanses us so that we may have perfect fellowship with God and with the community of the risen Christ.

Suggestion for prayer: *Take some time for personal confession. Be specific, and be confident of God's forgiveness.*

Remember Who You Are

April 15-21, 1985
Monday, April 15

James F. Koob†
Read 1 John 2:28–3:10;
Mark 10:13-16.

When the "elder" of First John writes "that we should be called children of God; and so we are," the elder reminds us that our ministry is not vested with rights we deserve (e.g., because we worked yesterday we get today off) nor is it necessary to redouble our efforts (e.g., this week I will get it right). All we are supposed to do is be ready for a once-in-a-lifetime encounter because, obviously, we have been on the same side as God in doing justice and being compassionate. Obviously!

That may have been obvious to the elder, but I am aware of acts of justice that have gone undone. I am painfully aware that somewhere around Thursday my bag of compassion seemed more empty than full. And whether I feel I deserve today off or have myself all fired up to try again, Jesus halts me and invites me to embrace something different.

He wants me to become a child again. The new life in the kingdom is to become like children who know they are loved. Loved not because of good grades or fine performances, but because loving parents created them and love their creation. Loved not because they deserve it or promise to do better, but because they intuitively and rightly know they can trust the Lover.

We are the children of God.

Suggestion for meditation: *In the quiet of your prayer time, go to a restful spot where Jesus will greet the child in you and bless you.*

---

†Minister, First United Church of Arvada (U.C.C.), Arvada, Colorado.

Tuesday, April 16   Read 1 John 3:2;
                                    2 Corinthians 3:12-18.

Someone once told me that growth is simply a change that has gone well. My first instinct when reading Paul's observation that we "are being changed into [Christ's] likeness," is to think: Oh, I understand that I am gradually changing into this image of Christ; it's a good personal growth experience, and I certainly hope there is enough time.

When we read the elder's affirmation in First John 3:2, it ought to occur to us that this change is beyond our power. The change of Paul and the elder is a radical transformation. The transformation that we will undergo is not like a decision we might make to increase the level of exercise this spring!

Like a lover, waiting for the beloved, I wait with tainted moments of unbelief for Christ, wondering when he will ever come. I am to be unveiled. It would be more comfortable if the unveiling was as a bridegroom carefully lifting the veil to lovingly behold the bride. Yet I sense that the unveiling is more like in the Temple on Good Friday—when that veil was torn in two. It is to be an almost violent stripping away of the curtains that have blinded me to who I am and what I am to be.

And who are we? The elder says that at the end "we shall be like [Christ]," and the apostle tells us that we now "are being changed into [Christ's] likeness from one degree of glory to another."

Like him. Transformed into his likeness. Yet only after the veil of blind ego has been lifted.

Suggestion for meditation: *In the quiet of your prayer time, go to a darkened room, bumping into things you cannot see. After awhile let the light of Christ come in to illumine your life.*

118

Wednesday, April 17   Read 1 John 3:3;
                                           Matthew 5:8.

Maintaining a clear sense of purpose, being faithful to the visions we have beheld, and staying the course of one's calling are hard disciplines.

We have all heard the story of the pastor who was constantly frustrated with not being able to get all the appointed work done because of constant interruptions. If it was not someone calling on the phone, or another crisis call at the hospital, it was someone who "happened" to be going by and thought she would just drop in for a minute to talk with the pastor. It was years before the pastor concluded that the ministry of Christ's servant was in the interruptions and not in the appointed and self-imposed tasks.

I have consoled myself with that story. It calls to mind the small ways of serving that Christ taught in the parable of the final judgment and the profound effects of that service.

Perhaps my eagerness to say yes to all agenda items is a stumbling block. Yet, as I listen to John the elder, "Every one who thus hopes in [Christ] purifies himself as he is pure," I am spurred to put an effort forth as a believer in order to conform to the ways of humanity Christ has mirrored. We respond with our unique gifts. We lead with our dreams and visions. Our pilgrimage is marked by seeking a balance between maintaining our human *sense* of what is important and the persistent voice of God who *says* what is important. Joyfulness arises from not abusing the freedom God has granted us in our walking together.

Suggestion for meditation: *In the quiet of your prayer time, journey to a lighted room in the middle of which is a scale with two trays. Balance what is important for you and see what God puts on the other tray.*

Thursday, April 18   Read 1 John 3:4-6;
Isaiah 53.

How easy it is to forget, while doing what is most important, that which is *ultimately* most important: "You know that he appeared to take away sins."

Daily I am reminded of my own sinfulness and confronted with the sins of many whom I see. Less obvious are the number of times I offer an assurance of reconciliation. Yet that is the most significant action a Christian has to offer.

Being the sort of person who enjoys beautiful objects, I wonder if I avoid the right of forgiveness because of the ugliness with which it is associated? Sins I can see as ugly; but forgiveness is another matter. The servant song of Isaiah that helps our understanding of who Jesus is, says, "We despised him and rejected him; he endured suffering and pain. No one would even look at him—we ignored him as if he were nothing" (TEV). How is it that God chose what is so unseemly, so unlike the Greek ideal of beauty, as the means for such a joyful and beautiful gift? Then again, God does not necessarily have to mimic my human aesthetics.

Perhaps in the difference of ways lies even more truth. Perhaps I fool myself about what people are wanting from their contacts with me. What if it isn't the compassion and wit that emerge so easily? What if it isn't the knowledge and wisdom I have nurtured? What if their unspoken desire is to hear again about God's folly of the cross, ugliness and all, and how it brings them to life again?

Suggestion for meditation: *In prayer, journey back to the empty tomb and discern how ugliness is transformed into beauty in the light of Easter Day.*

120

Friday, April 19   Read 1 John 3:7;
                                         Acts 5:27-40.

A mentor observed while I was arguing for a more open posture about some long-forgotten issue: "Jim, you can be so open-minded, your brains fall out!"

As I have learned ministry, I have been confronted with the need to be tolerant. I have found myself saying, "Nothing surprises me anymore." At the same time there has been a realization that I have increasingly desired to become more rigid. Paul's affirmation that nothing "in all creation, will be able to separate us from the love of God in Christ Jesus our Lord" (Rom. 8:39) prompts me to wonder if there are not some things that can separate us.

The elder is much less ambiguous: "Little children, let no one deceive you. He who does right is righteous, as he is righteous." Once again who we are to be is mirrored in the brightness of the Son. And once more the hard question comes: What is the mind of Christ?

The temptation to have no boundaries or to build lethal fences is always present. As I share the affirmation of Paul, I feel called further into my relationship with Jesus as the way to determine what is right. And often what I believe is right is at odds with either no fences or high fences. It is a paradox, and the only solace I have found is Luke's remembrance of Rabbi Gamaliel's words: "If this plan or this undertaking is of men, it will fail; but if it is of God, you will not be able to overthrow them. You might even be found opposing God!"

Suggestion for meditation: *In your prayer time, go to the place where you meet the Christ and inquire about how you mirror his righteousness.*

Saturday, April 20   Read 1 John 3:8;
                                    Matthew 13:24-30, 36-43.

I have enjoyed the atypical snowstorms we have had in our region in recent years. The joy comes from the halt of the routine, the forced hibernation, and a great excuse for canceling meetings! There is also a curse that comes with it when the melting snow refreezes into sheer ice. When that begins, and I start taking steps very carefully, I experience the curse with no blessing. It doesn't take many spills to make me a much more cautious person.

There is rock-solid hardness to an uncontrollable landing on an icy sidewalk. Not only is it painful and dangerous, there is something of a disgrace for having been such a klutz in the first place.

I think of the hardness of falling when I feel the very adamant judgment of the elder in First John: "He who commits sin is of the devil. . . . The reason the Son of God appeared was to destroy the works of the devil." Equally disturbing is Jesus' warning in the parable of the weeds and the wheat. To sin is to fall hard on the word heard from Jesus the Christ.

The hardness of these judgments is a caution for us who enjoy God's new springtime called grace; for us who have heard the word and nothing is routine anymore; and for us who have emerged from our tombs. A word of caution: Don't slip on sin!

Suggestion for meditation: *In the quiet of your prayer time, sit on something hard or hold something hard and meditate on the hardness that slips into your life.*

altar moments 7/19/05

Sunday, April 21　　　　　　　　Read 1 John 3:9-10;
　　　　　　　　　　　　　　　　　Luke 24:35-48.

Those with whom we celebrate today are the witnesses of all that has happened. We are the Easter people who bear witness to Christ's victory over the grave.

I have observed my daughter's curiosity over the years about who she is and how she came to be a daughter. The first inquiries began with an exploration of her baby pictures which we had zealously taken. As time has passed, she has heard the oral traditions we have established with family and friends surrounding her birth. During the last few years, her curiosity has shifted to the physiology and biology associated with her being born. As much as she will come to know about where and how she came to be a daughter in a human family, and as intriguing as the pictures are about how she once was, I believe what she will always remember are the stories. They are the enduring witness to who she is.

A colleague once told how his father never said to him when he was going out as a teenager, "Be good," or "Be careful." Instead he would say, "Remember who you are."

In the Gospel of Luke this day, we hear again who we are. And because we know who we are, the wise elder of First John observes: "By this it may be seen who are the children of God, and who are the children of the devil: whoever does not do right is not of God, nor he who does not love his brother."

We should live according to who we are: children of God, born to God.

Suggestion for meditation: *In your prayer time, go quietly to an upper room and remember stories that tell you who you are.*

MY CUP RUNNETH OVER

April 22-28, 1985 **Norma Woodward Haist†**
Monday, April 22 Read 1 John 3:18.

People whose cups overflow show their love in what they do.

Bert and Mary are a radiant couple who trust and take delight in the Lord. Because of their commitment to God, they have helped others and been active members of our church for many years.

We knew they had no children, so some of us asked if we could have a 50th wedding anniversary celebration for them. We printed the invitation in the church bulletin and held the event in the fellowship hall between two church services. Volunteers set a lovely serving table with lace cloth, candles, and centerpiece. Others served the punch and cookies people had furnished. One took photographs and donated his work. Another bought an album and put the photos and mementos in it for them. Joy filled our hearts and continued even after the last dish was washed. Mary's sister and a few nieces and nephews, their only relatives, came. Mary and Bert were pleased. We were, too.

Your deeds may be quite different. Perhaps they include shaving a sick man in the hospital, laying a carpet for a divorced mother, taking an elderly person to church weekly, being foster parents, serving on community service projects. The list could go on forever, but as long as we serve in love, we are serving God.

Prayer: *Lord, help us find more ways to cheer people. Help us love in deed and in truth and not just in word. Amen.*

---

†Teacher and free-lance writer, Hastings, Nebraska.

Tuesday, April 23   Read 1 John 3:18-24.

People whose cups overflow love one another.

Sometimes our hearts condemn us. We hear from inside us, You're guilty . . . guilty . . . guilty. We know we have spoken sharply, exaggerated, or have been callous, and we feel sorry about it. But "God is greater than our hearts, and he knows everything." Our minds cannot imagine that God is omniscient—knowing everything that has happened since the beginning of time, everything we will do today and all the events of the future. But as we become more mature Christians, this is not a frightening concept but a comforting one. God knows all about us and still loves us. We cannot pretend with God or hide our foul deeds and mistakes. God already knows.

We all meet people who are not perfect. Neither are we. As a teacher of young children, I seldom keep them indoors at recess as they need to run and exercise. One day when a child did not have his work done, I kept him in to help him. After school his mother came into my room and screamed at me, "You hate my child. You're unfair. You keep John in for recess every day!" At that point it was hard to love that parent. After I had reacted in what I hope was a positive, loving manner, she calmed down and left. Then I began to wonder why she needed to act that way.

Maybe everything had gone wrong for her all week, and she just had to explode at someone. I happened to be the one. (It might have been the grocer who dropped her eggs or the jeweler who did not have her watch repaired.) I must forgive myself for feeling guilty, then forgive her and take it all to God who teaches us to love one another.

Prayer: *Lord, help me to show your love each minute of every day. Amen.*

Wednesday, April 24   Read John 10:11-13.

People whose cups overflow become shepherds.

"I am the good shepherd. The good shepherd lays down his life for the sheep." Can we imagine dying for anyone? Probably we would give blood and maybe a kidney to save a child or a sister, but would we even consider dying for a stranger? Jesus died for us. Those words are easy to say, but when we try to realize how much he did for us, we cannot comprehend.

"He who is a hireling and not a shepherd, whose own the sheep are not, sees the wolf coming and leaves the sheep and flees; and the wolf snatches them and scatters them. He flees because he is a hireling and cares nothing for the sheep." Are we a hireling or a shepherd? Do we love Jesus so much that we want to lead, guide, love others into the kingdom? Or do we start out as a hired hand with good intentions and when the wolves of life come—ridicule, pride, hard knocks—do we run away and leave our budding Christian friends on their own?

The shepherds of the church are the ministers, and we expect them to have their lives so grounded in Jesus that they do not become preoccupied with salaries and parsonages. There are lay shepherds too, on the mission commission, the boards of the church, teaching children and adults. We must watch our priorities.

Once I belonged to an education commission that constantly quibbled over what time the church Christmas program would be and whether the children would wave palms on Palm Sunday. Now I serve on one that is different. These people give priority to the spiritual growth of children, teachers, and adults. What a joy to serve on this commission and to do our best toward being good shepherds.

Suggestion for meditation: *Concentrate on the many ways you can serve your church and your Lord wherever you live.*

Thursday, April 25   Read John 10:14-18.

People whose cups overflow become cup fillers.

"I am the good shepherd; I know my own and my own know me." The good shepherd led the sheep near the clear water, and the sheep could sense the shepherd's care. "He leadeth me beside the still waters. He restoreth my soul" (Ps. 23:2*b*, KJV). We need to be led near the cool springs to drink.

Have you ever visited a friend and felt thirsty? The friend might say, "How about a cup of coffee?" You refuse, so she says, "Then I'll make you tea." But what you would really like is a drink of good clear water.

We also need spiritual water. We need a rousing sermon that stirs us into action, a Sunday school class discussion in which our horizons are widened, a longer period of prayer, a weekend retreat or time of renewal. These can give us refreshing spiritual water.

"I have other sheep, that are not of this fold; I must bring them also, and they will heed my voice." Our lives cannot touch people in the whole world, but we can do some things to bring the other sheep to hear the good shepherd's voice. Over a period of time, four foreign students have spent two years in our home. Although we were not sure that any of them became Christian because of us, we did our best to share our Christian lives and home with them. Perhaps, in the long run, something we did or said will influence their lives toward Christ. Our cup-filling can help support a friend in Ecuador and a friend's son, a pilot, who flies missionaries into remote parts of Mexico. We feel our tiny bit of financial support may be helping when we read their thrilling letters telling of those who have accepted Christ.

Prayer: *Thank you, Lord, that some day "there shall be one flock, one shepherd." Amen.*

127

Friday, April 26   Read Psalm 23.

People whose cups overflow may walk through the valley of the shadow.

Shadows—they fall across our paths suddenly as we walk, and we are startled. I drive my car into the garage at night, and a shadow in the corner makes me look again to be sure I am alone. A day is sunny and bright, then clouds shadow the earth. Will it rain on the clothes I just hung on the line? My friend seems healthy and suddenly a spot appears on her nose that needs X-ray treatments. A shadow comes over her life. Another friend has lymphoma and for a time is healthy and strong. Then the lumps reappear, and she must face the shadows of pain and illness that come with the chemotherapy. I carry our baby a full nine months, and she is stillborn. A dark shadow of childlessness covers our lives.

In all of these situations we walk through the shadows; we don't remain under them forever. We walk through the valley where the shadows of fear, death, pain, illness, and separation are, but if we love our Lord, we know we are not alone. We may be afraid, a few minutes or a few months, but God offers a rod and staff to comfort us. We come out of the shadows into a new day, into the bright sunshine. If we are Christians, we see life in a new perspective. The shadows may return momentarily, but God's love is greater and dispels the shadows of our lives.

Prayer: *Dear God, who gives us more sunshine than shadows, we thank you. Thank you for the still waters and the restoration of our soul. Thank you for the promise that we may dwell in your house forever. Amen.*

Saturday, April 27   Read Acts 4:8-10.

People whose cups overflow are filled with the Holy Spirit.

Peter might not have uttered these brave and profound words if he had not been "filled with the Holy Spirit" (Acts 2:4). An "uneducated, common [man]" (Acts 4:13), Peter was one who was sometimes afraid, who spoke before he thought and sometimes lied. Now he was so full of the Spirit that he spoke right up to the rulers and elders.

It must have been a dramatic scene. On one side were Annas the high priest, Caiaphas, John, Alexander and others of the high priestly family in their rich robes. On the other side were Peter and John in their ordinary clothes, perhaps somewhat rumpled and dirty from spending the previous night in a jail. Despite their looks, the rulers recognized that Peter and John had been with Jesus.

A central figure in the drama was the man, more than forty years old, who had evidently been crippled most of his life. He was well known in the community and had obviously been miracuously healed since he was now standing and walking by himself. When the questioning began, one of the priests asked, "By what power or by what name did you do this?" Peter looked his questioners boldly in the eye and replied, "Rulers of the people and elders . . . be it known to you all, and to all the people of Israel, that by the name of Jesus Christ of Nazareth . . . this man is standing before you well." Then he accused the rulers of crucifying Jesus Christ and told them that God had raised Christ from the dead. What boldness the Spirit gave Peter!

Prayer: *We are thankful for the Holy Spirit who led Peter and John and countless others to do your will, O God. Let us, too, be open and ready to serve. Amen.*

Sunday, April 28   Read Acts 4:11-12.

People whose cups overflow let the Spirit lead.

The drama continues from yesterday's setting. Peter tells the rulers that this Jesus is "the stone which was rejected by you builders, but which has become the head of the corner." He is boldly telling the authorities that they are the builders and they treated Jesus, the stone, in despicable ways. Now Jesus has become the head of the corner. My dictionary says that a cornerstone is one that unites two intersecting walls and is the indispensable and fundamental basis of the entire building. The *New English Bible* says that Jesus has become the keystone, which is the "central wedge-shaped stone of an arch that locks the others together." Jesus can be either the keystone or the cornerstone of our lives.

Peter continues, "Salvation is to be found through him alone; in all the world there is no one else whom God has given who can save us" (TEV). What a testimony the Spirit led Peter to give! The rulers did not know what to do with these outspoken men and finally turned them loose.

How much do we believe that Jesus Christ is the only means of salvation? Enough to pray daily? tell a close friend? tell a person who is without hope? visit newcomers in town and invite them to know Jesus? visit people in prison and tell them the good news? go as missionaries? teach a Sunday school class?

It was dramatic for Peter to speak courageously to the leaders. The Spirit may or may not lead us to do anything so daring. But we need to begin by building our lives on Jesus, the stone which the others rejected.

Prayer: *Thank you, Lord, for your word. May we hear and obey. Amen.*

RISEN LORD FOR A WAITING WORLD

April 29–May 5, 1985   **Robert K. Smyth†**
Monday, April 29   Read Psalm 22:25-31.

Only three weeks ago Christians gathered in the early hours on Easter to join in the glorious refrain "Christ is risen! He is risen indeed!" We know the day as the spring of souls, the time for new life arising within us just as spring flowers push through the soil.

It is virtually impossible for our thinking capabilities—imaginative, inventive, and inclusive as they are—to encompass the resurrection. It is God's initiative, interceding at the right time through the risen Son, to lay claim to our eternal spirit. God confirms that the cross is not final. The resurrection reforges the link of inseparable love, declaring that nothing can separate us from God's love.

The beginning of Psalm 22 is more familiar to Christians than the closing verses. The pilgrimage of each Good Friday reminds us of Christ's haunting cry of forsakenness. We hear the words from the resurrection side of the cross. We know he is not forsaken, nor are we.

We celebrate him as the risen Lord for a waiting world, the one who reigns to all the ends of the earth, who calls all the families of the nations. By faith, we tell our children of all the things God is doing. We teach them to believe and hope, too.

Prayer: *Thank you, God, for loving us forever. Amen.*

---

†Senior Pastor, St. Andrew's United Methodist Church, Cherry Hill, New Jersey.

Tuesday, April 30   Read Acts 8:26-35.

God places an inquisitive nature within all of us as part of our intellectual gifts; it begins working in the earliest days of our life. As we reach out in curiosity or exploring or questioning or earnest searching, we create "teachable moments." We are ready to receive, to hear, to find, to be challenged. Children provide many teachable moments. If we are parents or teachers, we need to be alert to seize these times to instruct or guide. Christians are to be ready to share the faith when other persons open teachable moments for us.

Philip was provided such a moment when the Ethiopian official admitted his need for guidance in understanding the prophecy of Isaiah. Philip seized the opportunity, for he was thoroughly committed to the good news of Jesus. His life had a new reason for being because of the risen Lord. His spirit and his mind were permeated with the love, light, and truth of God. He was one of seven deacons—Stephen was another—appointed by the church (see Acts 6:5). He was an evangelist to the waiting world.

Philip soon surmised the Ethiopian was not born to Judaism. This man had come to Jerusalem as a seeker, as one thirsting for both a consistent moral standard and a certain faith in God. The soil of his spiritual life was prepared for receiving the seed of the word, and Philip was ready to be the sower. It must have been an exhilarating experience for Philip to have this great opportunity. It must have been a joyous occasion for the risen Lord to know his commandment to teach and baptize was fulfilled. We know Ethiopia was an early site for Christianity. Was it the fruit of this official's faith that was the seed?

Prayer: *Whether one seed or many, Lord, lead us to see the teachable moment and to sow. Amen.*

Wednesday, May 1   Read Acts 8:36-40.

In our spirit is a characteristic that motivates us to make some response to Christ when he inspires us. We communicate our gratitude through some confirming action. One man takes up his pallet and walks, another goes to the Temple to offer praise after being cleansed of leprosy, Mary Magdalene sins no more, a man born blind praises God because once he was blind and Jesus enables him to see.

When a sermon, solo, prayer, or anthem brings love and hope alive, we confirm our feeling with an amen or applause, a hug or a handshake. These become our response, making our conviction even stronger.

Philip must have been a compelling, convincing teacher as he rode in the chariot with the Ethiopian. After all, he had firsthand experience with Jesus and was simply passing along all he had seen and heard. A seeker such as this official would be an eager learner. The Ethiopian was seeking and waiting in a world of expectation when he heard of the risen Lord. Some confirming action had to happen to give outward expression to the inwardly warmed heart.

Seeing water, he commanded the entourage to halt. One can imagine the Ethiopian hurriedly pulling Philip toward the water, with joy too full to be contained. Buried with Christ in his immersion, raised with Christ in his new life! The Ethiopian could never be the same. He was now a follower of the Way.

Prayer: *O God, empower us to remember that "there is none who can help or deliver me or make me safe save You, Lord God, my only Saviour, to whom I commit myself and all that is mine."* Amen.

---

*Thomas à Kempis, *The Imitation of Christ*.

Thursday, May 2   Read John 15:1-8.

Only a limited number of plant species are able to survive without some form of roots or similar connection with basic nourishment. Air plants are able to absorb the moisture and raw materials that they need for food directly from the air. But most plants have a root system. Our human intake of air and food make up our system to supply bodily need.

As Christians, we realize our fundamental spiritual need for inner nourishment; and this is supplied as we abide in the risen Lord. We choose to be united totally with Jesus by faith. We press our hungering and thirsting spirit against him for inner satisfaction, just as a branch must be united with the vine to grow and bear fruit.

When Jesus describes himself as "the true vine" or "the real vine" (TEV), he employs an analogy already in the minds of the hearers of his time. Until God became incarnate in Jesus, Israel was considered the vine. Prophets such as Isaiah, Jeremiah, Ezekiel, and Hosea refer to the vine, but in their images the vine is degenerate, wild, without fruitfulness. Jesus reveals that God has a new planting, the real and true vine, rooted and grounded in the fertile soil of God's grace. The one for whom the world has been waiting has come.

With Jesus as Lord, we graft ourselves to the vine; our nurture flows from God through the Son. Whatever fruit we bear is because the Son is in us. Whatever love we bring to the waiting world is because of this adding relationship, and to the glory of God.

Prayer: *O God, "abide with me; fast falls the eventide."* * *Amen.*

---

*Henry F. Lyte, "Abide with Me," the United Methodist *Book of Hymns*, no. 289.

Friday, May 3   Read John 15:1-8.

Our previous pastoral appointment was to a district super-intendency in a section of southern New Jersey that is extensively agricultural. The travels involved in that ministry regularly took us through areas where apple and peach orchards, vineyards, and blueberry fields produced their fruit. The winter routine of farmers required deliberate, prudent pruning of trees, vines, and bushes to force the strength of spring and summer growth into fruit rather than into nonproductive branches. Homeowners follow a similar discipline in their yards about this time of year to help with the growth and beauty of shrubs and bushes.

The teaching of our risen Lord in this lesson instructs us to cleanse our lives of the extraneous, the unnecessary, the unacceptable. Just as farmers prune trees and bushes, we must purge our life, spirit, and mind of all that is sinful, of all that hinders us from knowing and fulfilling the Creator's will. We are to discard actions or attitudes that are abrasive.

The word of Jesus makes clean all persons who truly hear him, who understand and obey his loving admonition. Sometimes his word calls for tough choices, when we know a long-practiced habit or lack of self-discipline requires radical pruning in order to permit a fruitful discipleship. Only so is God glorified: not simply by what we say, but by what we are and do. We choose to let an active piety be the fruit of a holy love.

Prayer: *Thank you, Creator, for putting a new and right spirit within us. Amen.*

Saturday, May 4   Read 1 John 4:7-8.

The motion picture *Oliver* begins with scenes depicting the Dickensonian orphanage where Oliver and the other boys were kept. A badly faded inscription on the dining hall wall, where all the orphans can read it, says, "God is love." The unfortunate aspect of the setting is that the stern, cruel behavior of their keepers contradicts the biblical affirmation. There soon follows the plaintive song "Where Is Love?"—a valid question for the film story's setting and for times of similar contradictions in our life.

The premise for Christian belief lies in the passionate plea in today's scripture: "Beloved, let us love one another." This is God's word, for God is love! Love is God's nature, and the nature of Christian character. God's love is alive in God's people, who center faith, hope, and witnessing on all that God is doing for us. When we hear of brutalities, atrocities, and the warrings of people upon people, we realize how widespread is the need for love. The grace of God persuades us to patiently keep at living love each day, making certain that "God is love" is inscribed on Christian conduct.

God's love is present in the world, albeit in more quiet ways than daily headlines. It is embodied in our love as Christian neighbors, remembering Jesus' teaching that anyone in need is this neighbor. It is alive in missionaries called to world service, and in leaders who offer the example of Christ-led love in every sphere of influence. God continues to expect us to use every opportunity to affirm that the world needs this love now.

Prayer: *O God, help us to be Christ to our sisters and brothers each day of our lives. Amen.*

Dial a Devotion
10/22/06

Sunday, May 5   Read 1 John 4:9-12.

Does God send letters? This scripture implies God does. God sends the clearest, most extensive, most lasting communication in the most dependable courier, God's Son. Even more significant than the method God chooses is the message conveyed. The one concept God wishes us to know and believe personally is the dimension of divine love. God perceives we have difficulty in understanding this, so it is packaged in a person.

God takes the initiative, makes the primary move, loves us first. God comes to us to live love like one of us. God doesn't even expect us to come partway. The epitome of grace, which is the nature of God, becomes incarnate in order to give us a way to live—through the Son. God also takes the step to assure us our sin is forgiven. The heart of the gospel is captured in these verses.

Whenever this love permeates our whole being, then God abides in us. When God's love is our center, it is able to expel all lesser loyalties and affections. The risen Lord is resident in our spirit and reigns in us. He perfects our character so that day by day we become more like him, we move toward the fulfillment of God's will, and we have God's love to offfer as our best gift to a waiting world.

Prayer: *O dear Lord, help us to see thee more clearly, love thee more dearly, and follow thee more nearly, day by day.* Amen.*

---

*From Richard of Chichester.

GOD'S ENDURING VICTORY

May 6-12, 1985   **Woodrow A. Geier†**
Monday, May 6   Read Psalm 98:1-3.

In Christopher Fry's play, *The Dark Is Light Enough,* the heroine and her household stand under military guard because she has harbored a refugee. Countess Rosmarin Ostenburg seeks to relieve her boredom by asking the guards to sing a song. They burst out with words calling up images of their "valiant steel," vengeance upon a fallen foe, and rivers of blood. The countess stops them. She learned their shabby war song in her childhood. She demands a love song. The old songs cannot do justice to new realities.

This incident is a parable of our human existence. The Israelites of old needed a new hymn for the enthronement of the new year. So the psalmist summoned them to sing of God's presence. The Eternal is here, victorious over all the chaotic powers of earth, victorious in bringing about the salvation of his people of Israel. Only a new song would do— one that would celebrate God's steadfast love and faithfulness.

These three verses of Psalm 98 proclaim God's victory over the cynicism and despair that afflict our world. We are called to sing it though nuclear holocaust impends. The song points us toward divine love that culminates in Jesus Christ.

Prayer: *Eternal God, you have proclaimed to us your steadfast love in the life, death, and resurrection of Jesus Christ. Teach us this hymn anew, that our lives may tell others of your ever-abiding victory. Amen.*

---

†Free-lance writer, Nashville, Tennessee.

Tuesday, May 7   Read Psalm 98:4-9.

God's enduring victory is apparent in all things that praise their Creator and Redeemer.

All nature praises the Lord today—the roaring seas and the creatures that surge therein, fields and forests and streams that shelter and feed insects and animals and birds. They "make a joyful noise to the Lord," and they summon us to praise.

Human nature responds with praises to the Lord with the sounds of musical instruments, which symbolize how human nature lifts its best song.

We have seen this high human response in a thousand ways—
• men and women and children seeking in their families the good life;
• people in churches celebrating the beloved community and reaching out in love and healing to the world beyond;
• prophets proclaiming the divine will in society;
• poets and artists and writers and teachers bringing wisdom into our lives;
• legislators fostering just and humane laws;
• farmers and grocers laboring to feed and clothe the world.
So let us praise God today for seedtime and harvest and for the mysterious working of the order of creation.

Let us continue our praise by remembering unsung individuals we name here who bless our lives:

Prayer: *We give thanks to you, gracious God, for the sheer wonder and beauty of your unceasing blessings. In all these we see how you have come to judge the world and to set righteousness as the foundation for our living. Amen.*

Wednesday, May 8   Read Acts 10:44-48.

God's encompassing victory is evidenced by the gift of the Holy Spirit to the Gentiles.

Our scripture tells us "the Holy Spirit fell on all who heard the word." So far so good. But some persons within the group of "all" were Gentiles.

Peter had been telling the people, Jews and Gentiles, of the central event of God's revelation to the human race in the life, death, and resurrection of Jesus Christ—the event that evidences supremely God's enduring victory over sin and death.

Peter had just said that *everyone* who believes in Christ receives forgiveness of sins. Would the church try to perpetuate a localized, restrictive, nationalistic faith, or would it become captive of the Holy Spirit and freed to proclaim a universal faith?

The Jewish Christians were amazed that God had sent the Holy Spirit upon the Gentiles. Would not these "outsiders" have to be subject to and qualified by the ancient law before they could become Christians?

Did God really care about the Gentiles as much as he did about the Jewish Christians? Does he really care as much about the Russians, the Cubans, and the Iranians as he does about the Americans?

Peter commanded that the Gentiles be baptized in the name of Jesus Christ. Here history took a new turn. God's triumph was evidenced in a new outreach to the Gentiles. Now neither race nor nation nor class would be paramount. The God of surprises had acted again. The church would be catholic, universal, reaching out in love and compassion to *all* people.

Prayer: *Thou Holy Spirit, who came to liberate the church from narrow loyalties, free us today to be the church amid clashing tribalisms and nationalisms that the kingdom of God may come. Amen.*

Thursday, May 9 Read 1 John 5:1-5.

God's enduring victory is evidenced in the love that overcomes the world.

Suppose a disciple today should say to Jesus, "I love you, but I do not love the riffraff you associate with—criminal types, women of no virtue, beggars, drifters, ne'er-do-wells."

We have reason to believe Jesus would respond as he did to the Pharisees and Sadducees when a scribe asked him which is the greatest commandment. Jesus said, "You shall love the Lord your God with all your heart, and with all your soul, and with all your mind. . . . You shall love your neighbor as yourself" (Mark 12:30-31).

John the elder catches the meaning of Jesus' response in our scripture for today. Hatred for God is shown in hatred for God's children. We cannot love God without loving God's children. The elder repeated a popular saying, "Love the parent, love the child."

To love God and God's children—this is our faith, said the elder, that overcomes the world. It vanquishes tribulations. Love of God and love of God's people: one love.

Jesus made this love the main business of his life. He came to express the love of God to us. He demonstrated God's love, involving himself in the pains and sufferings of people. This is the victory, then—Jesus living, teaching, suffering, dying, rising from death. He demonstrates God's enduring victory.

Love God, love God's people, the riffraff included. Jesus commanded us to do this daily.

Prayer: *Enlarge our sensitivities and sympathies, O God, that we may demonstrate your love today. Amen.*

Friday, May 10   Read John 15:9-11.

God's enduring victory is evidenced in the joy of Christians.

Writers Friedrich Nietzsche and D. H. Lawrence, as well as others, have chided Christians for being so sorrowful. Lawrence could not abide the sad hymns the Christians sang in his time, and he deplored their denial of Christ's resurrection. Other writers have wondered why—if our church life is healthy—we could be so gloomy. They have sometimes questioned whether we worship a Lord who lies in the tomb.

I have often thought of these charges during Holy Communion. What solemn, masklike faces we show at the Lord's Supper where we are guests! How dismal we are at this celebration of Christ's final triumph over sin and death! Like the artists who painted the Man of Sorrows on European cathedral walls, we have become captive of an image of Christ's humiliation and death.

Have we forgotten the central focus of the revelation of God in Jesus Christ? On the night of his betrayal, Jesus reviewed with his disciples all the bitter experiences of humiliation and defeat. Then he said, "These things I have spoken to you, that my joy may be in you, and that your joy may be full." The overwhelming note he struck came in John 16:33: "In the world you have tribulation; but be of good cheer, I have overcome the world."

Our final image is not of the suffering Savior but of the risen Lord—alive and bringing joy to all who in faith will cast their lot with him.

Suggestion for prayer: *Let us ask ourselves why our lives so often do not evidence the joy that overcomes the world. Then let us pray for courage and confidence that come with Christ's joy.*

Saturday, May 11   Read John 15:16-17.

God's enduring victory is proclaimed in Christ's choice of us for discipleship in his name.

I imagine that in the semi-darkness of the upper room a disciple leaned toward another and asked, "What am I doing here?" Be that as it may, Jesus spoke to such a question that was on the minds of all the disciples.

"You did not choose me, but I chose you." Jesus knew what was in the minds of the disciples—their yearnings, self-doubts, anxieties, fears, and failures. Yet he assured them he had brought them here—the right place at the right time.

"That you should go and bear fruit." Jesus had trusted ordinary people with his mission. He came to call disciples—learners, persons who would be humble, teachable, responsive.

"That your fruit should abide." Though the disciples wondered, Jesus knew the seeds of permanence were in his mission. Future generations were to see that the "divinity that shapes our ends" would not fail.

"So that whatever you ask the Father in my name, he may give it to you." We are never left alone. If we take up our vocation in Christ's name—after his nature and purpose—we shall ask for the right things.

For reflection: What am I doing here? I have been brought here by the eternal mercy and purpose of God. I am here to face the frustrations and failures of my life in the light of God's love extended to me in Christ. I am here because I have Christ's own pledge that the work he has called me to do will prevail. I am here to proclaim the victory that overcomes the world.

Prayer: *Hear our prayer, O God, for courage, sanctified imagination, patience, strength, and the ability to serve. Amen.*

Sunday, May 12   Read John 15:12-15.

God's enduring victory is proclaimed when we love one another as God loves us.

And how has God loved us? In the Incarnation, God took the risk of human nature. Jesus came as God's supreme gift of love for us. He came from beyond the human realm to call us into friendship, and he laid down his life for his friends.

We were lost and alone, craving a demonstration of the divine, an evidence of the good life that we could affirm with our whole being. To our despair Jesus brought hope; to our seasons of doom, he brought confidence that God's mercy is everlastingly available.

And what did Jesus ask of us? "Love one another as I have loved you." An impossible standard? Could we love each other as Christ had loved us? Could we see the image of God in the person who despised us? Could we exalt love of God and love of neighbor as the *magna carta* of our freedom from evils that blight and kill?

Yes, said Jesus. The kingdom of God is founded on God's love. In it you have divine aid. In it the poor in spirit, the ones who mourn, the meek, the ones who hunger and thirst for righteousness, the merciful, the pure in heart, the peace-makers, the ones persecuted for righteousness' sake—these all find their home. God is love. When our lives say that, we proclaim our confidence in all that Jesus said and did.

And we are rewarded—rewarded in terms that Christ promised. We become more loving, more courageous, more kind, more faithful. We grow because we become more Christlike and therefore more truly human.

Prayer: *Gracious God, help us to remember that you first loved us that we might love one another and proclaim your enduring triumph in the world's life today. Amen.*

KEPT BY THE POWER OF GOD

May 13-19, 1985   **Thomas R. Albin**†
Monday, May 13   Read John 17:11b-12;
                                                          Acts 1:15-17.

God can keep us in his will.

When Jesus prayed that his disciples be kept in the name which God had given him just as he had kept them in that name, their minds must have flashed back to the time that Jesus fed them along with the multitudes (Matt. 15:33-38) or the time he stilled the raging sea (Matt. 8:23-27). What do you think it means to be "kept" in God's name? Recall the times you have been kept by the power of God in the past.

Jesus' prayer in John 17:11b had a purpose greater than just personal protection from harm. What was it?

To be one, to be united in harmony, peace, and blessing in the same way that Jesus was one with his Father, can only be accomplished by the grace and power of God. Apart from God there is no peace, no unity, no lasting harmony.

These verses in John and in Acts make it clear that although we can be kept by the power of God, God will not keep us against our will. Judas was numbered among the twelve, was allotted his share in the ministry, and was protected by the power of God. Yet, he willed to turn his back on it all. How will we respond? With repentance, faith, and forgiveness, or with self-condemnation, despair, and destruction?

Prayer: *O God, have mercy on me. Enable me to repent of my sin and to put my hope and trust in you. Keep me each day in your name. Amen.*

---

†Minister of Discipleship, First United Methodist Church, Tulsa, Oklahoma; Ph.D. candidate, University of Cambridge, England.

Tuesday, May 14   Read Psalm 1;
                                                        John 17:17.

God can keep us in his word.

The Psalms are essential reading for every person who desires to know God and to grow in grace. Psalm 1 draws a sharp contrast between the person who makes the word of God his or her foundation for life and the person who refuses to heed God's revealed will.

In scripture one finds the term "law" with two very different meanings, one positive and the other negative. Here the psalmist speaks of "law" in the positive sense that we find in Deuteronomy 4:1: "Give heed to the statutes and the ordinances which I teach you, and do them; that you may live."

The term "law" can also have a negative connotation— most often in contrast to "grace." We find this in John 1:17 and frequently in the writings of Paul (Rom. 4:15*f*; 6:14; 8:3-6).

Psalm 1 describes the blessedness, prosperity, and joy of the one whose delight is the law of the Lord. What does it mean to delight in the law of the Lord? (See Ps. 119:9-16.)

The man or woman who would prosper in all that he or she does is one who not only delights in God's law but also meditates on it day and night. This implies a regular pattern of consciously putting the word of God into one's heart and mind, taking time to think and reflect—allowing the words to become insights through the operation of God's Spirit breathing life into one's personal understanding and actions.

Prayer: *O Lord, this day I will choose the way of blessedness. Teach me to delight in your law. Enable me to sink my roots deep into your word through regular times of meditation. Amen.*

Wednesday, May 15 Read John 17:14-19, 25-26.

God can keep us in his world.

It is important to let the Bible determine our attitude toward life. Jesus asked his Father to keep the disciples *in* the world and to keep them *from* the evil one. This has been misunderstood many times in church history, and Christians have tried to keep themselves *from* the world.

To avoid the world in order to escape its nastiness, preclude persecution, or to keep ourselves clean is simply wrong. Jesus' words are too clear: "My prayer is not that you take them out of the world . . ." (NIV). Christians can be *in the world* but not *of the world*. In fact, we must be. How often have you sung "This Is My Father's World"? Meditate on the final verse of Maltbie Babcock's great hymn:

> This is my Father's world,
>   O let me ne'er forget
> That though the wrong seems oft so strong,
>   God is the ruler yet.
> This is my Father's world:
>   Why should my heart be sad?
> The Lord is King: let the heavens ring!
>   God reigns: let the earth be glad!*

Now reread John 17:18, 25-26. Our mission is to make Jesus known to the world in order that the love of God might be made known to all.

Prayer: *Dear Son of God, forgive me for living all too often in a heaven of my own making rather than on the path to heaven you walked—caring for children, helping the poor, the infirmed, and the powerless, and loving your enemies. Amen.*

---

*The United Methodist *Book of Hymns*, no. 45.

Thursday, May 16   Read 1 John 5:11-12.

God can keep us in his Son.

Although Paul's letters are full of references and insights concerning what it means to be "in Christ," our reading today takes us to the First Epistle of John. In a few concise words the writer sets before us the very essence of life, both here and hereafter:

> And this is the testimony, that God gave us eternal life, and this life is in his Son. He who has the Son has life; he who has not the Son of God has not life.

These words are almost like a New Testament echo of Moses' words in the Old Testament:

> I call heaven and earth to witness against you this day, that I have set before you life and death, blessing and curse; therefore choose life, that you and your descendants may live, loving the Lord your God, obeying his voice, and cleaving to him; for that means life to you and length of days, that you may dwell in the land which the Lord swore to your fathers . . . (Deut. 30:19-20).

The entire Epistle of First John describes what Christians believe about the Christian life. This letter was one of John and Charles Wesley's favorite books of the Bible. As an act of discipleship and a means of spiritual growth, read the entire book sometime this week.

Prayer: *O Lord, teach me more of what it means to be in Christ. Help me to understand that this is the central issue of life. In Jesus' name. Amen.*

Friday, May 17   Read John 17:13.

God can keep us in his joy.

Jesus' desire is that his followers "may have the full mea-sure of my joy within them" (NIV). Sometimes we confuse joy with happiness and think that genuine joy is the absence of difficulty.

The word *happy* is defined by Webster as "favored by luck or fortune—enjoying well-being and contentment." It is in-teresting that the words *happy* and *happiness* are rarely found in scripture.

What kind of joy does the Bible speak of? Joy is a by-product of the life of God in the souls of people. Jesus endured the pain of death on the cross for the joy of reconcil-ing us to God (Heb. 12:2). We know that the disciples were filled with joy when they saw the resurrected Christ ascend into heaven (Luke 24:52). James tells us to "count it all joy, my brethren, when you meet various trials . . ." (James 1:2). Obviously, the kind of joy the scripture speaks of is not dependent upon the absence of difficulty or some fortuitous event.

What is the source of true joy? How could Paul and Silas still sing and pray in prison at midnight after being severely beaten and thrown into prison?

Christian joy is not dependent on outward circumstances but on the condition of the inward life of the spirit. It is time for us to rediscover this essential insight so that our experi-ence will be like that of the first disciples who were "filled with joy and with the Holy Spirit" (Acts 13:52).

Prayer: *Lord Jesus, fulfill your promise in me today. Forgive my sin and enter in. Fill me with the genuine joy that comes from the Holy Spirit. Amen.*

Saturday, May 18   Read 1 John 4:7–5:3.

God can keep us in his love.

There is nothing in you or me that can earn, deserve, or merit God's love. God loved us first (1 John 4:19). "While we were yet sinners Christ died for us" (Rom. 5:8). The love of God is the key to all of life, both here and hereafter.

Being kept by the power of God means that we are preserved and protected by the power of love. The mystery of how divine sovereignty and divine love interact will always be beyond our comprehension. The same thing is true concerning the will of God and human freedom. However, what is important for us today is to know that God is love. The issue that faces us is how to respond to God's love and whether or not we choose to share that love with others—for the primary characteristic of divine love is that it is always giving.

To be truly Christian, love must first of all be dynamic: "God so loved the world that he *gave*. . . ." Secondly, it must be relational: ". . . he gave his only Son, that whoever believes in him. . . ." And finally, it must deal with the very essence of life: "whoever believes in him should not perish but have eternal life." (See John 3:16.)

As Christians, we are kept by God's love, but we cannot keep God's love unless we are willing to share it with others through meaningful spiritual relationships.

Prayer: *Lord, make me an instrument of your love this day. Help me to put my faith into action by showing me when, where, and how to give. Amen.*

Sunday, May 19   Read 1 John 5:9-13.

God can keep us eternally and give us an assurance of our salvation.

One of the immeasurable joys of being kept by the power of God is the freedom from fear either about this life or the life to come. Our lesson for today was written to believers "that you may know that you have eternal life."

Assurance of salvation is a fundamental doctrine of the church. John Wesley wrote and published two sermons on this topic specifically. Here is an excerpt from the second sermon:

> By the testimony of the Spirit, I mean, an inward impression on the soul, whereby the Spirit of God immediately and directly witnesses to my spirit, that I am a child of God; that Jesus Christ hath loved me, and given himself for me; that all my sins are blotted out, and I, even I, am reconciled to God. . . . He so works upon the soul by his immediate influence, and by a strong, though inexplicable operation, that the stormy wind and troubled waves subside, and there is a sweet calm; the heart resting as in the arms of Jesus, and the sinner being clearly satisfied that God is reconciled, that all his "iniquities are forgiven, and his sins covered."*

Prayer: *Grant, O God, that this day I may have a deep assurance that I am yours and you are mine. From that base of deep calm, let me minister your healing love to others. In Jesus' name. Amen.*

---

*The Works of John Wesley (Grand Rapids, Michigan: Zondervan) vol. V, pp. 124-125.

WIND OVER MATTER

May 20-26, 1985   **David R. Hunsberger†**
Monday, May 20   Read Acts 2:1-4.

A newspaper cartoon pictured the stereotyped politician, a senator who welcomed the reporters but who never gave them a straight answer. On his desk lay his own book entitled *Wind Over Matter.* In that cartoon's clever twist of a familiar phrase the church long ago found sober, yet exciting truth.

The Bible often portrays the Spirit of God by the striking figure of wind or breath. What the Genesis narrative related as the dawn of human consciousness (2:7), Paul the apostle applied in Romans 8:2 to celebrate the blessing of the gospel.

Acts contains the Bible's witness to the triumph of wind over matter at Pentecost. The occasion became a sort of church birthday, coming fifty days (*Pentecost* means "fifty") after its Lord's resurrection.

The onset of our warm weather suggests the Palestinian wind's dependable summer relief for any who face that climate's heat. The prevailing sea breeze reaches the hill country by late morning. Shortly after noon, pedestrians clutch their hats. By late afternoon, the wind may rise to what feels like gale force.

But the wind in Acts 2 struck in the morning. The onrush of the divine presence proved powerful and uncontrollable. Wind prevailed over matter.

Prayer: *Almighty God, in the heat of our work, refresh us by the Holy Spirit. Through Christ, our Lord. Amen.*

---

†Pastor, Spring City United Methodist Church, Spring City, Pennsylvania.

Tuesday, May 21   Read Acts 2:5-21.

Wind over matter guarantees new management for the church. It answers the question posed in Acts 2:12.

If a restaurant or gasoline station announces new management, its customers expect quicker and better service. How long that can last no one knows. But for a while, at least, it may promise a welcome change.

Pentecost serves notice that the church needs that sort of management change permanently. To some congregations this will seem easy: simply get a new pastor. Their pastors may counter with an equally facile solution: get a new congregation.

The church requires both. But Pentecost answers that need with no change in personnel. Management belongs to the one who alone holds the right to assume charge, namely the Spirit of God.

This new management requires certain changes in the church. Unwillingness to act amounts, by itself, to a decision. Whatever the choice, its result will show as plainly as any sign hanging out front.

The common expression "my church" illustrates the ease of forgetting this. To refer to one's own congregation, parish, charge, circuit, or denomination is one thing. But "my" church? No.

The institution belongs to its Founder. Its first members did not take over after he ascended. Pentecost made clear that those followers acknowledged who was in command.

Whatever any church building's outdoor signboard may read, it actually announces either "Under New Management" or "Out of Business."

Prayer: *Eternal God, prompt us to let the Spirit take over. Through the Lord of the Church. Amen.*

Wednesday, May 22   Read Ezekiel 37:1-14.

A well-known preacher of an earlier generation had to move unwillingly. Worse, many of his less cooperative parishioners followed him. Yet that unwelcome transfer marked a turning point in his career. Had he not moved, we would never have heard any more from him.

One day that preacher—Ezekiel the prophet—stood on a battlefield where the soldiers apparently fled in such haste as not even to take time to bury the bodies of their fallen comrades. Meanwhile, the jackals and vultures finished their grisly job. Only whitened bones—thousands of them—remained, strewn all over the open valley.

First, the prophet took a survey of the human wreckage that littered the landscape. Then came a divine command to preach to that dead congregation. Ezekiel obeyed, listened, and watched a remarkable change take place.

Behind this parsonage stands a backyard pole supporting a weather vane. Its arrow veers to the slightest shift in wind direction. The gentlest breeze starts those blades turning.

But God's wind over matter concerns no ordinary atmospheric disturbance. When Paul warned against useless, changeable teaching in Ephesians 4:14, his word for wind differs from the ones that announced the Spirit's coming in Acts 2:2 and 4.

Ezekiel summoned the breath of life from the four winds. The weather bureau would call that unlikely. Was the prophet only exercising poetic license? Perhaps. But his words pointed to another method in the operation of wind over matter.

Prayer: *Infinite God, turn us to the gospel's truth. Through the Pioneer of our faith. Amen.*

Thursday, May 23   Read Psalm 104:29-30.

God's wind over matter accomplishes more than just a maintenance function. The divine breath confers life on every created being.

Some 270 miles up the Nile, a peasant woman uncovered a heap of cuneiform tablets back in 1887. Their wedge-shaped characters proved to be royal correspondence registering complaints from petty princes in Canaan. The site turned out to be the seat of the Egyptian government during that brief interval historians call the Amarna Age.

One of those Amarna tablets preserved a hymn to the sun god. Its translators wondered what relation, if any, it held to the Old Testament nature psalm, 104. That psalm cites the need of all living things for Yahweh's creative breath. "Hymn to Aton" extols the solar deity, whose breath bestows life.

The church expresses that idea in Christian terms with the ninth-century hymn "Veni Creator Spiritus"; in English, "Come, Holy Ghost, Our Souls Inspire."

The Bible uses the word *create* more carefully than does average English speech. That word occurs more than forty times in the Old Testament, nearly always with God as its subject. Its personal meaning sounds in the prayer for a clean heart in Psalm 51:10. But it takes on cosmic force in the promise of new heavens and a new earth in Isaiah 65:17.

The church's life depends on the Holy Spirit's life-giving breath. Otherwise, nothing else avails. To remain the church of Christ, God's people have no choice. The divine wind must prevail over matter.

Prayer: *God of all creation, by the Spirit's breath of life renew creation within us. Through the High Priest of our confession. Amen.*

155

Friday, May 24   Read Romans 8:22-27.

Wind over matter stands among the most important, yet easily most neglected beliefs. In a sentence: Sin against the Christ may be forgiven, but not one against the Holy Spirit, says Matthew 12:32.

God's wind holds authority over all matter, including any institution or book. In the third century, Cyprian of Carthage asserted that no one can "have God for his Father who has not the Church for his mother." Others report that Jerome suggested that not knowing the scripture means not knowing the Christ. But Irenaeus of Lyons had preceded them both by insisting that neglecting the Holy Spirit means ignoring the Creator and lacking Jesus Christ, the life. Without the Spirit, worship sinks into idolatry and faith fades into intellectualism or hardens into legalism.

Instead, the Spirit brings life. Paul's words recall the law's command in Numbers 28:26 to consecrate the first fruits of the wheat harvest. The church appropriately presented a Pentecost thank offering of about 3,000 conversions.

Then the apostle cites the kind of firm hope that, in the New Testament, does not invoke wishful thinking. The business person *hopes* the economy will improve. The farmer *hopes* for adequate rainfall. But New Testament hope confidently awaits God's promises. It confronts the Christian with positive assurance in the face of complete insecurity. This brings joy (Rom. 12:12), confidence (Heb. 10:23), comfort (2 Thess. 2:16) and security (Heb. 6:19). All because it centers in Jesus Christ, our hope (1 Tim. 1:1).

Prayer: *God of all truth, illumine the sacred page and revive the church. Through the living Word. Amen.*

Saturday, May 25   Read John 15:26-27.

God's wind over matter offers unity to the church. Acts 2:14 cites that unified apostolic witness.

The Nicene Creed describes the Holy Spirit as proceeding from the Father, as described in John 15:26. But a western insertion "and the Son" drove a wedge between East and West in the medieval church.

In the country where the church took its start, Christian unity may sometimes assert itself with surprising force. Nowadays tours to that land have grown popular. If you go, take your time and use your legs.

Two visitors did that when a North Carolina student offered his companionship on a hike starting from the coast at Haifa across lower Galilee. The second day's tramping brought us to Nazareth, but entering that town from the west caused confusion when certain familiar landmarks failed to appear. Two Arab residents came along and kindly gave directions.

After asking whether we were Jewish or Christian, one of them said, "I am Orthodox and my friend here is Protestant." Then, seizing my arm with a viselike grip he added, *"But we are one in Christ!"*

Whether the Holy Spirit proceeds from the Son as well as from the Father apparently did not concern those two Arabs. Something more pressing occupied their minds.

Christian unity means nothing as a vapory hope. Like the incarnate Lord, it must take expression in flesh and blood.

Those fingers on my arm left no doubt about that.

Prayer: *God of peace, seal our unity in Christ for a solid witness. Through him who before Pontius Pilate made the good confession. Amen.*

Sunday, May 26 (Pentecost)
Read John 16:4*b*-15.

God's wind over matter fulfills a promise. Yet that same benefit may loom as a threat.

Diggers who excavate the land of the Bible sometimes contend with a breeze that greets them with more force than they find agreeable. Dusty whirlwinds may blind the workers or scatter their tools.

At the 1972 Beersheba expedition the surveyor needed help to read and record elevations in meters above sea level. A tripod supported a theodolite to take readings at any angle. An idle moment brought the urge to turn the instrument around and gaze off in the opposite direction. At perhaps two kilometers across the Negeb's bleached expanse, the lens focused on a Bedouin harvest scene. A draft animal dragged a sledge endlessly around a makeshift threshing floor. The wind whisked the chaff away.

No one disputes the church's need to discard its chaff. But what (or even *who*) is that chaff?

Every Bible reader recalls the winnowing of chaff described in the first psalm. But what the Spirit really does on coming (John 16:8) may not set so well.

And, if the Spirit addresses all society, why not the church? The congregation stuck in its own rut may find this gale more than distracting. Wind over matter promises—or threatens—a winnowing.

Prayer: *God of all grace, enable us to face the Spirit's prevailing wind, whatever the risk. Through him who in every respect was tempted as we are. Amen.*

Changed!

May 27–June 2, 1985
Monday, May 27

Ruth Brunk Stoltzfus†
Read Isaiah 6:1-8.

A changed view

It was no ordinary experience that day. The temple was shaken to its foundation and Isaiah to the core of his being. When Isaiah saw the Lord, he saw himself as hopelessly unclean and undone, in the midst of a people likewise in ruin.

Isaiah was likely a priest or a prophet at the time. Do religious leaders sometimes need a self-shattering experience before the Lord? Isaiah belonged to the aristocracy, but of what importance were social standing and economic or political success before an awesomely holy God? In that awesome presence he had a changed view of the Lord, of himself, his people, his mission.

Do you and I ever see the Lord? Moses saw the One who is invisible (Heb. 11:27, NIV). Jesus said anyone who had seen him had seen God (John 14:9). Paul said Christ is the image of the invisible God (Col. 1:15). Peter said, "Though you have not seen him, you love him . . . you believe in him and are filled with an inexpressible . . . joy" (1 Pet. 1:8, NIV).

There is a sure seeing by the eyes of faith, a knowing by a renewed mind, a believing by a surrendered heart that goes beyond any ordinary perceptions. This seeing can change our approach to all of life.

Prayer: *Lord, I want to see you and see myself in life-changing ways, through Christ. Amen.*

---

†Mennonite speaker and writer, Harrisonburg, Virginia.

Tuesday, May 28   Read Isaiah 6:6-7;
                                            John 3:1-17;
                                       Ephesians 4:22-24.

A changed self

Isaiah was well-educated and capable, but before a holy God he cried, "Woe to me! I am ruined!" (NIV) Only when he came to the end of himself could he find forgiveness, inner peace, and God's direction for his life.

In Jesus' time, a learned, influential Jew came for a night-time interview. Jesus said to him, "You must be born anew," explaining this second birth as being "born of the Spirit." Nicodemus did not understand what Jesus was talking about. As a good, upright Jewish leader, wasn't he all right just as he was? With all his theological learning, he was not aware that human efforts are not enough, that the human heart is sinful and in need of changing by God's power.

Since we do need a healthy sense of self, how do we reconcile that fact with the Bible teaching that we must die to self? (Rom. 6:2*f*) I struggled for years with this apparent contradiction. Ephesians 4:22-24 was to me a flash of light in the darkness when I saw the answer of the two selves. We die to the old, sinful, deceitful, self-centered self and realize a new, Christ-centered self "created to be like God in true righteousness and holiness" (NIV).

Then there is a continuing work of the Spirit in us for God's glory, not ours. We "reflect the Lord's glory . . . being transformed into his likeness with ever-increasing glory, which comes from the Lord, who is the Spirit" (2 Cor. 3:18, NIV).

Prayer: *Lord, help me to die to self, then to live a new life of love by your resurrection power. Amen.*

Wednesday, May 29   Read 2 Tim. 3:2-5; Psalm 29.

Changed talking

Timothy describes the ungodly as "boastful" and "lovers of themselves" (NIV). They have a form of godliness but deny its power, says the Letter to Timothy.

The power has not changed us deeply enough until we boast about the Lord rather than ourselves. (Affirmation is quite another thing, and we all need it from each other.) The changed Paul said, "May I never boast except in the cross of our Lord Jesus Christ" (Gal. 6:14, NIV).

Isn't it amazing that we sometimes try to squeeze in impressive words about ourselves while serving as messengers of God? The story about ourselves that will inspire others is one in which, like others, we had or we saw a definite need and God met that need.

The psalmist boasts that way: "I will exalt you, O Lord, for you lifted me out of the depths . . ." (Ps. 30:1, NIV). Psalm 29:1 says, "Ascribe to the Lord glory and strength." After telling of God's mighty power over nature, the psalm shows such a God abounding in love and power on behalf of people.

Some of us may wish to write our personal psalm of praise for the way God has watched over our pilgrimage and undertaken for us. I will share one part of mine:

"You sustained me when crisis struck. With tiny infant in my arms, I knew I might not live. You gave me grace to say, 'Your way is best.' And then you snatched me back from the gates of death! I thank you, God of strength!"

Prayer: *Forgive us, Lord, for being too quiet about your acts of love and care. Amen.*

Thursday, May 30   Read Romans 8:12-17.

A changed center

Once we are born of the Spirit, we live according to the Spirit and not according to our sinful nature. We humans, weak on our own, now have more than a "want-to." We have the "power-to," by the indwelling Holy Spirit. But this is not automatic, coming without effort on our part.

Note Paul's action words for us in the Romans passage. Paul often refers to the continuing tension between living by the sinful nature and living by the Spirit. Those who are led by the Spirit are sons and daughters of God! Jesus prayed, "Abba, Father" (Mark 14:36, NIV). Now, through the work of redemption, God is also *our* Father. By the real presence and prompting of the Holy Spirit, we can say with feeling, perhaps with tears of joy, "Father, my Father." Being in God's family means we are heirs of God and have a common inheritance with Christ!

But wait. This is not an easy Christianity that calls us to personal salvation so we can sit back while asking God to bring on the blessings. If we are co-heirs with Christ, sharing Christ's sufferings must precede sharing Christ's glory. Distinct from those afflictions common to everyone, these sufferings come to us because we belong to Christ. We must go counter to customs and commands around us when they are contrary to Jesus' way. That goes along with being in the family.

Prayer: *Father, my Father, I thank you that through Jesus I can be in your family and experience the presence, power, and joy of your Holy Spirit, even in the midst of pain. Keep me close to you and true to you in times of suffering for Jesus' sake. Amen.*

Friday, May 31   Read Luke 14:25-33; 1 John 2:6.

A changed loyalty

There is a first loyalty and there are lesser loyalties. Jesus made it clear that loyalty to him is absolute and every other loyalty is like hatred in contrast. He said, "Any of you who does not give up everything . . . cannot be my disciple" (NIV). EVERYTHING! What fierce loyalty Christ demands, in contrast to our puny ideas of easy Christianity! Jesus said also, "Anyone who does not carry his cross and follow me cannot be my disciple."

What is our cross? Draw a vertical line on a page to represent ways of our culture that are contrary to Jesus' way. One-fourth of the way down the page from the top, draw a short line across to represent the fact that we must go counter to those ways because we belong to Christ. That is our cross, a place of pain and joy. Like Paul we are "sorrowful, yet always rejoicing" (2 Cor. 6:10).

What does it mean to "follow Christ?" John says, "Whoever claims to live in him must walk as Jesus did" (NIV). There go our materialism, nationalism, and militarism, the idols of our time in which we trust.

A Catholic bishop was once asked how members of the faith in one country could kill members of the faith in another country during war time. He answered that it can happen only when loyalty to nation is put above loyalty to God.

Some of us yet have a cross to take up in obedience to Christ and the new order Christ came to bring.

Prayer: *Lord God, give us courage for our time. Help us to be faithful to you and willing to take the consequences of obedience to you in the spirit of Christ. Amen.*

Saturday, June 1   Read Isaiah 6:8; 2 Cor. 5:14-21.

A changed mission

After a view of the Lord, of himself, and of his people, Isaiah soon heeded a call from God for mission. As a prophet, Isaiah spoke hard messages to the people and their leaders, for they had forgotten God and forsaken justice. He spoke of hope, too, as he prophesied of the coming Messiah.

Paul had had a quick change of mission when he saw and heard the Lord on the road to Damascus. The persecutor-turned-servant-of-Christ-and-the-church gave the secret of his incredible strength: "I labor, . . . with all *his energy*, which so powerfully works in me" (Col. 1:29, NIV, italics added).

The Holy Spirit gifts, calls, and enables each one in the church for a unique part in its ministries, both within the church and in a world of physical and spiritual poverty.

Once we are changed, we no longer live for ourselves but for Christ who died for us and was raised again (NIV). Imagine! God "has committed to us the message of reconciliation"; we are Christ's ambassadors! Paul says, "Christ's love compels us" (NIV).

Years ago when I discovered those little strips of correction paper for covering my typing errors, I wanted to tell everyone about it. I called friends in area offices and asked, "Do you know about . . . ?" I was excited enough about this mundane thing to make sure others knew about it.

If we are excited about Christ's wonderful act of covering our sins, we will want to tell everyone!

Prayer: *Lord, take my mind and think through it, my heart and love through it, my voice and speak through it, my hands and help through them, my feet and walk through them, through your energy in me. Amen.*

Sunday, June 2   Read 2 Corinthians 5:1-5.

A changed address

Thank God we have "an eternal house in heaven, not built by human hands" (NIV). We would not want this earth with its ills to be our permanent address.

The Bible describes our short time on earth as "a fleeting shadow" (Job 14:2, NIV), "swifter than a weaver's shuttle" (Job 7:6, NIV), "a mere handbreath" (Ps. 39:5, NIV). Often we have a reminder that our stay here is brief and uncertain: the death of a loved one, a narrow escape in an accident, a medical test, an alarming X ray, or a serious operation and statistics that say we likely will not live.

Let us look now at our hands. One day they will lie still in death. This need not alarm us if we understand God's plan. Jesus Christ lived and died to "destroy him who holds the power of death—that is, the devil—and free those who all their lives were held in slavery by their fear of death" (Heb. 2:15, NIV).

When this meaning breaks through to us, we can actually graduate from fear to longing. Paul says that our body is an earthly tent, that we long "to be clothed with our heavenly dwelling" (NIV).

In Christ and because of Christ, we are "incurably" full of hope. Jesus said to the troubled disciples, "I will come back and take you to be with me" (John 14:3, NIV). That is still the plan. When Christ comes or death comes, we will be home at last!

Prayer: *Lord, for all of time and eternity we want to praise you that you became the way for wanderers like us, the truth for doubters like us, the life for dying people like us. Amen.*

TRUSTING THE WAYS OF GOD

June 3-9, 1985   **David Randell Boone**†
Monday, June 3   Read 1 Samuel 16:14-23.

The narrator has made it clear in the preceding section that Saul is on his way out as king, to be replaced by David, the Bethlehem shepherd. Samuel the prophet has effected this transition by anointing David in the presence of his brothers. From now on, the reader understands that God's spirit rests upon David.

With tragic irony, the newly anointed David is brought in as Saul's court harpist and armor-bearer. Saul has unwittingly allowed himself to be positioned to witness the swift rise of the figure who will displace him.

God's role in this text may seem startling. God is a personal agent who causes historical events: *God* transfers favor from Saul to David, and *God* sends the evil spirit that troubles Saul.

Hebrew religion courageously recognized the implications of the personal sovereignty of God. It affirmed that God is ultimately responsible for evil as well as good. We recall that Saul had disobeyed God by sparing Agag and the best goods after Israel's destruction of the Amalekites. But later kings disobeyed God without losing their thrones. Why, then, such arbitrary treatment of Saul?

Prayer: *O God, with sovereign freedom you direct the history of humankind into the channels of your own purposes. When trouble strikes, give us grace to trust that those purposes are ultimately good. Amen.*

---

†Pastor, Harpeth Presbyterian Church, Brentwood, Tennessee.

Tuesday, June 4   Read 1 Samuel 16:14-23.

A satisfying answer to the question posed at the end of yesterday's meditation may be beyond us. This ancient text about Saul and David addresses some of our present theological perplexities, the perplexities of those who ask why God causes or allows unjust suffering and the uneven distribution of good life.

One may deny that God is all-powerful. One may believe that God does not cause or allow nuclear wars or the deaths of children because God is powerless over a random universe of chance happenings.

This perspective—that God does not cause unjust suffering nor allow evil because God's only option is impotently to suffer with us—has never been embraced by a majority of Christians. The prevailing Christian understanding has always been that what God does and allows to happen reflect God's reasons, reasons that may and often do baffle us. God loves Jacob but hates Esau, hardens Pharaoh's heart, and transfers favor from Saul to David. God knows why; we can only trust in God.

Some of God's ways are past tracing out (see Rom. 11:33-36, where this thought leads to a doxology). And this is, after all, what we should expect if God is really the sovereign God of the Bible and of us finite creatures with limited powers of understanding. On the other hand, we need never fear asking—even, with some of the psalms, demanding—God to give us an explanation for the messes we're in, the injustices we see, the doubts we cannot dismiss.

Prayer: *Eternal God, we adore and own your all-wise sovereignty. Enlighten our minds to your will and ways as far as our capacity will allow. Amen.*

Wednesday, June 5   Read Psalm 57.

This psalm is prefaced by a reference to David's fleeing from Saul and seeking refuge in the cave at Adullam (1 Sam. 22:1), and so traditionally has found a place in the Saul-David drama. But precisely who the psalmist is—it may or may not be David—is not important, for the psalm itself tells us that its author is beset by fierce and dangerous enemies. The first part of the psalm, therefore, is a desperate cry to God for help and justice, the second a hopeful thanksgiving for the relief and vindication that the beleaguered one hopes will come soon.

The theological bases for the appeal are God's covenant love, firm and unchanging, and God's purpose for the psalmist. If the author is David, he would surely be thinking of his just having been anointed by Samuel for the purpose of leading Israel.

Anyone who has ever felt led by God to a particular task understands that there are moments when opposition can cause the person to doubt that the response is to a genuine call of God. The lions seeking to trap us are varied: competing commitments, physical threats, financial barriers, illness. To be faithful to our calling we need solid roots in God's steadfast love for us. Then *our* hearts, too, will be steadfast in the awareness that God's purpose for us will not fail.

Prayer: *O God, from whom all holy desires, all good counsels, and all just works proceed: Give to your servants that peace which the world cannot give, that our hearts may be set to obey your commandments, and that, defended from the fear of our enemies, we may pass our time in rest and quietness. Through the merits of Jesus Christ our Savior. Amen.**

---

*Adapted from "A Collect for Peace," *The Book of Common Prayer*, The Episcopal Church (Church Hymnal Corporation and The Seabury Press, 1977), p. 123.

Thursday, June 6   Read 2 Corinthians 4:13-15.

Paul interprets his catalogue of apostolic sufferings (2 Cor. 4:7-12) as a living out of the death and resurrection of Christ. Continually afflicted, perplexed, persecuted, struck down, and given up to death, Paul is never defeated or destroyed. He never gives up. Why?

The answer lies in the nature of Paul's faith. Paul is a man of faith who is often puzzled about the meaning of things. He is not usually victorious over his enemies. He prefers to list sufferings, not resounding success stories. His opponents often get the better of him. And in the midst of this human weakness, Paul says that this is the way life in the world under the cross is until the Lord comes. The treasure of the gospel is contained in earthen vessels, and God's power is perfected in human weakness.

Paul's apostolic style is not that of a triumphant general who wins campaigns by brilliant strategies. He is rather more like the faithful and true field sergeant who daily muddles through in the hope that headquarters will forward the needed supplies and in the humble confidence that if he does his part well and faithfully, the fighting will one day end.

Paul says that he and his converts have the same spirit of faith as the author of Psalm 116, whom he quotes. The psalmist had kept faith in the goodness and loving purposes of God during a bad time when he was afflicted and depressed. Paul says *that* is the spirit of faith: loyalty and trust that God's promises are true in spite of setbacks and crosses and the routine anxieties of life.

Prayer: *O God, I thank you that my salvation does not depend on my successes, and that what you want most from me is loyalty. Keep me faithful. Amen.*

Friday, June 7   Read 2 Corinthians 4:16-18.

To lose heart, to give up on the entire Christian enterprise, was an occasional temptation even for those who lived in the first dawn of the church. For a faith that was only a generation old, this pang of doubt and discouragement must have sometimes been acute.

The problem of walking by faith and not sight, in that era or this, is that there is no immediate, practical principle to test its claims. David must have wondered periodically whether the promise of his anointing would ever be realized, for Saul held the reins of power. Who would not be tempted, in a moment of weakness, to question the promise?

A similar uncertainty made many early Christians nervous. Jesus had not returned. Sporadic persecution of Christians by the authorities had broken out. And Christians wrangled among themselves about the true interpretation of the faith. Paul's gospel, in particular, was controversial, and was not approved by many Jewish Christians living in Palestine. Some even questioned whether he was a genuine apostle.

So one could easily lose heart and doubt the promise. But Paul didn't, at least never for very long at a time, because the one thing that he could not doubt was the evidence of his own Christian experience: outward bodily suffering accompanied by a daily inward renewal and transformation into the likeness of his Lord. His inmost life was being re-formed by the power of God. Like it or not—and I'm afraid many of us don't like it—the evidence of inner personal renewal is still the best testimony of the authenticity of Christianity. And to God be the glory.

Prayer: *O God, may the pentecostal fire of your love burn out my sins and refine me daily into a holier person. Through Jesus Christ. Amen.*

Saturday, June 8   Read Mark 3:20-27.

This passage surely represents an authentic historical tradition from Jesus' ministry, although the other two synoptic gospels report the setting as the healing of a mute demoniac (Matt. 12:22-32; Luke 11:14-23). All three references remind us that Jesus was renowned as a healer and an exorcist, as well as a teacher. Jesus was concerned with body, mind, and soul together; and the modern medical profession inherits his mantle as legitimately as educators and ministers.

Jesus had just come down from the Galilean mountain where he had commissioned the twelve whom he had called to be with him. Back at home he found the still-clamoring crowd, anxious for healings and exorcisms, an impatient family, and a group of critical scribes visiting from Jerusalem. What a reception!

Jesus' conversation with the scribes contains two opposing interpretations of his ministry. The scribes, perhaps put off by the crassness of crowd behavior and Jesus' sympathetic response, said that the only way Jesus could cast out demons was to be himself possessed by a demon.

By way of response to the scribes' interpretation of what was going on, Jesus said, "Nonsense." If Satan is at war with Satan, then his forces against good are compromised. But if you look around, you see that this is not so. Evil, in the forms of illness, mental disorder, cruelty, injustice, is yet oppressing. When you see the forces of evil checked, therefore, the only adequate explanation is that a stronger force of good has prevailed.

Prayer: *Strong Son of God, come in power today to bind the powers of evil wherever they oppress. Amen.*

171

Sunday, June 9   Read Mark 3:28-35.

Some sayings of Jesus are more difficult to understand than others, and some are more liable to misinterpretation. This passage and its parallels have arguably caused more grief and unnecessary anxiety to faithful Christian people than any other passage in the New Testament. This is unfortunate, because the true import of the section on "the sin against the Holy Spirit" is to offer comfort and assurance to disciples of Jesus.

To begin with, notice the important introductory assertion that "all sins will be forgiven" and "whatever blasphemies they utter." That is a categorical promise that *nothing* humans do or think or say, including the most horrible thoughts and terrible atrocities, are beyond the bounds of God's forgiveness. And Christians must never lose hold on that promise. It's the gospel.

To grasp the meaning of the next phrase that begins "but whoever blasphemes against the Holy Spirit" requires that we remember who evoked this saying: those critical scribes who said Jesus was possessed by the prince of demons. They had witnessed the spiritual power of the kingdom of God in Jesus' ministry, power that could heal and drive out demons, and they had interpreted it as evil.

And the point of Jesus' saying about the "eternal sin" of blasphemy against the Holy Spirit is that there are some people whom not even God can forgive. Not because God is not willing to forgive them, but because they persist in resisting his love and in perceiving good as evil.

Prayer: *God of compassion, cast out our demons and do not let them triumph over us, for the love of Christ. Amen.*

To Be Led by God

June 10-16, 1985   **Sally Dyck†**
Monday, June 10   Read Psalm 46:1-7.

Looking out over a congregation still unsure of what to make of a woman pastor, I began my ministry with the words of the psalmist: "We will not fear though the earth should change . . . the mountains shake . . . waters roar and foam." If we claim to have faith in God in the midst of all kinds of earth-shattering experiences, surely God remains our rock and our salvation even though a tiny woman has become the pastor! Fear of the unknown causes us to lose all perspective and courage.

Asking suburbanites to attend district leadership events at the downtown church after dark brought looks of terror and incredulity to their faces. Surely the God who promises to be with us though "the nations rage . . . [and] the kingdoms totter" will be with those who venture into the inner city in Christ's name!

Psalm 46 is a song of courage and faith. It is not meant for the one looking only to comfortable experiences or the one who desires a convenient life, uncomplicated by the changes which come through growth and newness. It is not meant for the one who walks the well-trodden path. Psalm 46 is meant for the one who hears God's call to walk the less-traveled path into the unfamiliar and unknown territory of faith.

Prayer: *O God, who helps us "right early," may we not lose perspective but trust in the ways you are able to make us grow in faith. Amen.*

---

†Pastor, Church of the Redeemer, Cleveland Heights, Ohio.

Tuesday, June 11   Read Psalm 46:8-11.

The medical community is telling us of a new epidemic: that of stress-related illnesses. Stress affects people in all walks of life, from the custodian to the corporate executive and from the factory worker to the housewife. All suffer from stress and, therefore, have the potential for stress-related illnesses.

We usually associate stress with the big crises of our lives, but stress is most pervasive in our daily living. We feel hassled and harried. Life is out of our control even as we struggle to have control. Our values and priorities are out of balance with the ways of God. We feel the rub in our souls like a car that is out of alignment. We get worn-out and irritable.

The psalmist was a soul in distress. The world was crashing in around the psalmist, and it was a struggle to keep a good perspective on faith. The psalmist's situation is timeless. While the circumstances vary from age to age and from person to person, at some point we are souls in distress. We suffer from disease, spiritually and physically.

The psalmist had a solution to the problem. Even when the world is crashing in around us, we can trust that God is present. One thing is required of us in order to recognize God, however, and that is to "be still." Stopping our perpetual busyness and inner commotion is like stopping a locomotive going full speed. But it is only in turning to God that we find peace.

We often insist that we cannot afford the time to stop and be still and listen for God. However, we cannot afford *not* to "be still and know . . . God."

Prayer: *In the stillness of this moment, O God, I seek your voice. Calm me in the midst of life's busyness. Speak to me as clearly as my heart requires. Thank you for your eternal presence. Amen.*

Wednesday, June 12   Read 2 Samuel 1:1, 17-27.

David mourns the loss of Saul and Jonathan, who have fallen in battle at the hands of the Philistines. David's sorrow is great, and so he sings a song of both lamentation and courage in honor of these two fallen warriors. The warfare imagery of the Old Testament is disconcerting to those of us who are advocates of peace in a world that totters on the precipice of nuclear destruction. How do we explain or understand a God who commanded the Israelites to go into battle?

No matter what else we say about the role of warfare in the formation of the ancient Israelite nation, the one lesson that we can learn is that Saul, Jonathan, and David were people who put their lives on the line for God. God guided and protected them in their faithfulness; even when they fell, it was God to whom David turned in his grief.

In light of this context, the warfare imagery should not be cast aside. God calls us to be strong and valiant, not easily dissuaded by hard choices, unpopular stances, and self-giving opportunities of service. In service to others, our lives are no longer our own, but God's. We glibly sing and pray that we offer ourselves to God but are afraid to go to inner cities where love is needed, to touch the victims of sin, and to risk our time, conveniences, and reputations to minister to the hurts of the world.

As advocates for peace, we dare not compromise the courage it takes to put our lives on the line for our faith even when it involves sorrow and hardship. The same God who goes before us in such battles also comforts us in our personal losses.

Suggestion for prayer: *Think about what God has been calling you to do that you have been afraid to do. Ask God for courage to do it and for trust to be faithful.*

Thursday, June 13   Read 2 Corinthians 5:6-10.

The central theme along my journey of faith has been "to be of good courage." Courage is more than bravery in battle; courage is a virtue essential to Christian living. The English word *courage* stems from a word meaning "heart." The heart was considered to be the source of all emotional, intellectual, and spiritual energies in ancient thought. Courage is the mobilization of one's whole self to strive for good in the face of opposition, to be of "good heart."

My early Christian education was filled with the stories of the martyrs who courageously faced death for their faith. In order to fulfill one's calling, courage is necessary. We may not face the danger of death in our daily living, but we do face a multitude of threats in society which can kill our spirits and which threaten the good we seek in Christ Jesus.

Sexism, racism, and classism pervade our society. We need courage to resist their sin. We need courageous people of the faith who stand in opposition to society's systems—and sometimes even to the church—when violent blows are dealt against human equality.

Paul makes it very clear in verse 10 that we all stand in judgment according to the measure of courage which we show in the living out of our faith. As we live courageously, other Christian virtues blossom and grow. It requires hope to "walk by faith, not by sight." One can only be courageous if one is hopeful.

In a world that "just doesn't care," love is a courageous act. Loving those involved in sexism, racism, and classism, as well as loving the victims necessitates the mobilization of one's self to do the good.

Prayer: *O God of grace and courage, who strengthens our heart for the good: encourage us, make us hopeful and loving in a world broken by sin. Amen.*

Friday, June 14   Read Mark 4:30-34.

Speaking in parables may seem strange to us. Would it not have been better if Jesus had simply stated all his knowledge clearly and straight-forwardly to his confused disciples? Our problem begins with what a parable is. It is a story which describes a truth or a comparison of two things, one of which is well-known in order to give insight into what is less familiar to the listener. Therefore, a parable is not in a mysteriously-coded language but in everyday language using ordinary experiences.

Parables were the primary way Jesus talked to his disciples because the stories and comparisons helped them to unlearn and relearn concepts about God. They saw with new eyes and heard with new ears. New images of the ways of God and the kingdom of God broke apart old ways of thinking, and their hearts and minds were challenged. It was through the parables that "he explained everything."

The reason many congregations enjoy good children's sermons is because they are a form of the parable, or an object lesson. A good children's sermon describes something of God in light of a familiar object. A too lengthy or moralistic explanation of the comparison can be its downfall, but the simple comparison can provide new insight into the spiritual life.

Jesus seems to be encouraging his disciples to make their own object lessons and parables from their own experiences. This is how we learn to "theologize," that is, gain new understandings about God through what we know and see around us.

Prayer: *O God, creator of all that we see and know, help us to use our imaginations in such a way that we can come to understand what it is we do not readily see and know otherwise. Amen.*

Saturday, June 15　　　　　　　　Read Mark 4:26-32.

Gardening provides a needed experience for me each year: a reaffirmation in the Creator God. The garden in my backyard is an object lesson of faith, a "faith garden," if you will. Jesus compares the kingdom of God with the scattering of seeds on the ground and their stages of growth into maturity.

Planting seeds brings the doubt out in me. When I look at those dry, dead-looking seeds, I can hardly believe that much will come of them. The fact that a handful of seeds can produce more vegetables than a refrigerator, a freezer, and a storage shelf can hold is truly amazing! Perhaps it is not so much disbelief as a sense of awe at the abundance of God, the abundance which comes from sowing seeds.

Much of what we do in the church is akin to planting seeds. How can this routine, mundane task possibly have anything to do with the kingdom of God? we wonder. Our disbelief emerges when we forget the miracle and abundance of God. What seems like a small, insignificant act can become vital and essential in our own lives or in the lives of others.

It is through the faithful nurturing of small things that the great can happen. A phone call to a sick friend, a card to a shut-in, a few minutes to listen to a troubled teenager are all the small seeds that when sown produce an abundance of spiritual wealth in the recipients' hearts—and in our own. The mustard seed is very small, but it grows rapidly into a large bush. When we are doing small acts of kindness, we need to keep the vision of God's abundance in our minds.

Prayer: *Creator God, thank you for making me who I am because of small seeds sown in my life. Help me to believe in your abundance and thereby sow seeds of kindness and love every day. Amen.*

Sunday, June 16   Read 2 Corinthians 5:14-17.

If we slithered out of our skins periodically like a snake or walked out of our shells like a crustacean or burst forth from our cocoon like a butterfly, we might better understand what it means to be "in Christ" and a "new creation." Changing and growing are expected stages in the lives of God's creatures. These other creatures shed their outer coverings because the body inside has grown too big and is being restricted and confined. It is probably similar to wearing shoes that are too small for the feet.

When we open ourselves to the power, love, and grace of Christ, we are also expected to be growing inside, in our spiritual lives. Like God's creatures, we grow in stages until periodically we emerge as new creations.

As we are growing in Christ, we shed our restricting, confining behaviors, attitudes, and habits. These are our shells, and they are what keep us from being all that God calls us to be. Slowly, often painfully, we must break out of them, leaving them behind.

When we leave our old shells and skins behind, we feel vulnerable and uncertain until new behaviors, attitudes, and habits can be formed to replace them. It takes time to learn the ways of a new creation. Bitterness, anger, guilt, and resentment are hard to shed. We get easily discouraged in our effort to live in Christ. We must remember that we will *always* be growing, that growth is a process we strive for until all "the old has passed away, [and] behold, the new has come."

Prayer: *O God, who is the same throughout the ages, give us the courage to change and grow throughout the various stages of our life and faith. Amen.*

THE CHRISTIAN, A QUALITY LEADER

June 17-23, 1985   **Samuel Kamaleson†**
Monday, June 17   Read 2 Samuel 5:1-5.

Between leaders and followers there is a well understood relationship built on mutual consent.

The need for a new leader in Israel brought representatives of all tribes of Israel to David at Hebron. They identified the strands that make the leader-follower relationship.

1. "Behold, we are your bone and flesh." Leader and people share a common heritage that ensures confidence, commitment, and mutual consent.

2. "In times past, when Saul was king over us, it was you that led out and brought in Israel." David's qualities were already tested and proved.

3. "And the Lord said to you, 'You shall be shepherd of my people Israel, and you shall be prince over Israel.' " The leader has had a call. The call comes from the Lord who is the transcendent authority of both leader and followers, checking any unhealthy self-interests of the leader. As shepherd of God's people, the leader is accountable both to God and to the people. This three-party relationship with the Lord provides for balance and stability. Thus, their relationship can remain productive for a long time.

Prayer: *O Lord, may my loyalty to you, your people, and my relationship to your people remain clear in my mind today and always. In Jesus' name. Amen.*

---

†Vice-President, Pastors' Conferences and Special Ministries, World Vision International, Monrovia, California.

Tuesday, June 18   Read 2 Samuel 5:6-12.

One measurement of successful leadership is the period over which the leader-follower relationship remains productive.

David overcame opposition. He turned ridicule around to make it a proverb in his favor (vs. 6-8). The enemy's stronghold became his. He improved the city. His neighboring kings admired him and supported him. The sphere of the leader's influence expanded.

Can the leader's personal success strain the strands that constitute the leader-follower relationship?

"And David perceived." The leader understands personal success in terms of ultimate purposes. His engagement with history is a result of contemplative understanding of his identity in terms of the events of history around him. He handles success and failure with the same contemplative understanding of the original purposes associated with his identity as a called, committed, and consenting person.

David saw that the Lord had established him as king, that the Lord had exalted the kingdom, and that the Lord had done all of this for the sake of the chosen people, Israel.

Today's Christian leaders act out of their identity in Jesus Christ, made visible as expressed identity within the world where Jesus Christ is *now* Lord. By this contemplative action, these leaders also earn a right to be heard.

Prayer: *Dear Lord, teach me to understand that success is not what happens around me but what constitutes that happening, even your relationship with me and your people. Amen.*

Wednesday, June 19   Read Psalm 48:12-14.

David, the leader, creatively used his "space in history." Jerusalem, the concrete evidence of this fact, conveys the message to succeeding generations.

The Lord, who so miraculously and mightily acted in history to establish Jerusalem, is steadfast, loving, just, and triumphant. Leaders from every succeeding generation who share the commitment of David and his followers to this Lord would experience the same results within their historic setting.

To those who understand their identity in terms of their commitment to God, God will be their guide. Within this commitment God will become the Primary Cause. God will then determine the process by which each leader makes choices in history.

The nature of this covenanting God is steadfast. God will perform this kind of action in history through any leader of any succeeding generation forever and ever.

Every Christian leader has a "space in history." The church is a visible, definable, human community. Its covenant relationship to Jesus Christ and the realization of this covenant, within the context of present history, endorses its claim to a knowledge that the rest of the world is yet to know.

Prayer: *O Lord, may the pattern of your action proven by David, Peter, John Wesley, and others, be the guiding principle in my life as well. Amen.*

Thursday, June 20   Read 2 Corinthians 5:16-19.

The leader of quality is strongly motivated.

The scripture shows that the leader has a new way of measuring people: not by their social birth but by their new birth; not by their advantages, but by their activities; not by themselves, but by Christ; not by what they have, but by what they do; not by what they were, but by what they are.

This new means of measuring others arises because the leader is also a new creation, who lives in a new state. This new personhood results from a new relationship; it does not begin with a personal resolve to be good or to study religion, but begins "in Christ," where the leader is.

The leader understands that the reconciliation this relationship has brought carries the call to bring others into the same reconciliation. In and through Jesus Christ, God has taken the initiative to bring humankind into fully reconciled relationship. The leader, who has verified the truth of this historic action, now must be the initiator in the process of reconciliation. Jesus Christ is the model for this process.

Since "God was in Christ reconciling the world" (KJV), the message and ministry of reconciliation to which the leader is called spells *incarnation*. The leader's response demands personal engagement; and as the leader transforms history, the leader is transformed.

Prayer: *Master, you are my model. Forgive me for having shifted my eyes from you. I hear you call to me to relate to you. Transform me to become like you. Amen.*

Friday, June 21   Read 2 Corinthians 5:20.

There are at least three possible attitudes toward life. We can rebel against existing conditions, against others, ultimately, against God. We can live in resignation and become a pawn in the hands of designing perpetuators of inhuman political and economic dictatorships. The Christian leader's attitude is one of reconciliation. Through Jesus Christ, such a leader is reconciled with God, with self, and with the world. Because Jesus Christ is alive, the leader's reconciled relationship is devoted, dynamic, and relevantly renewed day by day.

Thus, the leader is an envoy for Jesus Christ. Such an appointment as leader carries with it a clear sense of purpose, responsibility, and accountability. Contemplating this aspect of the appointment can serve as a strong antidote if a leader becomes depressed.

The appointment also provides privileges, such as the privilege of representing others. This representation transcends national, racial, and other divisions. The appointment carries resources. In Ephesians 1:11-14, the leader is reminded that God sends the Holy Spirit to provide renewable, enhancing, enlightening energy for the leader.

Prayer: *Master, so often I set my eyes on scriptural definitions of appointment and task. Enable me to see the more basic realities. Enable me to know that I must serve as an ambassador for you—to your people and to the world. Amen.*

Saturday, June 22   Read 2 Corinthians 5:21–6:2.

The leader's personal insignificance wins new meaning in the light of the possibilities that arise because of the initiative that Jesus Christ took on our behalf.

"All have sinned" (Rom. 3:23) and hence none can redeem another. People, boxed into the cause-and-effect sequence, reap the wages of sin as death. The One who alone could act on behalf of humankind had to be the One who was not caught in the same cause-and-effect sequence himself: He "who knew no sin" became sin for us. He "reaped" what we had "sown" (see Isa. 53), so that we may "reap" what he has "sown."

The leader understands this relationship "in Christ Jesus" as the final release from having to act properly in history. The leader becomes co-worker with God. The leader understands the nature and the content of God's rule and, hence, is able to identify the presence of God's rule in history. The leader's involvement in history thus becomes creative. Change is no threat because the leader knows the mind of the One who controls all change. Such a leader pleads for responsible commitment in history and to history with an emphatic *now.*

Prayer: *O Lord, may the urgency of time and history dawn upon me. May your control and presence in my life heal my panic. Lord, teach me the urgency that is without panic. Amen.*

Sunday, June 23   Read Mark 4:35-41.

The Christian leader understands the urgency of the *now* movement in history. The Christian leader must also understand the posture that permits acting without panic.

Jesus initiated the move to go to "the other side." The disciples "took him with them in the boat, just as he was. . . . And a great storm of wind arose."

All of life's engagements with history are characterized by these qualities. No Christian leader is exempt from such anxieties. But Jesus was in the stern, asleep on a cushion, and this irritated the disciples. They understood his indifference as a lack of concern for their plight. He was awakened, and he first rebuked the wind and demanded that peace and calmness return. After the calm had been restored, Jesus challenged the disciples to examine the cause of their fear and the meaning of faith in the face of life-threatening situations.

To the disciples, then and now, the evidence of Jesus' care and concern for them would be for him to enter into their state of panic. But to the Master, then as now, the evidence of the disciples' identification with the Lord of history is their entering into his calmness during moments of stress. This reality not only heals us from the consequences of sin and enables us to share in the benefits of Jesus' life, but it also involves our moving from panic to confidence within the test of day-to-day history because Jesus Christ is Lord! "Wind and sea obey him."

Prayer: *O Lord, teach me day by day to escape from my panic and my fear and to know your calmness and your confidence. In your name, Lord Jesus. Amen.*

A TOUCH OF WINGS AND THINGS

June 24-30, 1985   **Joan P. Berry†**
Monday, June 24   Read 2 Samuel 6:1-15.

About 35 years ago, Massachusetts Institute of Technology held an exhibition of scientific marvels, some of which, like the microwave oven, have become commonplace. Another of the exhibit's wonders was a luminous globe that remained stationary wherever it was positioned. The homeowner could have light wherever it was needed without extra lamps and switches.

Children noisily pointed out the obvious: "It's gonna fall down!" Adults smiled indulgently, knowing that electrical forces held the globe in place, but they, too, felt, "It's gonna fall down!" They looked back frequently on the chance that the invisible touch on the globe would drop its burden. Then they could say, "Told you," even though they hadn't dared to tell any such thing to anyone.

Uzzah, tailgate guard for the journey of the Ark of the Covenant, had a similar problem. He knew, but he didn't. He believed, but not really. And when his gut said, "It's gonna fall," he grabbed and died.

The point isn't whether God was being peevish or whether a taboo was broken. The point is that the touch of God's power is enough—is untiring—and it will support God's own.

Prayer: *Lord God, please never tire of touching me. Never let me mistrust your power and cause my own fall. Lift and touch me, Lord. Amen.*

---

†Free-lance writer, El Paso, Texas.

187

Tuesday, June 25   Read Psalm 24:3-6.

The fortress at Salzburg, high on its hill above the city, isn't a beautiful place, like some of the magnificent Austrian palaces, for instance. Rather, it is awesome in the strength of its design, its forceful character, the antiquity of its stone.

As my foot touched upon stone steps that were curved and worn by the touch of other feet over the centuries, my thoughts turned to those feet: children and dogs, young knights and lords, ladies and doxies, prisoners and soldiers, the wealthy and the poor, healthy and sick, God-fearing and evil. All of those feet had passed these halls lightly in innocence, sprightly in love, swiftly in guile, heavy in malice.

How dared we add our steps to those others, when all we had to give was curiosity or boredom? How dared we so casually and carelessly leave our touch, making ourselves one with the past and with the future?

But of course, all have the right to enter this place, to see what is to be seen, to feel what is to be felt. And to a few will be given that special gift of knowing that they stand in a special place. A few will be touched by time.

The psalmist asks who has the right to ascend the holy hill, who has the right to enter the holy place. He is answered by the Christ, who says that all may enter to see what is to be seen, to feel what is to be felt. And to a few will be given that special gift of knowing that they stand in a special place by the grace of God.

Prayer: *My God and my Lord! I will proclaim your holy and healing touch to all who will hear, to the end of my days, to the ends of the earth. Amen.*

Wednesday, June 26   Read Psalm 24:7-10.

It was back in the 1940s. Our Girl Scout troop was invited to spend an afternoon at the Perkins Institute for the Blind to play with the children of our own age. Probably, in the thinking of all the adults concerned, it was just as important that we be sensitized to the capabilities of blind children as it was that they be exposed to the thoughtlessness of the sighted.

We made many mistakes, but we learned a great deal about patience and good humor. We swam and laughed in the swimming pool; we ran and played in the playground; we sang and danced around the piano in the lounge, all according to the rules for the handicapped children. We frequently broke the rules. We helped them understand that, because we couldn't refrain from using words of sight, they should be able to use them, too. We laughed a lot about trying so hard. And we made friends.

I went back several times to visit my friend and to play with her, and just walk around and talk. One day she said, "I like you so much. I want to see who you are. Do you mind?" We sat on a bench, on the beautifully landscaped lawn which I so much regretted her not being able to see. And then she opened the eyes of my heart. She passed her fingertips lightly over my face and hair, translating her touch impressions into a mental image of me. Through touching me, she saw who I was.

Prayer: *Master of my handicapped spirit, I praise you for allowing me to see you and who you are every time I touch or am touched by one of your creation. You are the Almighty, the Lord of hosts, magnificent in your power and love! Amen.*

Thursday, June 27   Read Mark 5:25-34.

A recent animal health article noted that the family pet that is handled lovingly and touched frequently is happier, eats better, and lives longer than the animal who is rarely petted. We learn also in basic psychology courses that infants who aren't caressed deteriorate. Something about touching is essential to life.

Basque sheepherders relate that at the end of the day's migration, when the shepherd relaxes beside the fire, the sheep have a ritual of their own, centuries old. Though scatterbrained, each sheep apparently knows its place in the flock. The leader is first to approach the shepherd in the dusk, coming alone to be spoken to, checked for burrs or cuts, medicated if necessary, but to be touched. When the leader moves on, the next animal in the invisible order comes forward, to be touched.

There is something dynamic, something vital, about touch: especially the caring touch. There is an exchange made between need and source of comfort that is as delicate as a butterfly wing, as powerful as a battery charge. "Who touched my clothes?" (NEB) the Christ could ask, knowing that the power of his love had leapt to meet a need, as surely as power leaps between cathode and anode.

One might suppose that, having felt that energy drawn, the Christ was thereby diminished. But we know better, and scripture witnesses to the fact that the more love and energy distributed, the more there is built up at the source.

Prayer: *Source of all love, as you have blessed me that I might be a blessing, touch me that I might touch others in their need and in your name. Amen.*

Friday, June 28   Read Mark 5:35-43.

Our congregation has a benevolence called, for want of a better name, the Pastor's Fund. It exists for the purpose of aiding anyone in the community who comes for help. Not adequate to all needs, sometimes it runs out. But typical of its working is what happened a while back.

A young woman in blue jeans and T-shirt came to the office and announced herself by saying, "I was told you're the church that helps." She had a job interview lined up, but no money for clothes. She was wearing what she owned.

The church secretary could have given the woman a check or cash. But instead, the secretary called two church women who came and took the young woman shopping. Together, they bought a coordinated outfit that could be worn in different ways, with shoes and purse to match.

Although she wasn't a member of our congregation, that young woman continues to send a dollar or two now and then to "the church that helps." She did get the job.

There have been other similar experiences with the Pastor's Fund, but the fund itself isn't nearly as important as what is happening through it. Jesus could have said to the girl everyone said had died, "Little girl, I tell you to get up." He didn't have to go to her house, enter her room, send out the weeping relatives, take her by the hand. He could have said it; and it would have been done. But he took her by the hand.

Prayer: *O God, remind me: My hands are your tools, powered by your grace and love, to touch and to hold others. Amen.*

Saturday, June 29 Read 2 Corinthians 8:7-12.

A young bride followed her husband to America as soon as he found work to support them both. They came from a European village which, at that time, was so poor that people scrabbling in the dirt thought themselves fortunate to find a potato, a wild onion, a few wormy nuts. Such were eaten out of hand, or were cooked over an open fire at best. Recipes were for the wealthy who had a choice of food.

The bride brought only the clothes on her back, love, pride, and the determination to be a good wife and a good American. In a spartanly furnished company house, she set out to learn homemaking. The women who lived nearby were also immigrants, but from other countries. How could she learn from them without a common language? She watched.

If the other women were hanging wash, she washed. If they were beating rugs, out came her rugs. If they were airing bedding, her quilts appeared over the window ledges. But, best of all for her purposes, her kitchen window faced the kitchen window of the next house. Doggedly, and not without mistakes, she learned to bake bread and to make soup by watching and copying every move the next-door neighbor made.

In later years, her excellent bread only one of her many arts, her own children learned her skills by watching closely. There was no way she could have explained to anyone why this step followed that: it was the way the thing was done in America. How kind of God! How fortunate for her husband! They could so easily have lived next door to a terrible cook.

Prayer: *Kind God, as one of your tools, I know that I will be used in your own time for your own purpose, in ways I may never notice. Thank you. Amen.*

Sunday, June 30   Read 2 Corinthians 8:11-15.

A dear friend of ours vowed he would punch the pastor in the nose if the pastor tried to shake hands with him during the passing of the peace, a ritual recently added to our worship service. The whole idea of such a display during worship enraged him beyond reason. However, being educated, he questioned his own reaction; and, being devout, he spent much time on his knees over the matter.

The Holy Spirit reached him somehow, for one day our friend rushed into the pastor's office with radiant face, announcing, "I see it! If I cannot touch my brothers and sisters here—the ones I know—then how can I hope to touch the ones out there—the ones I don't know?"

From that point on, the passing of the peace found him all over the sanctuary, greeting, touching, even hugging his brothers and sisters. It became the high point of his week.

This is the stuff of faith: feeling God's touch in all the dusty corners of life—in new things we don't understand, as well as in traditions; in the thump of a good dog's tail, as well as in the shoulder-slapping camaraderie of old school chums; in the thrust of a sheep's muzzle, as well as in the impersonal sign on the parking lot bin for cast-off clothes; in feeling the pride of the child in her new accomplishment, as well as the thrill of the handicapped person in his. To feel God's presence in the touch of wings and things—and then to pass that touch on wherever, whenever, and however we can: this is the stuff of faith.

Prayer: *Almighty, magnificent, worthy of praise are you, our God! Amen.*

Strength through Weakness

July 1-7, 1985   **Greta L. Schumm McDonald†**
Monday, July 1   Read 2 Corinthians 12:1-10.

"When I am weak, then I am strong."

These words do not rest easily on our twentieth-century ears. We see weakness as inferiority, not as an avenue to strength.

We want to be strong, whether it means possessing more missiles than a neighboring nation, owning the most impressive home, or dominating a conversation with our point of view. We want to be strong in ways that help us escape failure, vulnerability, and pain. Yet these are inevitable—and often important—aspects of our human growth. A vital faith needs to help us face and embrace our humanity, not escape it.

In this passage, Paul addresses a group of people in the Corinthian church who used their faith to escape their humanity. The "super-apostles" claimed to have received a superior wisdom from the Holy Spirit and preached about a hardly-human Jesus for whom life held no suffering and death held no threat. They offered to make "superpeople" out of the Corinthians and interpreted their wealth and popularity as a sign of God's blessing on their message.

Paul rejected these claims, "for the sake of Christ," in favor of a faith that faced life as it is. "For when I am weak, then I am strong."

Prayer: *God of life, help us to face and embrace our humanity today and, for the sake of Christ, to be lovingly involved in the needs of others. Amen.*

---

†Pastor, First United Methodist Church, Elizabeth, Illinois.

Tuesday, July 2   Read John 9:1-5.

Strong in grace

Several years ago, Harold Kushner wrote a book about a personal tragedy in his life, *When Bad Things Happen to Good People*. It was a best seller, for it spoke to questions we often ask in the face of life crises: Why did this have to happen to me? and Why can't God take this problem away? Deep down, we often assume that we somehow should be excused from the usual ailments of human life.

God does provide us with moments of great joy. Paul tells of an experience of spiritual ecstasy in Second Corinthians 12:2-4 which was a moment of great joy for someone he knew. But Paul also knew that God's grace was just as present during an experience of suffering.

When Paul was stricken with his thorn in the flesh, he begged the Lord to remove it. But it remained.

Yet Paul did receive an answer to his prayer that gave him much reason to rejoice. The answer he received was, "My grace is sufficient for you, for my power is made perfect in weakness" (2 Cor. 12:9).

That answer redirected Paul's attitude toward his suffering. He no longer asked for his problem to be removed. He wrote to the Corinthians that he had embraced his suffering. He could even boast about his suffering as a way in which he had come to know Christ's presence with him, sustaining him and using him with purpose.

Prayer: *O God of our past and our future, help us to gratefully receive the truth that nothing in all creation can separate us from your love in Christ. Amen.*

Wednesday, July 3   Read 2 Corinthians 1:3-7.

Strong in service

The grace of Jesus Christ enabled Paul to see fresh meaning in his suffering. He knew that Christ's power could emerge through his weakness.

Our sufferings also take on new meaning as we offer them up to Christ's power. Often we find that through our weakness Christ is able to reach into the life of someone who is suffering.

A man was diagnosed as having cancer. At the hospital, in preparation for his first treatment, lines had been drawn on his face and head to define the areas where the radiation should be directed. The lines were still visible on his skin when he and his wife stopped at a restaurant on their way home.

While they were there, someone they barely knew recognized them and, understanding what the lines meant, sat with them for awhile. This person had also had cancer and had undergone similar treatments. Very simply he shared his experience with the couple. Those words of empathy and encouragement provided the husband and wife with strength for days to come.

In the opening verses of Second Corinthians, Paul reflects upon the truth that we can be channels of grace for each other. We are able to serve others in their suffering because we have been helped by God in our suffering. In our weakness, we are given the strength to serve.

Prayer: *O God, you have loved us and sustained us all our days. Help us to discover anew what a gift it is to be able to serve others. Amen.*

Thursday, July 4   Read Mark 6:1-6.

Strong in healing

When Jesus ministered to people with illness, he often asked them to name the problem they had. To be clearly aware of and able to admit what specific area of their lives needed healing sometimes seemed to be part of the healing process.

In today's passage, we read that Jesus was able to touch a few sick people and heal them. That does not surprise us. What is remarkable is that except for those few healings, he was unable to do miracles in his hometown.

As Mark tells it, the people in Jesus' hometown reacted to him with jealousy and hostility. Far from being able to admit their areas of need to Jesus, they shut themselves off from the care and healing he could offer. They were not willing to admit their weaknesses to Jesus. Their false strength prevented the miracles and healing that could have been a part of their lives.

When we are unable to admit our areas of need to Christ through prayer, or through sharing our need with others, we can prevent the emotional, spiritual, and, sometimes, the physical healing that might occur in us.

The question John Wesley asked each week of each member of his classes was a perceptive and potentially healing one: "How is it with your soul?" We need to ask that of ourselves and each other more often, and to be "weak" enough to allow Christ to touch us and heal us.

Prayer: *Help us, God, to rekindle in ourselves the assurance that you desire good for us. May our lives be open to your healing today. Amen.*

Friday, July 5   Read Luke 10:25-37.

Strong in love

The title "Good Samaritan" has taken on a noble ring in our day. We hand out Good Samaritan awards and initiate Good Samaritan programs and institutions. A person unacquainted with the parable of the good Samaritan might assume that a Samaritan was generally admired by his or her contemporaries.

Of course, nothing could be farther from the truth. Samaritans, in the time of Jesus, were outcasts—half-breeds of questionable background with crude religious practices. Most Jews definitely disliked Samaritans.

In the parable Jesus tells, the weakness of a Samaritan's low social standing becomes a strength for love. While the priest and Levite were concerned about ritually defiling themselves by touching a wounded and possibly dead person, the Samaritan was himself considered unclean. He knew what it was to be scorned and abused. In compassion he lifted the wounded man upon his own animal, took him to an inn where he could recuperate, and paid the bill for his expenses.

Like the Samaritan, our experiences of injustice and exclusion can deepen our compassion for others. Our weakness, when offered to Christ, becomes the strength to love.

Prayer: *God of love, we lift up to you the moments of pain and unfairness that live in our memories, asking that you would transform them into gifts of compassion for others. Amen.*

Saturday, July 6   Read 2 Samuel 7:1-17.

Strong in accomplishment

David, fresh from victorious battle and from bringing the Ark of the Lord to Jerusalem, contemplated another great project—building a house for the Lord.

But through Nathan the prophet, God asks David, "Are you the one?" (NIV) David learns that the temple will be built by one of his offspring, not himself. Instead, God will build David a house, a covenant of love with him and his descendents.

Later is his life, David committed the destructive acts of adultery and murder and experienced the agony of losing an infant son to death. We read that God's love and forgiveness sustained David in spite of his sin and tragedy, and that David was able to recommit himself to God with new integrity. Generation after generation has received encouragement from David's life to claim God's love in spite of their sin. That may have been a more significant part of the house God was building through David than any physical structure.

We, too, need to ask, "Am I the one?" in prayer and reflection before we begin projects that require our time and commitment. "Am I the one for this task, or is there another area of my life that needs attention, from which this task would pull me away?" "Are there people in my family or community who need my presence more than my performance?"

Prayer: *Eternal God, make us aware of our weaknesses and our limits, that through them your strength can lead us to make the best use of the opportunities we have. Amen.*

Sunday, July 7   Read Psalm 89:20-37.

Strong in living

Of all the limits we experience as human beings, the most powerful is death. The time we have to accomplish goals, develop our talents, and use ourselves for service is finite.

When David considered building a house for the Lord, God led him to understand that it was a project that would be carried out after his life was over. David himself would not see the completion of that dream.

In today's Psalm reading, we hear words describing God's covenant of love with David. An aspect of that love is that it will continue beyond David's life. David's time to live would be limited, but God's love would be eternal.

Our most common thought about our own death is about what we will lose. Our precious experiences—witnessing a sunrise, being embraced by a child, hearing the truth of a beautiful poem or song—will be over in the way we know them now. Yet, in God's eternal love, death can give meaning to our lives.

A woman in our church has symptoms of multiple sclerosis, though that disease cannot be diagnosed until all other possibilities have been eliminated. Facing a future whose limits she does not know, she finds that she is being given life in a new depth. After a year of dealing with her illness, she could say, "It's strange, but I am almost grateful for this. Now I know so much more than before what is important to me, and to what I must give myself."

Prayer: *We thank you, God, that as we face our mortality, your presence helps us live for eternity. Amen.*

HOUSE BLESSINGS

July 8-14, 1985   **Cornish R. Rogers†**
Monday, July 8   Read 2 Samuel 7:18-29.

The ancients had a craving for blessings. They felt that the world was filled with spiritual forces, both friendly and unfriendly. So they turned to their sources of spiritual power to protect them from evil. In the Hebrew tradition, blessings were the transmission of divine vitality to the person or place blessed.

Although our modern culture does not admit of things of the spirit, offically, there is a pervasive uneasiness among people that reflects a deep desire to be assured of the avail- ability of invisible resources to combat whatever there is out there unseen.

In today's scripture, David, although he possesses great power as king, appeals to God for spiritual protection, a protection not against physical harm alone, but against evil spiritual forces that threaten both body and soul.

It is interesting to note that blessings are invariably related to place. The house in which one dwells is the arena of one's close relationships with others; so God's blessings cover not only the individual but the individual's intimate relationships also. This understanding of blessing frees us from selfishness of motive and lifts our appeals to a higher plane of interper- sonal concern. That is why it is proper to pray as did David:

Prayer: *"O Lord God, thou art God, and thy words are true . . . now therefore may it please thee to bless the house of thy servant, that it may continue for ever before thee."* *Amen.*

†Professor of Pastoral Theology, School of Theology at Claremont, Clare- ment, California.

201

Tuesday, July 9   Read Psalm 132:11-18.

House blessings are not as popular as they once were. Still there remains a deep longing among many Christians to have their homes "blessed" by God if only by having their pastor, as a living reminder of God's blessings, visit in their homes. Lay leaders or visitation teams also convey God's blessing when they visit in the name of the Lord.

The vital link between the church and the home is sustained by God's blessings which flow back and forth between them through the individuals who claim both as their dwelling places.

The psalmist discovered that when we invite God to our dwelling place, God may choose it for a habitation! We must be careful, therefore, when we ask God to "come by here"— God might decide to stay!

> The Lord has chosen Zion;
> he has desired it for his habitation:
> "This is my resting place for ever;
> here I will dwell, for I have desired it."

What an awesome and fearful experience it is to be under the close scrutiny of God in our own home, to live under God's inescapable presence! But that is what God's blessings are about. They are both judgment and grace.

God's spirit, however judgmental, is always tempered with grace. What makes God's spirit so fulfilling is the fact that it is God's spirit, not whether it reveals judgment or grace. "In thy presence there is fulness of joy," exulted the psalmist (Ps. 16:11). One need not fear, then, the blessings of God.

Prayer: *Come into our hearts, Lord Jesus. Come in today, and come in to stay. Amen.*

Wednesday, July 10   Read Ephesians 1:1-5.

The house we inhabit ought to be a reflection of the habitation of God. The 'doxa' or glory manifested in church should find some expression in our homes. When our homes are blessed, they have been chosen as outposts of the temple of God. The spirit of sanctuary, of peace, of love and forgiveness should pervade our dwellings. A visiting, sensitive spirit should be able to recognize that "surely God is in this place!"

Remember that God can be recognized in storms as well as in the "still, small voice." It is not how piously we live but under whose roof we live that determines whether or not we are living under God's blessings. Even when we have transgressed the will of God for us, we are still under God's blessings as long as we can say with the psalmist, "I know my transgressions, and my sin is ever before me" (Ps. 51:3); and as long as we move to do the work of repentance, having received God's forgiveness through Jesus Christ. Awareness of God's blessings is itself the best reminder of our transgressions and the surest stimulator of our confession of sin.

It is the person of Jesus Christ who permits us to live under the blessing of God: "[God] destined us in love to be his sons through Jesus Christ."

Jesus is the link between God's house and ours. Since Jesus himself *is* the blessing of God, his presence in our homes makes them truly blessed.

Prayer: *We thank you, O God, for Jesus Christ's presence in our midst, for through him we are blessed. Amen.*

Thursday, July 11   Read Ephesians 1:6-10.

When we acknowledge and submit to God's rule in our lives, we are blessed. Those blessings enable us to gain a new perspective on ourselves. We are able to plug into God's essentially mysterious will for us and thereby gain a yardstick for measuring our spiritual development.

We are energized by Jesus Christ from whom we gain wisdom and insight. But what we receive most from him is the assurance that God's blessings will not be given and taken back according to our deeds, for in Christ, "we have redemption through his blood, the forgiveness of our trespasses, according to the riches of [God's] grace."

Jesus is not only our assurance of being blessed, but also our supreme example of one who was so faithful to God's will that he became God's blessing for us. No longer do we have to wonder about the right way the blessed of God should act; we see in the life, death, and resurrection of Jesus the decisions, actions, suffering, and rewards that are in the offing for us when we respond fully and faithfully to God's blessings.

When God's spiritual vitality is conferred on us, we can do all things in Christ who died for us. In Christ is God's plan "for the fullness of time, to unite all things in him, things in heaven and things on earth." To be a part of God's plan, to do our part in advancing that plan, is to be truly blessed.

Prayer: *You bring to us the fullness of joy, Divine Spirit, when we submit to the outpouring of your blessings in our lives. Teach us to respond in radical obedience to your will. May it be so. Amen.*

Friday, July 12   Read Mark 6:7-8.

One of the popular signs on the cluttered desks of busy workers reads, "Bless this mess." It acknowledges the mass of confusion that often results from our frantic pursuits, the lack of order and purpose that often accompany our half-hearted attempts to complete our assigned tasks, and the desperate hope that somehow all our vain efforts will still count for something good in the economy of God. "Bless this mess."

At a deeper level, it constitutes a prayer that God will find a way to make victorious our failures, to make straight our crookedness, and to give direction to our aimlessness. "Bless this mess."

The deepest mess we're in, however, is our penchant for sin. So Jesus, in today's scripture reading, gives the disciples "authority over the unclean spirits," a blessing that enables them to confront sin in themselves and others in such a way that its sting is rendered harmless and its effect is transformed to be used for God's ultimate purposes.

When we ask God to "bless this mess," we are invoking Christ's presence into our disordered lives to provide a new center around which to reorder our priorities so that what we do is done for the glory of God.

Prayer: *Forgive the mess we have made of our lives, O God, and bless our efforts as we do what we can for your coming kingdom. Amen.*

Saturday, July 13   Read Mark 6:8-11.

The good news of God's blessing is inevitably counter-balanced by the bad news of our rejection of God's offered gift.

Jesus supplies his disciples with all the spiritual powers needed to offer to those they visit two by two on their missionary journey. He makes it clear that the disciples do not need to be concerned about such ordinary physical accoutrements as food, bags, or money. He knew that they could depend upon hospitality for food and shelter—hospitality from those who accept God's blessings communicated through the disciples' hands and hearts. So in a real sense, the physical security of the disciples was linked to the responsiveness to the gospel of Jesus Christ of those they visited.

Knowing that they would be rejected by some, Jesus directed the disciples to move away deliberately from those who refuse to hear them, but to stay as long as necessary with those who are receptive: "Where you enter a house, stay there until you leave the place."

The power of Christ as God's blessing can be entrusted to those who will be his emissaries into all the hurting areas of the world. What a responsibility and a joy to be a disciple empowered by Jesus Christ to be a blessing to others!

Prayer: *Empowering God, give us the faith that when we bring your good tidings to others, we need not be concerned about ourselves. Amen.*

Sunday, July 14   Read Mark 6:12-13.

God's blessings cannot be made known except through repentance. That was John the Baptist's cry in preparing the way for Jesus Christ, who became the blessing of God.

So the disciples "went out and preached that people should turn away from their sins" (TEV). They knew that unless people became aware of the marvelous spiritual resources of God, they would perish in their attempt to defeat the thick forces of sin and death. And the only way to become aware is through an act of repentance.

There is something about "coming clean" with our shortcomings which clears our spiritual lenses so that we can perceive the awesome blessings God provides for us to overcome the vicissitudes of life.

The scripture records that those who did repent as the result of the preaching of the disciples had their demons cast out and were healed of their sicknesses.

God's blessings can be conferred on all who repent of their sins, accept Jesus Christ as Savior, and respond to God's will.

Prayer: *O Divine Redeemer, come into our hearts and help them to beat in consonance with yours. Open up our horizons so that we can enlarge our vision of what is possible for us, and give us the courage to be faithful to your purposes for us. Amen.*

GOD IS OUR PEACE

July 15-21, 1985   **Patricia E. Coots†**
Monday, July 15   Read 2 Samuel 11:1-15.

What does the story of David and Bathsheba say to me? I don't have David's power to have everything I want. I would never let a peson die because I desired her spouse. David was a great leader. How could he have done this—and why is this story in the Bible?

The Bible is honest. Stories were not chosen to glorify any individual—only God. Many people in the time of David were corrupt and self-serving, just as people are today.

It is easy for us to identify self-service on the part of civil servants with whom we do not agree politically. It is easy to see it in a boss, a complaining neighbor, a loved one with whom we are annoyed. It is less easy, however, to see it in ourselves when we cheat on our income tax, tell "harmless" little lies, or exaggerate stories about our neighbor. It is less easy to see it in ourselves when we want what we want when we want it even though it is not good for us—like eating or drinking too much or desiring someone else's spouse.

We don't understand ourselves, but we know these things cause us inner strife. Our God at the center of our life can bring us peace.

Suggestion for meditation: *At what place in my life are things out of control? God can help me bring discipline to that area. I will try to work with God today.*

---

†Assistant to the President for Administration, School of Theology at Claremont, Claremont, California.

Tuesday, July 16   Read Psalm 53:1-5.

In California, most days are fair. We expect to go for daily walks without raincoats, to garden, and to drive on a crowded-but-dry freeway. There may be months of beautiful weather followed by a week of blustery rains. And then we wonder how nature can do this to us, bewailing the fact that we can't trust the weather anymore. Complaining comes easy.

Psalm 53 expresses no pleasure. If David wrote it, it would seem to picture his feelings about himself and his relationship to God.

Sometimes it is difficult to trust people or to see anything good in them. Some friends of mine have a house which has three times fallen prey to burglars. After three invasions of their home, they find it difficult to trust anyone they do not know. They have come to the realization that only God can restore their lack of hope for people.

Some of us have reason to mistrust people. Many of us have experienced times when we felt cheated or let down by someone we love or admire. When that happens, we may embrace the inner turmoil and decide not to trust anyone. Then comes the realization that we can trust God and that God can restore our sense of trust in people.

One definition of peace is freedom of the mind from annoyance. Lack of trust disturbs our minds. Trust in God can bring peace, for God is our peace.

Suggestion for meditation: *Where in my life do I need God's help in being able to trust? For what loving relationships can I rejoice and for what gifts of God do I give thanks today?*

Wednesday, July 17   Read Psalm 53; Eph. 2:11-12.

God does restore our lives. Without God, our world is without hope.

The psalmist describes many unlovable people, unfaithful and uncaring. The wonder is that God loves the unlovable and is continually working toward restoration—of people and of the world. The Bible is a book about God's work of restoration and our part in that. In union with Christ Jesus, we "who were once far off" have been brought near.

How do we work with God in restoration? Prayer can be a powerful force for change. If we truly communicate with God and spend time in prayer, lives can be changed—the lives of those for whom we pray, and our own lives, as well.

We can share God's work when we work with people who need to be restored to wholeness. That can mean the prisoner or the ex-prisoner, and it can mean ourselves and the one who sits next to us in the church pew. It can mean working in situations which appear hopeless and with people who seem lost to us but surely not to God. It can mean working where hope is high and people openly acknowledge their tie to God. God knows us all and loves us. This knowledge can bring us hope and peace if we ask.

Prayer: *Dear God, today I want to be in communion with Christ Jesus. I want to know how I can be a co-worker in your task of restoration. Guide me to what I am to do. Amen.*

Thursday, July 18   Read Ephesians 2:14-22.

People in the community where I live have great concern for education. An interfaith group works for many kinds of changes. An important one of these is improving education. All ethnic groups and many nationalities are represented in workshops that deal with English as a second language. The need for education in many languages is explored. The group also works to improve prison conditions, to preserve human rights everywhere, and to find ways of alleviating world hunger.

Our scripture today posits a difference between those far off and those nearby. In some ways the difference is real. Even one hundred years ago, missionaries who went from the United States to India or China or many other places had little hope of returning. Today, those far-off places are a day's travel away or within speaking distance by telephone.

But although people in all nations may have common goals, we don't often work together. Perhaps for the survival of the world we may need to find ways we can share concerns with those far-off members of God's household. Peace far-off and nearby can depend on such enterprise.

God is our peace, and God is a key to peace among nations, peace within families, and peace within ourselves.

Suggestion for meditation: *I am a fellow citizen with those in God's household around the world. What can I do today to work with other citizens of our world in the cause of peace?*

Friday, July 19   Read Mark 6:30-34.

In the scripture passage for today, Jesus invites the apostles to come with him to a place where they can rest quietly. They were all weary of involvement with people and with much coming and going.

What a universal need was expressed in that invitation—to go to a place to "rest quietly" (NEB). None of us leads a problem-free life. Problems are a part of living. Involvement with people is a part of living, and involvement always brings some stress.

It is popular to talk about stress, about what it is and who has it. The answers are varied. It comes to those with too little power and to those with too much—to those surrounded by too many people, and to those with too few people nearby. The answer to any stress must always be to come to a place where we can rest quietly with Jesus Christ. Through Christ, we come to know that God is waiting to lead us through the problems we face. Jesus Christ has much to teach us if we want to listen. Christ has peace to bring us if we really desire it.

Suggestion for meditation: *Today, I may feel there is more to do than I can do, or that I can't measure up. God can help me if I share these feelings in prayer. Or will I be too busy?*

Saturday, July 20   Read Mark 6:35-43.

In a special weekend retreat experience, the Walk to Emmaus, a small group of Christians gather together. One of the highlights of the weekend is delicious food prepared by a loving group of volunteer cooks. Another highlight is the opportunity to share in the Lord's Supper on a number of occasions. After those meals, we feel well fed—often too well fed—and after the Communion services, we feel well filled.

There are explanations of the parable of the feeding of the multitude that suggest that those present were inspired to share the food that they had brought. Whatever the explanation, we know that the people were fed.

Our society is food-oriented. Supermarket ads are an important part of our newspapers. Cookbooks proliferate (as do diet books). Books about being filled in the act of Communion haven't made many best-seller lists, but a small piece of bread shared with others and with God can satisfy our hearts.

There is great joy when we are filled with God's love. It is easy to appreciate God's love and be grateful for it when we share an exciting experience with others. Often, though, when life seems darkest and loneliest, we experience that love and our lives can be changed. We know that Christ Jesus is our peace and that God can fill our lives.

Suggestion for prayer: *The crowds who heard Jesus were filled, as were the apostles when the Holy Spirit came to them after Jesus had departed from their midst. Pray that today the Holy Spirit will fill you and use you to do God's will.*

213

Sunday, July 21   Read Mark 6:44.

We cannot read this familiar story without being made aware once again of Jesus' compassion for all. His physical condition mattered little when he saw a need he could satisfy. He must have been concerned about the apostles' physical condition, but he expected them to be of his mind. We are not told how they felt.

Jesus could never leave anyone out. All needed to be fed. The last word in this passage, *men,* sparks our awareness of how Jesus' followers have often left people out. We talk glibly about the feeding of the five thousand. When we read the word *men,* we may not realize that there must have been women and children there also. The woman's movement and other special groups are raising our consciousness about those who are left out. All of a sudden, we realize that some people can't attend church because there are steps to climb or because they would not be accepted because of their color or their clothing.

The crowds of people who came to hear Jesus must have included many who were always left out. Education, sex, color, wealth, or physical appearance had nothing to do with Jesus' concern for all people. Some of those people probably gossiped and were occasionally dishonest, and perhaps they weren't much fun to be around. But Jesus accepted them all and wanted to be reconciled with them all. One of the ways we work for peace is desiring to be reconciled with all peoples and including all in our life as the community of faith.

Suggestion for meditation: *How do I measure up as a follower of Jesus? Do my words or my actions exclude others more often than include them?*

GOD SATISFIES OUR NEEDS

July 22-28, 1985   **Hugh Irwin†**
Monday, July 22   Read 2 Samuel 12:1-14.

God satisfies our need with the gift of insight.

Notice that I say *needs* not *desires;* for desires are often not in accord with God's best wishes for us. Indeed, our desires are often contrary to God's will. That we have abundant life is very important to God. Insight into ourselves, so essential for integrity and wholeness, is necessary for abundant life. Robert Burns, the Scottish poet, prayed for it, and so should we; that through a God-given power we might see ourselves as others see us. We feel sure that God answers such a prayer.

We believe that is what happened in this story concerning King David and Bathsheba. David looked, lusted, and sinned; yet when Nathan spoke of David's sin in the story, David did not recognize it. Instead, he became very angry, promising drastic action against the culprit. Patiently, Nathan showed him that the despicable action which so aroused his anger was the very one which David as king had taken. Fortunately, David saw the light and in true humility confessed his sin, repented, and sought God's forgiveness. This he received, even though, as always, he had to pay for his sin, and he had to see others suffer as a result of his sin.

Sin is seldom, if ever, confined to the sinner.

Prayer: *Give us insight, our God, to discern our sins, seek your forgiveness, and, receiving it, turn from those sins. Through Jesus Christ our Savior. Amen.*

---

†Retired pastor, White Rock, British Columbia, Canada.

Tuesday, July 23   Read Psalm 32.

God satisfies our needs with forgiveness and a restored relationship.

This psalm is both a beatitude of forgiveness and a vivid description of the burden of unconfessed sin. Sin is regarded as willful disobedience to God's commands, a "missing of the mark" which includes sins of both omission and commission, sins of inequity, deceit, and wrongdoing. And guilt is one result.

When David laid bare his heart before God, acknowledging his sin and seeking forgiveness, he received forgiveness, and his burden was gone.

Augustine considered this penitential psalm his favorite. He had it written on the walls of the room in which he died. Doubtless, it reminded him of his early life—sometimes a bit tumultuous—and the graciousness of his Lord's forgiveness and redemption. To Martin Luther also, this was not a psalm of cheap grace but an acknowledgement of the depth of sin which ever wounds a heart of love. It also spoke to him of the costliness of forgiveness.

The ultimate confession here, as always, is to God, for in all our lives there are some matters which are for God's hearing alone.

"Confess and be saved" seems to be the psalmist's gospel. As Christians we see God's redeeming love continually. We should see also God's sorrow for our individual and collective sins. As revealed in Christ, God seeks ever to save us from sin and folly. How greatly we need this assurance of God's loving care today as we march ever forward to the possible destruction of our world—God's world.

Prayer: *Creator God, forgive what we have been and are; order what we shall be and do. Save us from ourselves by your grace. Amen.*

Wednesday, July 24   Read Psalm 32;
                                                        Luke 17:11-19.

God satisfies our needs with a restored fellowship evoking a witnessing faith of gratitude.

As the essence of wrongdoing is alienation from God, so the essence of forgiveness is the restoration of fellowship with God. This restoration, freely given to the truly penitent, causes a change of conduct.

Following the assurance of God's forgiveness, mercy, and continuing love, there should come a witnessing faith. So says the psalmist in witnessing to others of his saving experience.

A very necessary but often forgotten postlude to the great experience of receiving God's forgiveness and a restored relationship of communion with God is that of thanking God in joyous living. The psalmist urges us also to be glad in the Lord and rejoice, indeed to shout for joy. He reminds us of a few of the many reasons why rejoicing should be our instinctive response—God surrounds us with steadfast love and either preserves us from trouble and distress or delivers us in times of trouble.

In this life we are on a very difficult assignment, especially as we face the possibility of total annihilation by the nuclear bomb. In such a time we should recall and hold close to our hearts Paul's assurance in Romans 8:28: "We know that in everything God works for good with those who love him, who are called according to his purpose." Knowing that God works *with* us for good, we, too, as forgiven sinners, should surely work faithfully for justice and peace.

Prayer: *Our God, we sincerely thank you for your continuing love which surrounds our lives. Remind us always that we are not alone in this life. You are with us. Amen.*

Thursday, July 25   Read Ephesians 3:14-17.

God satisfies our needs with the gift of the Holy Spirit.

Paul is praying earnestly that God will give Paul's readers the gift of the Holy Spirit. Not that God is unwilling to do so—indeed God has already done so. What Paul is really praying for is that the Holy Spirit may be more fully appropriated in the inner spiritual lives of his readers. The early Christians experienced the Holy Spirit and the continuing presence of Christ in the fellowship of the church.

Christ was and is indeed the exalted Lord, but he is not absent from us. Christ promised, "Lo, I am with you always" (Matt. 28:20). That promise is fulfilled in the presence of the Holy Spirit, strengthener, comforter, counselor, helper. To his distraught disciples on the eve of his death, Jesus said, "It is better for you that I go away, because if I do not go, the Helper will not come to you. But if I do go away, then I will send him to you" (John 16:7, TEV).

The Holy Spirit was and is Christ alive in the fellowship. As our ascended Lord, he is making intercession for us in heaven. Yet he is still with us spiritually in the Holy Spirit. As long as Jesus was a visible presence with them, his disciples would have remained dependent upon him to answer their questions, settle disputes, resolve difficulties; hence, they would not grow to full maturity. Nor would they fully exercise their faith and obedience until the visible relationship with Christ became an inner communion. Now Christ through the Holy Spirit is not limited to time or place.

Prayer: *Abide with me, O God, in light and in darkness, in sunshine and in shade, in well-being and in suffering, in joy and in sorrow, in life and in death. Amen.*

Friday, July 26   Read Ephesians 3:18-21.

God satisfies our needs with the gift of the church.

The inner power and knowledge imparted by the Holy Spirit and the abiding presence of Christ in the heart result in a life rooted in love. This love gives power to comprehend something of the breadth, length, height, and depth of the love of God, dimensions which words alone can never fully describe. Rather, that love is revealed supremely in the life, death, and resurrection of Jesus Christ.

The breadth of God's love is evident in God's concern for the entire creation. The length of God's love is revealed in God's repeated efforts to rescue and redeem us, culminating in Jesus' death on the cross for us all. Christ in our Creator's home continually making intercession for us demonstrates the height of God's love. The depth is exemplified in God's presence with us in our various hells, for God never leaves us but saves, stays, satisfies. Paul himself does not discuss in detail these dimensions of God's love. We know that he considered it limitless and inexhaustible.

And where is such love to be truly and fully known and experienced? Why, nowhere else as fully as in the church with all of God's consecrated people. There in its communion we find the love of God. As the extension of the incarnation of Christ, the church is to live out in all the world the love and mercy of God, creator, sustainer, redeemer, parent.

Prayer: *O God, we thank you for your church universal. Through your strength and guidance and its fellowship, make the church truly your instrument for the continuing expansion of your kingdom on earth. Amen.*

Saturday, July 27   Read John 6:1-11.

God satisfies our physical needs.

Accounts of this miracle turn many off. It could not have happened that way, they say, even with Jesus in command. They say, "Did not Jesus refuse to resort to spectacular means to turn stones into bread to win people to him in his desert temptation?" But this was a case of hunger, or need, something Jesus always responded to. It was *not* a spectacular show of power.

We freely admit that we do not know all that happened that day on that hillside. Regardless of our understanding of this incident, the truth is that the hungry were fed. So it is today— at least when we forget our selfishness. We have our so-called miracle wheat, corn, rice, and hybrids. These bountiful harvests enable us to feed the hungry of the world when we cooperate with God in nature. And what do we do? Sometimes we kill millions of chickens, pour unlimited milk on the ground (or pay millions to have it stored away as powders), and pay farmers millions of dollars *not* to grow wheat or corn.

We have put a human being on the moon and yet seem unable to answer the transportation problem that sending our overabundance to starving children poses. God has given us, directly or indirectly, sufficient food to feed all God's children, but it means sharing, planning, and unselfishness. To reach that stage we need yet another miracle.

Prayer: *O God, help us to be truly grateful for food to nourish our bodies. May we ever be sharers of your bounty to suffering people everywhere. Amen.*

Sunday, July 28   Read John 6:10-15, 32-40.

God satisfies our spiritual needs.

Notice that before distributing the food Jesus gave thanks to God. In his commentary William Barclay suggests that in so doing Jesus was acting as father of the family. The grace he used likely would have been that of all Jewish homes: "Blessed art thou, O Lord, our God, who causest to come forth bread from the earth."* Should we ever consider to be out of order a simple prayer of gratitude to God for food? I think not. The eternal goodness of God shown in the food we have is a gift for which we should be always grateful and in continual remembrance.

We should be grateful especially for our spiritual food—Jesus Christ, "the bread of life." In his *Confessions*, Augustine said in effect, "Thou has made us for Thyself, and our hearts are restless until they rest in Thee." These small physical hearts of ours, in the center of our feelings and emotions, will be satisfied with nothing less than God. In Christ we have just that—the eternal love of God. Only in God do we find that peace and satisfaction which the world can neither give nor take away. In God we find that fullness of life promised to us (John 3:16).

Truly, Christ is the bread of life. He alone satisfies our deepest spiritual needs. In great gratitude we sing joyfully: Thanks be to thee, O God, for the gift of thy love in Christ Jesus.

Prayer: *O God of all mercy, compassion, judgment, and love, we thank you for your gift of gifts, Jesus Christ, the bread of life. Amen.*

---

*The Gospel of John, vol. 1 (Philadelphia: The Westminster Press, 1955). p. 205.

COVENANT LIVING

July 29–August 4, 1985   **L. June Stevenson**†
Monday, July 29   Read 2 Samuel 12:15*b*-24.

Roots and Relationships

Even before the world was formed, God chose to have a holy people. Ultimately, God intended these people to be children through Jesus Christ. The Bible records the journey of God's children from ignorance toward understanding, from disharmony toward unity, from darkness toward illumination—all in God's time. Covenant life is rooted in history.

In the Old Testament, God's love is centered on the chosen people, the people of Israel. The covenant, which established unity between God and Israel, represented an act of power on the one hand, "I will be your God," and an act of humble submission on the other, "You shall be my people." Rooted in God's eternal love, we are irrevocably bound to God. And being bound to God means being faithful to God.

David has a unique place in that journey of a people toward God. Under his reign Israel achieved greater unity. But he who became the forerunner of God's true Messiah was not sinless. In fact, at times he sinned greatly, breaking covenant and separating himself from God.

But David understood what God demanded of him and of Israel. He sought to be faithful and loyal to God. He bowed to God's will. He was truly repentant when his sins were pointed out to him. When David repented the way was again opened for a right relationship with God.

Prayer: *Dear God, I want to be rooted in your love. Help me each day to keep the way open for a right relationship with you. Amen.*

---

†Editor, *Glad Tidings,* Women's Missionary Society, The Presbyterian Church in Canada, Don Mills, Ontario, Canada.

Tuesday, July 30   Read Psalm 34:11-22.

Redemption

"The Lord redeems the life of his servants." Who but David could speak with such conviction? David was a man of many talents and attributes. He was a musician and poet. He was beautiful to behold and faithful and courageous as a shepherd. But David suffered. A fugitive pursued by Saul at the time he wrote this psalm, David had lost—and regained—faith in God.

Out of the depths of his personal experience David is able to speak to others in words of faith and hope. Recognizing that God is the supreme and constant reality with whom people have to relate, David reminds his listeners of God's redeeming presence in their lives.

The covenant with Israel was made as God redeemed the people from bondage. God promised them guidance and protection. God was *their* God, and they were *God's* people. But being a covenant people meant establishing right relationships with *all* persons as well as with God. Being a covenant people meant being bonded to each other as they were bonded to God. It meant desisting from evil words and deeds and doing good. David, having endured alienation from God and other people, is so sure in his faith that he can affirm that no trouble is so great that God cannot bring us through it. Bound to God, we are redeemed by God. God's servants will be delivered from all affliction.

Prayer: *O God, what a beautiful word* redemption *is. This week, I will remember that you have set me free. In the name of Christ, my redeemer. Amen.*

Wednesday, July 31   Read John 6:24-30.

Recognition and Requirement

How great was the faith of the psalmists like David! They lived before Christ came, but their faith and hope were in the same God. They believed although they had not seen! What a contrast is presented by those who followed Jesus.

They demanded a sign that they might know he was the Messiah—although they had seen the sign the day before in the miracle of the loaves and fishes (see John 6:14). With the coming of Christ, God's purposes unfold more clearly. Yet, even in the face of concrete evidence, there are those who struggle against understanding and illumination. In John 1, the apostle makes the point that when the Word of God takes on human form in Jesus, the contrast between those who yearn for the revelation and those who love darkness is sharpened.

Jesus seeks to lift the crowd's gaze to the reality and presence of a God who not only gives life but sustains life through Jesus Christ. But the crowd is concerned only with material possessions. The "sign" he wished to convey has really made no impression on them. They understand only "getting" something. They can't (as yet) comprehend the unselfish love of Jesus Christ. Deprived of comforts through the hard labor and foreign oppression of their time, they cannot grasp the significance of "work" for a food which will last eternally—the kingdom of heaven.

Recognizing the living Word requires entering into a new relationship with God through Jesus Christ—channeling ourselves into selfless living. It means choosing a life of which Christ is the center.

Prayer: *Lord, I believe; help my unbelief! May I always be ready to recognize the living Word at work in my life and to allow you to work through me. Amen.*

Thursday, August 1   Read John 6:31-35.

Remembrance

The covenant we celebrate today comes through the past in the great heritage of our faith from Abraham, through Israel, through Jesus Christ to us here and now. Nowhere are we as vividly reminded of the acts of God which have led to this present moment—especially Christ's dying and rising for us—as in the sacrament of Holy Communion.

God comes to us through signs. As we celebrate Communion, we feel God's presence through the common elements of bread and wine. We are reminded of the roots of our heritage in the New Testament. We become part of that older group of Christians who, gathering to worship and to remember their Lord, said, "This cup is the new covenant in my blood. Do this, as often as you drink it, in remembrance of me" (1 Cor. 11:25). A new covenant was established.

It was difficult for the crowd at Capernaum to grasp the implications of a "bread of life," a bread that could feed the spirit in a world where the physical body aches for nourishment. It is God, and only God, through Jesus Christ, who took on human form and appeared "full of grace and truth," who is the true bread from heaven, the bread that alone can give complete satisfaction.

Jesus came to be food for our every need. We have his assurance that we will never again be hungry. Those early Christians who celebrated Communion together did more than remember—they communed again with Christ. Their celebration was a reminder of his presence, his sacrifice, and his coming again. So may our celebration be!

Prayer: *Jesus Christ, bread of the world, fill my life today that in all I do and say I may reflect your presence. Amen.*

225

Friday, August 2   Read Ephesians 1:1-10.

Reconciliation

The whole Bible tells the story of God's calling into being a people to be God's people. It tells how last of all God sent to them a Messiah. And so the people of God journey on, from disharmony toward unity, toward the fulfillment of God's great purpose, "to unite all things in him (Christ)." Christ is the long-awaited new covenant of God!

When we explore the historical roots of our faith, we discover Christ at the climactic point of God's many acts of redemption of Israel. When we examine our personal histories, we find our relationships with Christ at the center. He is the center in whom all things unite and the bond who unites all things.

What does it mean to live a life of which Christ is the center? What does it mean to be living in Christ, to belong to Christ?

Simply put, it means to understand that God has once more visited and redeemed Israel as was promised. Through Christ, God has been revealed. Salvation is ours. Now, until he returns to bring all things to completion, Christ has gone to be with God. And, in a new way, he lives with us, through the Holy Spirit—to guide, comfort, and encourage. It means that Christ reconciles us to God. Although we sin and are cut off from God, Christ restores us to that right relationship we have lost. Christ comes and makes us one with God again.

The new covenant for us is new life—in Christ.

Prayer: *Dear Lord, let us relive again our own experiences of being forgiven and restored, so that we may forgive our offenders and restore them. Amen.*

Saturday, August 3   Read Ephesians 4:1-3.

Response/Responsibility

Jesus' followers found themselves bound together because they were all united to him. As Christians we also are bound to God by covenant and bound to one another in Christ. Covenant life is lived in the community of God's people.

Paul, writing from prison, urges his friends to maintain the process of unification "until we all attain to the unity of the faith . . . " (Eph. 4:13). Only in Christ could society find its center and only by possessing inner unity as individuals could the church show others that same unity within itself.

Paul indicates that God's rich goodness obligates believers to walk worthy of the high positions to which God has called them. He specifies four traits that Christians themselves must show if the church is to live in unity: humility, meekness, patience, and love.

These virtues are not the qualities of namby-pamby persons. There is a gentle yet quiet strength in one whose life is Christ-centered. There is no turning away from conflict; rather, there is the ability to express anger at the right time. There is a patience that perseveres under stress, a patience with the struggles of others, a suffering without unjust complaint. There is that love of goodwill that seeks the highest good of every person.

From these four virtues comes a fifth—peace, right relationships. These relationships can happen only when Christ is at the center of one's life.

Prayer: *Lord, as your people, who have found our center in you, may we ever seek to work with others in your community. Amen.*

Sunday, August 4   Read Ephesians 4:4-6.

Reflecting on the resources of our faith

In Jesus Christ, God's ultimate purpose has been fulfilled. A new covenant has been formed with the family of God that constitutes all the nations of the world. In the New Testament, the boundaries of God's love have widened to include people of every nation. Persons of all levels of society are brought into a new way of relating—into an equality of being.

The unity achieved in the reconciliation between people and God in the Cross led to the establishment of a new unity in relationships between individuals, both among themselves and within society, as members of his body, the church.

As Christ is God's instrument of reconciliation, the church is Christ's instrument of reconciliation in the world. Thus, unity must be achieved within the church if it is to preach the Christ in whom unity alone is possible.

By enumerating the sevenfold unity of the Christian church, Paul outlines the fundamental moral principles which are embodied in Christ and so are of the essential being of his church. The general theme of the Epistle to the Ephesians is the glory of the church as the society which embodies in history the eternal purpose of God revealed in Christ. Paul condemns factions and points to the need of a unified church. He stresses that "one-ness" which is the great resource of our faith. We are all parts of *one* body, led by *one* spirit, all consumed by *one* hope, all in the service of *one* Lord, united in *one* faith, possessing *one* baptism, and worshiping *one* God.

Prayer: *As an individual member of the body of Christ, dear God, may I ever strive to live my life in relationship with all who confess him as their risen Lord. Amen.*

GOD'S WAY

August 5-11, 1985   **Jonah Chang†**
Monday, August 5   Read 2 Samuel 18:9-15.

A world without God

The life and death of Absalom reminds us of the life and death of Jesus Christ, except that the goals and purposes of the two lives went in two completely opposite directions. Jesus humbled himself, and Absalom claimed for himself a crown, a kingdom.

Absalom was handsome, wise, gifted with leadership skills, full of strategies and adored by many people in Israel. He rode on his mule like a king, like a commander-in-chief. He epitomized success. However, there was no room in his heart for God. His rule illustrated the intensity of expectations on himself and his domain, but lacked the slightest trace of the hope which comes with knowing God. On that fateful day, his head was caught fast in an oak tree, and eventually his body was pierced by three deadly spears.

Jesus Christ was nailed to the cross, yet he turned to the people and to God to make everything new. He chose not to grasp the highest honor which was his right, but emptied and offered himself as an instrument of God's revelation and as a servant for all.

Prayer: *O God, in thy steadfast mercy, forbid us from straying toward self-righteousness and self-exaltation. Lead us to walk humbly with thee. Amen.*

---

†United Methodist minister and Executive Director of the National Federation of Asian American United Methodists, San Francisco, California.

Tuesday, August 6 Read 2 Samuel 18:1, 5.

Integrity

Who was this Joab? What courage he had! Being a general required that Joab obey the creed of the king; yet he dared to kill King David's son, Absalom, against David's orders. Joab managed to find the strength to overlook temporal consequences by obeying the voice of the One who was infinitely superior to King David—God.

Courageous people throughout time have heard and obeyed the command of the supreme God. When the high priest of the Jerusalem Temple charged Peter and other apostles for filling Jerusalem with the teaching of Jesus, Peter boldly remarked, "We must obey God rather than men" (Acts 5:29). Whether kings or high priests, no one can undermine God's authority without suffering grave consequences. Recognizing God's autonomy should be the foothold for human obedience and relationships. Let God be God, and let individuals be obedient creatures. Through obedience believers can begin to participate in the kingdom of God.

Although the sinfulness of humankind is fashionable, handsome, tempting, smart, and thrifty to me, I must "bruise my own body and make it know its master" (1 Cor. 9:27, NEB). Joab said, "I will not waste time like this with you" (2 Sam. 18:14). Our obedience to God is not a matter of gradual progression but of an eternal life which begins presently. For Christ's followers, obedience is the ultimate goal—"Be faithful unto death, and I will give you the crown of life" (Rev. 2:10).

Pryer: *O God, teach me to take delight in faith and obedience to you, from small matters to major issues of life. Amen.*

Wednesday, August 7   Read Psalm 143.

Teach me the way

Buddha taught that this world is filled with pains and tribulations. His advice, however, requires taking a static attitude toward life's destiny to eventually find harmony with the universe. The psalmist, on the other hand, takes an activist view of the universe, requiring rest in God. The psalmist experiences an enemy who has made him "sit in darkness like those long dead." Like the psalmist, today's prisoners of conscience—incarcerated for their struggles to advance freedom and human rights—can easily lose hope. Sorrow and despair may well overwhelm their hearts. However, the face of God has provided many of them with solace for their disheartened souls. The memory of God's past reign with the people of Zion has encouraged many of those in jail to stretch out their hands to God. Many have placed their trust in God; and in response, God has lifted up their souls.

Those who have been called to minister justice have actually engaged in a world of horrors. But the psalmist can see that God's hand is to be trusted, even in the face of those horrors. "Let me hear in the morning of thy steadfast love." What an effective prayer! One little stream of God's gift is enough to carry you and me on through this new day. Despite the seemingly overwhelming forces of holocausts and nuclear arms proliferation over the powers of construction, peace, and love, God can strengthen us to work for justice.

Prayer: *O thou mighty and righteous God, refresh hope for the meek, handicapped, mistreated, and imprisoned. Give us vision to see above the mushrooming clouds of fear and destruction. Amen.*

Thursday, August 8   Read Ephesians 4:25-32.

Mutuality in the gospel

Over the years many and various strategies have been created to expand the witnessing and missionary work of the church. However, too often the structures and legislations of the body of Christ have replaced the vision and commission of Christ.

Paul urges us to concern ourselves with being the *ekklesia*—the called of God, the church. As such, we are to speak the truth with our neighbor, "for we are members one of another." Under labels such as "evangelism," "social awareness," "missionary vision," "growth orientation," and "action orientation," people have been plagued with strife and the body of Christ has been divided. Paul advises the body of witnesses, "Be angry but do not sin; do not let the sun go down on your anger."

The truth directs the church. The world will know and will be "salted," or influenced, by Christ's church. God's people who stand firm and are zealous in obeying the Bible's teaching are capable of confronting the world without vindictiveness because they know of God's ultimate victory. *Laos,* the body of Christ, will be mutually complemented and coordinated on such genuine concerns as evangelism, education, employment, housing, family life, environment, energy, nuclear threats, gender and racial/ethnic considerations if each of us listens to God's call.

Prayer: *O Lord of the one, holy, catholic church, teach us to rejoice for the members who are united in thee though scattered throughout the world. Amen.*

Friday, August 9   Read Ephesians 4:30–5:2.

Prolific life

A Chinese saying states, "It takes 10 years to cultivate a tree, but it takes 100 years to shape a human character." One difference between a tree and a person is that the former remains stationary while the latter has freedom of movement. The kingdom of God may require several generations to materialize within a family, a community, or a church. It is a slow process, like the growth of living creatures, but it is also as alive and sure.

Paul wrote, "Be imitators of God, as beloved children. And walk in love, as Christ loved us and gave himself up for us, a fragrant offering and sacrifice to God." Since Christ abolished the old mode of worship—sacrificial offering—life itself has become the sacrifice. It is the sacrifice of living, *walking* as Christians, that is acceptable to God (see Rom. 12:1). The flame of the living sacrifice is the Holy Spirit, and the fragrance is the love seen in people. The gift of salvation cannot be better introduced by believers than through participation in families and communities. Through living a life of worship and service, the followers of Christ—the "imitators of God"—assure the world that Christ's reign, the reign of love and sacrifice, has begun and will endure forever.

Prayer: *O Holy Spirit, who links the roots to the branches and nourishes the tree, help us to be better imitators of God and to bear the fruits of love, joy, peace, patience, kindness, goodness, and self-control. Amen.*

Saturday, August 10   Read John 6:41-47.

Stop, watch, and listen

In your pilgrimage through this world, stop, watch, and listen!

Jesus said, "No one can come to me unless the Father who sent me draws him." The Jews rejected Jesus because they saw this gift from God come wrapped in an earthy, ordinary appearance. They wondered how "the son of Joseph, whose father and mother we know," could have come down from heaven.

Every television and radio station today wants people to listen, and we all want others to hear our point of view. But no one wants to listen to God, to search for God's will. Modern people simply cannot seem to endure solitude. Throughout history, many who heard God's word and repented changed the course of their lives and influenced the world dramatically. When Jesus came, he revealed and extended God's earnest invitation. However, without a response from hearers, the voice from heaven remains meaningless, the bread of life sits uneaten—and life slips away into an abyss.

Can anyone ignore this invitation while knowing Jesus' promise? Jesus said, "Truly, truly, I say to you, he who believes has eternal life." Have you heard? Have you believed?

Prayer: *God, draw us closer to you that we may hear your still, soft voice, see the life-giving Messiah, and accept eternal life. Amen.*

Sunday, August 11   Read John 6:35, 48-51.

Come to the banquet

Come, let us celebrate with a banquet! Food is plentiful, and everyone who has accepted the invitation is prepared to enjoy life together with God. This celebration of the bread of life is the ultimate party.

Some of us might feel that our worship services become cumbersome from time to time—probably because we often find ourselves chained to all the baggage we think we must carry along with us all our lives. We may be burdened with excess body weight, mental stress, or endless demands on our possessions. In such an imperfect world, leaders continue to toy with the notion that humanity can exist or coexist with arms and military might, thereby adding to the confusion of our days.

Christ does not come to satisfy such appetites. Christ comes with the invitation, "I am the bread of life; he who comes to me shall not hunger, and he who believes in me shall never thirst." But we don't have to accept the invitation. We can ignore this call and stay in a world of confusion and physical and spiritual hunger. We can eke out a meager existence for ourselves. But that is not what God wants for us.

Life does not involve merely existence. Life has meaning, and is, therefore, to be celebrated with a banquet of food, drink, joyous dance, exciting songs, and heart-touching fellowship. Christ, the bread of life, is the one who provides the banquet guests with nourishment for their lives. And partakers of this feast will never again hunger or thirst.

Prayer: *O Lord Jesus Christ, thanks and glory be to thee for the feast of bread and wine—the feast of eternal life. Amen.*

LOOKING CAREFULLY

August 12-18, 1985   **Mary Lou Redding†**
Monday, August 12   Read Ephesians 5:15-16.

When was the last time you stubbed your toe? Or hit your
thumb with a hammer or bent a fingernail back? Even small
pains can so fill our consciousness that they displace nobler
thoughts. We hit our thumb driving a nail—and suddenly all
the blueprints and specs for the dream house are forgotten.
We run up against some frustrating daily annoyance, and
ushering in God's reign of justice and love seems like a
fantasy.

"Look carefully" says the letter to the Ephesians, " . . .
because the days are evil." How so? Evil does not swagger up,
dressed in black, brandishing the mortgage paper and brag-
ging of having tied Polly Pureheart to the railroad track. If that
were so, avoiding it and foiling it would be greatly simplified.
No, evil is something far more palatable and inconspicuous.
Somehow, the very fabric of the systems we use mitigates
against the will of God being done in the world and in our
lives. Like little pains that divert our attention from bigger
plans, tiny lapses of faithfulness lead us away from God's plan
for transforming the world.

How do we "redeem the time"? How do we counteract the
human tendency to move in ever-smaller circles around ourselves? By *looking carefully*. Where is there pain? Where is
there need for reconciliation? For challenge of hurtful systems? Where is God's power needed to buy back what is about
to be lost?

Prayer: *Dear God, it is hard to keep what you want uppermost in
our minds. Help us to see where you want us to act on your behalf.*

---

†Managing editor, *The Upper Room*, Nashville, Tennessee.

Tuesday, August 13   Read Ephesians 5:17-20.

At some time, most of us either gradually or suddenly came to a decision to follow Christ. We were resolute about doing what we understood God to be asking of us. But somehow that resolute mind-set does not always last. Take the parable of Pockets:

> Her given name was Emily, but everyone called
> her Pockets.
> They called her that
> because she insisted over and over again
> that people shouldn't own anything
> they can't carry in their pockets. . . .

But, finding the four pockets of her jeans soon filled, she added coats with many pockets, and

> . . . Emily was last seen in Southern California
> standing very, very still
> She was wearing (several layers of clothes
> under) a woolen Army greatcoat
> on which she had sewn large pockets
> to hold
> her folding bicycle
> a television
> and
> a complete set of the Great Books of the
> Western World.*

Suggestion for prayer: *Look carefully at yourself today. What have you kept of your original vision? What have you let go? What keeps you standing still by weighing you down?*

---

*"Pockets" by Pat Ryan first appeared in *Images: Women in Transition*, ©1976 by The Upper Room.

Wednesday, August 14   Read 2 Samuel 18:24-33.

David waits for news from the battlefield. Absalom has gathered an army to overthrow him, and their opposing forces are fighting in the hills. For two years David and Absalom have lived in the same city without seeing each other. The rift between them is deep, and David feels it. Now he is worried that his son who is estranged from him will be hurt.

When the first runner comes, David asks, "And the young man Absalom? Is it well with him?" (AP) When Ahimaaz does not answer, David turns to the second messenger, interrupting the victory story to ask, "But is it well with the young man Absalom?" (AP)

The newsbearer replies, "May all your enemies be as he is!" (AP) In other words, Absalom has been killed.

Absalom's death means dissarray in the rebel forces, an end to the rebellion. Politically it is a time to rejoice. But David sees beyond short-term political goals. The real issue is the long-term good of reconciliation and forgiveness. And his chance for reconciliation has died with Absalom in the battle.

David saw what we must see—that political realities must be secondary to relationships. Believers struggle now perhaps as never before about political matters—nuclear proliferation, sexual and ethnic inclusiveness, how to spend the church's money. We spend time trying to win acceptance for a particular program or point of view. But is winning God's first consideration? Whether we're talking about our homes, our jobs, or government policy, if we win our point in a way that destroys relationships, if the chance for reconciliation dies in the battle, we like David are right to grieve. For God always sides with relationships.

Prayer: *O God, help me to look carefully at relationships. May I love as you do, unfailingly. Amen.*

Thursday, August 15   Read 2 Samuel 18:16-27.

The behaviors of the two messengers raise some questions about how carefully we look at those we deal with. Ahimaaz gets to David first and reports that the insurgent troops have been routed. When David asks about Absalom, Ahimaaz stalls. Then the second messenger, the Cushite, arrives. David asks about Absalom and is told his son is dead.

Contrast Ahimaaz's unwillingness to speak with the eagerness of the Cushite messenger. The second man was so caught up in the news of the victory that he couched even Absalom's death in positive terms.

It is easy for us, like the Cushite, to become so caught up in the news we bring, the ideas we've birthed, that we respond according to our wishes. We look at others from the basis of our presuppositions and expectations about what they want and need, rather than listening and looking to see what they reveal.

You've probably heard the story of the child who asked, "Mommy, where did I come from?" Mommy, who has been expecting the question, launches into an elaborate lecture, complete with drawings and moral guidelines. When she pauses, the child says patiently:

"Well, that's not exactly what I meant. See, Jennifer came from New Jersey, and Ricardo came from Illinois. And I just wondered where *I* came from." The mother missed the question because she thought she already had the answer.

Do we really look at those we encounter, to see where there is pain and where there is joy? And do we respect both, holding them up to the light of God's love?

Prayer: *God of all comfort, help us to wait today to let others say what they truly need. And then let us respond in love. Amen.*

Friday, August 16   Read Psalm 102:1-12.

This psalmist could have written country music. All the right ideas are there: "I can't eat," "I'm wasting away to nothing," "I don't fit in here," "Even God has thrown me out." The psalmist wrote, "I forget to eat my bread," "I have mingled my drink with weeping," "My bones cleave to my flesh," "I am like a pelican of the desert," and God has "taken me up and thrown me away."

We may think at first reading that this psalmist is one of the true pessimists of all time. But remember the last time you had a virus? Or the last time you were really depressed? If what we say at times like that were recorded, it would probably sound a great deal like today's reading.

We all have times like the ones the psalmist described here. To say that we don't is to deny how life really is. To expect our days to be all sweetness and light is as unrealistic as wanting to wake up without bad breath in the morning. The less-than-pleasant is simply part of being human. The psalmist sums up the railing, the aching, the bitterness we feel at eating ashes when those around us are feasting.

Sometimes we have to look hard and long at life to find anything worth looking at. True, sometimes it is wonderful—challenging, exhilarating, fun. But sometimes it is only weariness. It is then more than any other time we must remind ourselves to "look carefully." Beyond the troubles of life, beyond the alienation and illness and failures, there is God's goodness, steadiness, mercy. When we look carefully we see that for us, as for the psalmist, God is enough.

Prayer: *Lord God, open my eyes to see and my heart to trust your steadiness and your love beyond even the bad things that happen in life. Amen.*

Saturday, August 17   Read John 6:51-58.

Jesus was at it again—stirring up trouble, talking about things no good Jew would dream of doing. This time he was talking to the crowd about eating flesh and drinking blood! And not just that of animals! He was talking about people eating his flesh and blood! These were people who lived by strict dietary laws, but Jesus seemed to be deliberately trying to anger them by talking about what sounded like cannibalism! How could he mean all those horrible-sounding things?

Indeed. Jesus said a lot of things that turned the established order awry. He talked about losing self in order to find self, dying in order to love, being last in order to be first, being weak in order to be strong. What was he talking about?

The "looking carefully" admonition applies on several levels to this passage. First, it was difficult for Jesus' hearers to separate the literal from the symbolic. He had been talking about literal bread (this passage follows a story about feeding a multitude) and about manna, which was also literal. And the shift was difficult to follow.

It is still tough for us. It might be easier if God didn't speak to us through ordinary things. If we had to go to some particular place and be in some particular attitude, it might be easier to see what God is getting at than it is when God just barges in through the ordinariness of our days, alongside trips to the dentist and frustrations with co-workers and problems with the car or the children. But the fact is, God does come to us through ordinary, obstinate, impossible, arrogant people. And in them we see the winsome love that permeates even us.

Prayer: *Let us look carefully, O God, at your presence in those around us today. Amen.*

241

Sunday, August 18   Read Luke 24:13-35;
                                              John 6:51-58.

Here is another story of Jesus breaking bread. Jesus in speaking to the crowd made it clear that somehow daily life and divine life are intertwined. In fact, one lesson in the passage from John is how inseparable God is from the fabric of day-to-day life. Jesus made no distinction between the source of physical and spiritual sustenance because for him it was no more possible to separate God from life than to separate the flour from the leavening after the bread is made.

After the resurrection, Jesus encounters the Emmaus travelers and walks with them. They do not recognize him. When Jesus asks what they are discussing so intently, they are shocked. "Are you the only one in town who doesn't know the things that have happened here this week?" they ask incredulously (AP). Jesus then begins to explain the scriptures that tell of the Christ—and still the travelers do not realize who he is. Finally, at the end of the day, they sit down to eat. And as Jesus breaks the bread, they realize he is the Christ.

This story shows us that looking carefully is not merely a matter of the intellect. These two had given their attention to Jesus; they had asked him to stay and eat with them because they were interested in what he was saying. But they didn't realize the spiritual significance of what was going on until "their eyes were opened." Knowing facts alone is not enough. We must continually give attention to knowing with our spirits, asking God to open our eyes.

Prayer: *Lord God, may the eyes of our spirits be opened that we may see how to use what we know and how to serve you more faithfully. Amen.*

THE SPIRIT OF THE LORD

August 19-25, 1985   **Robert N. Zearfoss†**
Monday, August 19   Read 2 Samuel 23:1-4.

The spirit of the Lord is available, ready to be caught. It is evident in the life of that group that is alert to the needs of the people. We know it when we sing, "We are one in the spirit . . . ." Pentecost dramatized it for the early Christians.

Spirit is an active word. It is lively. It is animated. We say, "That's the spirit!" speaking of someone who exhibits vitality. The Spirit speaks in all-pervasive, young, and contemporaneous terms. No wonder then that David could be credited with saying that the spirit of the Lord had spoken through him.

Looking back over a lifetime of rich experience, David realized that whatever he had completed that was worthwhile was not his doing but was the work of God. He credited God for the words on his lips. He was an instrument, interpreting to others the spirit of the Eternal.

Today there are those who work for such an experience in their lives. Looking back, as David did at the end of his life, it becomes clear that the high and low moments are saturated with God's spirit. In meditation, as Walter Rauschenbusch put it, "Big things become small, and small things become great."*

Prayer: *God of the word of life, open our minds and also our emotions to the vitality of your spirit. We would be doers of your will. Amen.*

---

†Minister Emeritus, First Baptist Church, Evanston, Illinois.
*"The Little Gate to God" by Walter Rauschenbusch. Privately printed as a prayer card, circa 1920.

Tuesday, August 20   Read 2 Samuel 23:5-7.

The spirit of the Lord innoculates the believer with the serum of faithfulness. "Surely my house is true to God; for he has made a pact with me for all time," sang the psalmist (NEB). Whatever difficulties present-day circumstances bring, the conditions and the times will change. The eternal word of God stands firm, urging the faithful to remain true to their deepest spiritual values. The skies do clear. There is that quality in the word of the Lord that is supportive of justice when all around seems deceitful.

The degree to which Christians center their lives in the activity of God's spirit determines the true significance of their lifestyle. Only as God's spirit is continuously sought does life become good and spirited. This is Rule One. It is the first commandment: saturate thought and action with a perpetual awareness of God's spirit. Work at it all the time. See God's spirit at work in the world around you. God's spirit is to be in your veins! Habakkuk (3:17-19) sang of this in a unique way:

> Though the fig tree do not blossom,
> nor fruit be on the vines, . . .
> I will joy in the God of my salvation.

Paul proclaimed this truth in a totally different manner: "I can do all things in him who strengthens me" (Phil. 4:13).

Prayer: *God of glory, I joy in you as my strength. May I seek your spirit in all that I do today. Make me alert to your presence in the simple, seemingly mundane tasks I do. O God, open my eyes! Amen.*

Wednesday, August 21   Read John 6:22-34.

The spirit of the Lord nourishes the believer. John designated the synagogue at Capernaum as the place where Jesus said to a large group of his followers, "The spirit alone gives life; the flesh is of no avail; the words which I have spoken to you are both spirit and life" (John 6:63, NEB). Earlier he spoke to crowds who needed to be fed. They wanted bread that feeds the body. Hungry, they followed him everywhere. They were probably outside the synagogue waiting at the time he spoke these words.

At the end of a short walk from the ruins of the first-century synagogue at Capernaum, one comes to a high hill rising above the Sea of Galilee. Tradition places the Sermon on the Mount there. A little further on stands the Church of the Multiplication, with its ancient mosaic floor depicting, among other things, a basket containing loaves of bread and two fish standing upright.

For Jesus the feeding of the body was important but it was not as significant as the nourishment of the soul. His words spoke not of temporal matters but of eternal truth. Spirited words convey the essence of worship, confession, compassion, and dedication to God's will. Words in the Lord's Prayer feed the believer in renewed endeavor to be faithful to God. Words in the Sermon on the Mount enrich minds as well as emotions.

The Christian begins to "know" at deeper levels of comprehension. Words in the parables call for a true evaluation of one's self. Words such as *seed, harvest, bread,* and *wind* were nourishing words when Jesus used them. They are meant for the enrichment and guidance of the soul.

Prayer: *O God, we cherish the nourishment of souls more than the delights of the body. Feed us, Lord. Amen.*

Thursday, August 22 Read John 6:55-69.

The spirit of the Lord awakens the disciple. Jesus in speaking of the spirit of the Lord referred to himself as the gift of God in spirit. If he was seen as the presence of the Lord, then those who knew him would also know the light. He said, "I am the bread of life" (John 6:35, NEB). He then spoke in shocking metaphor: "Whoever eats my flesh and drinks my blood possesses eternal life" (John 6:54, NEB). For us, as for them, Jesus meant this in a highly specialized sense. Surely Jesus did not mean these words to be taken literally. He was using the most useful of staples and the commonest of fruits as a way of emphasizing the energy-producing quality of the spirit of the Lord.

Evidently there were those who heard only the surface meaning, for they said, "We cannot stomach this kind of talk" (AP), and they departed. But Peter and the other disciples, with help from Jesus, came to understand the symbolism of the bread and wine. They were stimulated by the vitality of his words. They, too, were caught up in the spirit of the evidence that Jesus not only fed the multitudes bread but also gave to those who believed in him a much more significant gift, the bread of life.

The spirit of the Lord awakens any who, seeking communion with God, take the bread and the cup, and in the process sense a divine purpose in their own lives. This happens over and over again within the Christian family.

Prayer: *God of the Table, awaken us to a helpful experience of your spirit. Following the directions of Jesus, we take the bread and the wine. With renewed dedication we covenant with you. Amen.*

Friday, August 23   Read 2 Corinthians 4:1-7.

The spirit of the Lord flows through human beings. Jesus called to his side men and women who would be inspired to lead others to be disciples. The spirit of the Lord became available to others so that in each generation there would be those called to be interpreters of the word. While in the sixth chapter of John it is noted that some departed from Jesus, others stayed. As Peter put it, "Where else shall we go?" (John 6:68, AP)

David said it right: "The spirit of the Lord has spoken through me" (2 Sam. 23:2, NEB). *Through* is a significant word for him. "Yea, though I walk *through* the valley of the shadow . . . " (Ps. 23:4, KJV). *Through* is a flowing word. God communicates to each generation through the lives of those who acknowledge the presence of the spirit. Persons are conveyors of that spirit. Francis of Assisi prayed well, "Lord, make me an instrument of thy peace." Paul was right on target when he wrote to the church at Corinth, "We have this treasure in earthen vessels." Believers are containers, carriers, and also transmitters of the spirit of the Lord.

Even as the atmosphere has contained sound and light waves since time immemorial, so also the Holy Spirit has been constantly available. Christians are vehicles by which God's spirit is beamed into the life of this century. There is a place for insight that is more powerful than cognitive knowledge. It is to be found in the spirit of the Lord.

Prayer: *God, so saturate us with a yearning for the truth that we may be conveyors of your creativvity. Let our daily lives speak for your spirit. Amen.*

Saturday, August 24 Read Ephesians 5:21-33.

The spirit of the Lord equalizes. The advice here in Ephesians is for husbands and wives. "Be subject to one another out of reverence for Christ." While the wording of these instructions seems slanted in the husband's favor, the text does point out that all members of the family are to be treated as God's creation. All human life is sacred. This belief carries over into the intimacy of home life. The spirit of the Lord speaks as an equalizer in the thoughtfulness that arises between husband and wife.

An interesting exercise occurs when the wording is reversed, substituting woman where man is mentioned and husband where wife is given. Even though there is a slant in favor of one over the other, the intent is clear: we are to be loving and equal in all family relationships.

This was a strange new concept in Paul's day. Because women were considered to be property, the idea of status for a wife was an astonishing new development. One of the significant contributions of Christianity to social mores has been in this area. Wives and children have status. They are to be treated with equal consideration.

This concept of the uniqueness of human personality is given added emphasis by the reminder that Christ is Lord of the church. In the church where Jesus is Lord, something wonderful happens: The Holy Spirit descends upon all alike. Status symbols fall by the wayside.

Prayer: *O God, reveal to us the ways in which your spirit is available to all on an equal basis. Erase the distinctions that separate and demean. Amen.*

Sunday, August 25   Read Psalm 67.

The spirit of the Lord illuminates the daily scene. The psalmist makes it clear that the spirit itself is evident in the behavior of those who trust in God. The radiance of the Eternal, reflected in the faces of believers, tells everyone that God is around! The spirit of the Lord lights up the areas where we are. Insights develop. New knowledge evolves. This shows up in the ways we praise God.

But that is not to say we deal only with sweetness and light. "Let all nations rejoice and shout in triumph," says the psalmist, "for thou dost judge the peoples with justice" (NEB). God does work through all believers to create a just and equable environment in which the abused and the neglected receive fair treatment. Here *justice* is the word. Because the believer has been illumined by the spirit, personal self-interest no longer rules. Generosity in dealing with others and compassion for victims of tragedy are commendable Christian responses. We can do nothing better than be fair in our daily behavior. The light of God's countenance is upon us.

Stephen, apprenticed as a new Christian to care for widows and the hungry, speaking of his faith, radiated this spirit: "His face appeared to them like the face of an angel" (Acts 6:15, NEB). There is a charisma, an electrifying quality that permeates life when we let justice and honor bear fruit through the spirit of the Lord.

Prayer: *O God, illumine my life. Let your radiance be evident as each day unfolds. In Jesus' name I pray. Amen.*

GROW STRONG IN THE LORD

August 26–September 1, 1985   **Anne Wolf†**
Monday, August 26   Read Mark 7:1-8, 14-15.

We must grow strong in the Lord to overcome the unclean spirits in our hearts.

This pronouncement story shows Jesus' opposition to the code of unwritten law which the Pharisees so scrupulously followed. Like the Pharisees, we sometimes cling to our own unwritten laws of society—materialism, sexism, racism—rather than to the laws of God. While we attend church faithfully, pray faithfully, follow our government's laws faithfully, we also pursue too many material goods, deny justice to the poor, minorities, and women.

To overcome these unclean spirits, we must look inside ourselves to find what is unclean and admit our failings. It is only after we humbly admit our failings and ask God's forgiveness that we begin to realize that God is our strength. Then we can begin to grow strong in the Lord.

Prayer: *O God, help us to see our failings and to have the humility to admit them to ourselves and others. Especially help us see how we contribute to systemic injustice in society by following unwritten laws. Forgive our failings and help us to overcome them. In Jesus' name. Amen.*

---

†Free-lance writer and editor; former managing editor of *Salt* magazine; Oak Park, Illinois.

Tuesday, August 27   Read Ephesians 6:10-13;
Wisdom 5:7-21; Isaiah 59:15-17.

We grow strong in the Lord by arming ourselves with integrity, justice, and holiness. In the Old Testament, we find God so armed against the enemies of God. Integrity, justice, and holiness are the powers God uses to convict humankind.

Paul challenges Christians to arm themselves with God's weapons rather then the weapons of the world. Paul believes that these virtues are what make Christians strong and full of the power of God. Armed with these virtues, we are able to fight not only the spirits who, in Paul's time, were thought to move the heavens and to live in the space between earth and heaven; but with these virtues we are also able to work against the evils in our world: to speak out for justice, to live with integrity in our homes and in our work.

Suggestion for prayer: *Reflect on one area of your life where you believe you have already put on God's armor. Then reflect on another area in which you can begin to resist evil. Thank God for the strength you already have and pray for the power to resist evil in other areas of your world.*

Wednesday, August 28   Read Ephesians 6:14-17.

We must grow strong in the Lord in order to spread the gospel of peace.

How do we both "stand our ground" and "spread the gospel of peace"? In our world it is sometimes difficult to do both at the same time. In fact, the two seem to be mutually exclusive. Those who stand up for what they believe can be seen as strident and militant—hardly characteristics of those who spread the gospel of peace.

But for Paul, doing both is possible because of faith—the faith in Jesus Christ and acceptance of God's salvation that gives us the strength to stand our ground in efforts for peace and justice. It is also faith in Jesus Christ and acceptance of God's salvation which allows us to stand our ground peaceably, without violence, respecting the opposition and not demeaning those who think differently. This is true whether we are arguing politics with a friend or working in the political arena for world peace. Faith in Jesus Christ gives us the power to do what is right while respecting those who disagree.

Prayer: *God of peace, give me the strength to live a life of peace. Help me to stand up for what I believe in, and give me the ability to listen to those who disagree, to treat them with respect, and to learn from them. In the name of the Prince of Peace. Amen.*

Thursday, August 29   Read Ephesians 6:18-20.

We grow strong in the Lord when we pray for what we need.

It takes a great deal of strength to be in prison as Paul was when he wrote the Letter to the Ephesians. That he would ask others to pray that he might have opportunities to speak out—when the very act of speaking out put him in prison in the first place—shows the depth of Paul's strength and faith in the Lord.

Paul reminds me of a woman I know who fears the possibility of nuclear war more than anything. Because of her fear, she spends her spare time working to lessen the threat of nuclear war. However, she finds it difficult to talk about the issue of nuclear arms with others who disagree with her or whose position on the issue is unknown to her. To overcome this difficulty, she prays for strength and courage to "speak without fear." Like Paul, she grows strong in the Lord because of her faith that God will give her what she asks for in prayer.

Suggestion for prayer: *Think of a time when God has given you what you asked for in prayer. Then ask God for something you believe you can get only with God's help.*

Friday, August 30

Read Luke 6:36-38;
Colossians 3:12-15.

We must grow strong in the Lord to have the power to forgive.

The problem with power in the world is that it usually brings with it pride and self-righteousness. Those with power can come to believe they do not need compassion themselves, and so they forget to have compassion for others. They can begin to believe that the power they have comes from within rather than from God.

But we must continually remind ourselves that all power comes from God and that we must use the power we have as God would. When we stand before the power of God, we are humbled because we realize our failings and weaknesses. But we believe God loves us in spite of those failings and even that God forgives us. If God who is perfect forgives us, how can we not forgive those who, like us, are imperfect?

This does not mean we stand idly by while society keeps people poor and powerless. It means we humbly admit to ourselves and others the part we play in injustice even as we try to bring justice to the world. It means that we forgive others for the part they play as we call them to change their ways.

Suggestion for prayer: *Think about a problem in our world which you contribute to by the way you live. Ask God for forgiveness. Then write a letter to the appropriate governmental leaders whose policies also contribute to the problem. Ask them to change their stand.*

Saturday, August 31   Read 1 Kings 2:1-4;
                                           Psalm 121.

We grow strong in the Lord when we realize God is with us.

From the time of Noah, God has continually told human-kind that their Creator is with them. "You shall be my people, and I will be your God," God says in Ezekiel (36:28). The covenant between God and humankind has been expressed in countless ways throughout history. And the covenant has been passed down from generation to generation, much as David passed it on to Solomon in the reading from First Kings.

But despite the many times God has reiterated the cove-nant—even sending Jesus to live among us—we forget or fail to believe that God is with us. We sometimes find it hard to have the faith and confidence in God that the psalmist had.

When we believe God is with us, we are better able to feel God's presence, to see the hand of God in our lives. This in turn gives us the strength to live as God asks. This is the faith that moves mountains. If we trust God's presence in our lives and live accordingly, God will continually show us that our trust is in the right place. And each time we have evidence that God is with us, we grow stronger in our faith and in our power to move mountains.

Prayer: *O heavenly Creator, thank you for the gift of faith and the power that we have because of it. Help us to look for the little signs you give us daily of your presence in our world. Help us to pass on your covenant to future generations, that our children and our children's children may know your love and presence in their lives and in the world. Amen.*

Sunday, September 1   Read 1 Kings 2:1-4, 10-13;
                                  Psalm 121; Ephesians 6:10-21;
                                  Mark 7:1-8, 14-15, 21-23.

What does it mean to grow strong in the Lord?

In the United States, we think of the president and other political leaders as powerful people. Corporations and their executives have power. Jesus had power, too, but of a much different nature.

Christians may have the power of politicians and corporate executives, but they also have the power of faith. The crucial issue is how they use the power they have. Do they use it to serve God and their neighbors—whether the neighbor is next door or in Central America? Or do they use it to gain more for themselves? Do they use power to bring God's kingdom on earth? Or to build their own kingdom (whether that be a corporate kingdom, a political kingdom, or a kingdom's castle for a home)?

Jesus did not reign as David and his sons did. Instead he defined power in a new way, in a way that truly revealed what it meant to walk "in faithfulness" before God. Jesus' power had to do with being last, not first; with serving, not being served; with giving to others, not grabbing more for one's own self.

This is the power Christians have from God. And it is the power they must use to help others—whether or not they have political and corporate power.

Prayer: *God of power, help me to continue to grow strong in you and to use that power to serve others. In those situations where I am tempted to use the power I have to destroy others, help me instead to use the power wisely to build people up. In Jesus' name. Amen.*

September 2-8, 1985   **Gloria B. Sauke†**
Monday, September 2   Read Psalm 119:129-130.

Absorbant and Symbolic

This psalmist portrays an openness and receptivity which is perhaps the most basic of emotions threaded throughout this psalm. Attitudinally, it represents the maximum extent of our yearning for wisdom.

An important element in what we are depends upon our ability to absorb from the world around us. From the day we are born, we experience a never-ending process of expanding. Our world continually grows to encompass more people and greater depth of understanding of them and ourselves.

The text reiterates this process—a *keeping* and *unfolding* process. The word *cherish* brings to mind these seemingly contradictory actions. For instance, the newly engaged want to tell, but want to keep; want to display, but want to keep covered; want to shout, but want to keep to themselves.

We must live this paradox in our faith, being both sponge and flag. We must be as the rosebush which quietly beneath cover draws from the earth in winter and from the sun in springtime, and slowly unfolds each petal, symbolic of the perfection of creation and the fulfilling of its purpose.

We are to learn and keep the testimonies of the Lord. We are to absorb and be a symbol of all that God's wisdom can make of us.

Prayer: *O God, help me listen more patiently and hear the word more diligently. May my actions ever more precisely parallel the message of salvation as known through Christ's ministry on earth. Amen.*

---

†Development Counselor, Lutheran Social Service of Minnesota, Minneapolis, Minnesota.

Tuesday, September 3   Read Psalm 119:131-136.

Resilient and Resistant

The psalmist speaks openly and persuasively of the need for undergirding and endurance. Cognizant of weakness and the world's ways, he pleads with a yearning and opened mouth, panting for that which must come from God.

The village smithy knew resiliency. The workers in the steel mills know what makes the ore flow. The operator of the steam press found in every dry cleaning establishment can tell you what the necessary element is. It is heat.

Many times we have heard the admonishment to keep cool. Does that apply? The psalmist asks for steps that are steady and that no iniquity be allowed dominion over him. Can we see the intent of the biblical message of acceptance being so distorted in our day that our eyes actually shed streams of tears?

We must keep cool as ice and unbending as steel. If we are to be advocates on behalf of the most voiceless of God's children, we must speak without hesitation, reaching out though our arms are weary, not being dissuaded from our singular purpose to be Christ's disciples.

Letting no iniquity get charge over us means making a conscious effort to align priorities with preferences, promises with productivity, and practice with purpose. If life is so jammed full of time and effort expended on things of little importance, we become living contradictions of our very being. And, most of all, we are not what God intends us to be.

Prayer: *Come, Lord Jesus, make me strong. With the light of the gospel, grant me also the strength to hold it high—today, tomorrow, and all the days that are mine. Amen.*

Wednesday, September 4   Read Proverbs 2:1-5.

Pattern and Design

In this passage we read that the whole being is to lean forward in earnest pursuit of wisdom. The heart, the ear, the mind—every faculty.

The text speaks of crying out for insight. The words *wisdom, knowledge,* and *insight* have much the same meaning. But insight connotes something extra, especially for Christians. What is it?

Does insight reflect the kind of reaction we feel when root words give new meaning to some familiar phrase? Does insight represent reaction to new knowledge as would require a change of mind? More importantly, does insight effect an about-face, a change in our practice, a challenge to such action as may come under question by persons who don't understand?

New patterns in tapestry and in life are the never-ending proof that life is not an end to be reached but an expression of God's unsurpassable greatness and creativity in an ever-changing world.

Creative thinking, like creative living, has got to challenge the past in the light of the present, daring to call into question every practice that limits the full expression of God's forgiveness. It must contantly headline the unique complement of our varieties of gifts and our diversity of styles. Our point of judgment can be exercised nowhere but upon ourselves. Have we grown? Are we new today? Will tomorroow find us closer in purpose to God's will?

Prayer: *Lord, make me open to receive, weighing old against new, doubting only my hesitance to grow and my reluctance to dare. Make me reckless for your sake, Lord. Amen.*

Thursday, September 5   Read Proverbs 2:6-8.

Strength for Justice

In guarding the paths of justice, the tapestry of life must also be strong to absorb the truth, be symbolic of its intent, be resilient to temptation, and be creative in its message.

Justice is a term we hear frequently, a term which has experienced significant exposure today under the umbrellas of equality and rights.

In this text in the seventh verse the case is strongly made for those who do justly. The paths of justice will never be out of sight of God, the one who is wisdom and strength.

But what is justice today? Can we translate the justice seen in the stories of the prodigal son and the dying thief into today's headlines without feeling our own desire to bend the message? Can we pray for justice and enjoy the world's wealth? Can we support legislators with our vote but not with the persuasion of our own conscience?

Whether we are the guard or the guarded in the paths of justice, there is no question they are to be protected.

To seek justice is not a search for a statement of truth but a constant striving for the sake of the weak, the misguided, and the innocent victims of our day.

Prayer: *When I curl up in warmth, O God, make me aware of those who shiver; when I fill my plate, let me dare to imagine an empty bowl in the hands of a child; and when I sleep, help me forget not those for whom the morning holds no hope. And forgive us our trespasses. Amen.*

Friday, September 6   Read Mark 7:31-37.

Healing, Caring, and Warmth

Utilizing an ancient folk remedy, Jesus uses spittle in performing this miracle. Though in many instances the direct command was the vehicle, here he performs what some felt was a more believable act of healing. To the divine-human person, the word *ephphatha* ("be opened") *and* the spittle contributed to the total impact of this miracle.

Mother Teresa ministers to the sick and dying on the streets of Calcutta. Her life and work represent a graphic contemporary example of the axiom that one must feed the body and the spirit by giving both body and spirit.

This tapestry of which we speak—is it a blanket? How many can my life keep warm, anyway? I can't be everywhere. I can't change the politics of world powers. I can't make jobs for the unemployed. I can't intervene for all the battered and abused. Yes, there is a limit, but the limit can only be known if we reach it and then set ourselves to doing yet more.

I once observed an elderly lady in conversation with a ten-year-old paper delivery boy. As she asked his name and gave her words of encouragement, she gently placed her hand on his shoulder and predicted he would reach his goals in life. I watched with pride and joy this one who had taught me to touch. She was my mother.

Every person we meet needs strokes of admiration and confidence. We must not miss any chance to bring someone hope.

Prayer: *Make me gentle, make me kind, O God. Fill me with the desire to bring warmth and healing; yes, to overwhelm another with my confidence in them. In the name of the great Physician. Amen.*

Saturday, September 7   Read James 1:17-22.

Reflective

From whence comes goodness? From God. And how stable is that source? "No variation or shadow due to change." God does not change.

That which we have is from the Father of lights. And we are made in a deliberate process of being the first fruits, products of God's word of truth, meaning the gospel. We are the very prize of God's creation.

We hear and we reflect what we hear, inwardly and outwardly. James points to human failure to live as God intends and admonishes us to live in accord with the gospel. In awe we are to trust.

When we consider the number of people in whom and things in which we trust in one day, it boggles our mind. In spite of sometimes experiencing the feeling—after disappointment—that we really don't trust anyone anymore, we actually never stop trusting. We eat food prepared by others. We drive cars assembled by people who are occasionally tired. We walk inside many-storied buildings. In fact, we play the odds as best we can. And sometimes we lose.

But, James writes about being a winner. We listen, we hear the voice of God, we read the proclamation of God's plan of salvation. The golden thread that weaves its way throughout the tapestry of our day reflects that sure and certain hope that is ours in Christ. It is no foolish fantasy of being out of touch with reality. Rather it is an inner peace, the unquenchable glow fed by the knowledge of God's intended salvation for us and all humankind.

Prayer: *I hear your word, O Lord. The narrative and the act of love and concern of people for one another speak dynamically of your will in my life, O God. I cherish your love and my role in your creation. Amen.*

Sunday, September 8　　　　Read James 1:22-27.

Colorful and Responsive

Being not just hearers who forget but doers who act, we shall be blessed in our doing.

The writer boldly displays the contrast between Christianity and the old pagan religions in that there need be no worship attempts to win God's favor. God's favor is already complete and available. It is our conduct rather that must be brought into a harmonious blend with God's will.

The color of the tapestry is the open expression of joy and service to all God's creation.

I once heard it said that church members ought not to be urged to give until it hurts, but to give and give and give more until it feels good!

If we hear and freely respond, we cannot but shout in reds, oranges, and yellows as bright as the rising sun.

From one extreme of pious platitudes and tracts strewn about to be stepped upon to the other extreme of closed-mouth Christianity, there is a vast range of expression. You and I must surely find our rightful place in that expanse, so that when the appropriate time comes, and someone is watching wide-eyed and with great intent, we are not afraid to witness to our faith. In whatever words we have must come the declaration that we do this because we believe in God, the creator, the redeemer, and the sanctifier. My life is as intentional as the day God gave me breath. I do what I do because of my inner knowledge of God's intent for me and my life, here on earth and hereafter.

Prayer: *God, I am thine. I mean for every act to glorify thy name. I have failed, but, TODAY, I start again. Amen.*

DYNAMICS OF DISCIPLESHIP

September 9-15, 1985   **F. Gates Vrooman†**
Monday, September 9   Read Mark 8:27-28.

The people knew what a messiah should look like, but Jesus didn't fit the picture. However, they did think he had the characteristics of the forerunner. So, while they didn't see the salvation before them, yet there was hope; but it was off in the future. What about us?

Mortar shrapnel tears into the chest of a soldier. A hollow-eyed child with distended stomach stares blankly out from the news magazine. A twelve-year-old runaway girl joins a prostitution ring. A husband beats up his wife and walks out on the children. Sophisticated atomic weapons replace obsolete ones. A drunken driver runs a stop sign and kills two people.

There is so much pain, suffering, and sin that it is easier, sometimes, to believe that a messiah *will* come than that one *has* come. (After all, if the messiah has come, shouldn't things be much better?)

Perhaps that's part of the reason belief in the second coming of Christ always gets more attention when times are tough. The desire for a messiah intensifies. And we do hope for Christ's coming in final victory.

Perhaps, then, we're not so different from those people who thought Jesus was only the forerunner. We're still waiting, too.

Prayer: *Thank you, God, for having already sent us Jesus, your anointed one. Help us realize what that means for us and others. Amen.*

---

†Co-pastor, The First Unted Methodist Church, Sycamore, Illinois.

Tuesday, September 10   Read Mark 8:29-30.

Peter answered, "You are the Messiah" (TEV).

Even though our radio is tuned into Mark's station, we seem to pick up Matthew's account of what Jesus said in response to Peter: "Blessed are you, Simon Bar-Jona! For flesh and blood has not revealed this to you, but my Father who is in heaven" (Matt. 16:17). But neither Mark's nor Luke's (9:18-22) version of the story contains Jesus' commendation of Peter.

Peter seemed to understand—but did he? He had not yet witnessed the crucifixion or resurrection. His use of the title "Messiah" may have been correct, but Jesus had yet to define the term for the disciples. So instead, the disciples are ordered, or charged, not to tell anyone what Peter has said.

The verb translated "ordered" is also translated "rebuked" in verses 32-33. It implies strong negative judgment. Jesus tells the disciples that he will be rejected and killed. Peter, showing now his misunderstanding, rebuked Jesus for saying these things. In turn, Jesus rebuked Peter in strong terms, saying, "Your thoughts don't come from God but from man" (Mark 8:33, TEV).

What about us? Do we let Jesus be who he is, or do we slap a "man-made" label on him? Can we really describe the divine in human terms with our limitations of thought and language? If all our language is necessarily metaphorical, then what we say about God is that God is like something we already know—like a father, like a mother, like a friend.

For us to say what Jesus is like still requires some encounter and relationship with him, some fresh, contemporary, firsthand religious experience. Then we can try answering the question, "But who do you say that I am?"

Suggestion for meditation: *Quiet and center yourself. Be open and receptive to God. Let God do the speaking and revealing.*

Wednesday, September 11   Read Mark 8:31-32.

In Daniel 7:13, "son of man" refers to a symbolic representation of Israel (a faithful remnant) who is finally vindicated after extensive suffering and hardship. If this is what Jesus meant by the term, then the "son of man" is a corporate entity which certainly would include the disciples. They, too, would suffer much, be rejected, and put to death. No wonder Peter reacts negatively! Not only should the Messiah not suffer like that, Peter doesn't want to either. Are we modern-day disciples any different?

Another interpretation of "son of man" is based on the prophet Ezekiel. The term is applied to Ezekiel innumerable times. Ezekiel used it to describe himself as one commissioned by God to serve in lowliness and suffering on earth, and later to see glory in a restored temple and land.

The parallel to Jesus' life is striking. "Suffer," "rejected," "death," "rise"—there are three negative strokes and one positive. Note the ratio. Three acts of downward mobility and one upward.

Why is it, then, so many of us expect that the ratio should be reversed once we are baptized, or converted, or enter fulltime Christian service?

We are not merely passive recipients of salvation. We are incorporated into the Son of man, a faithful remnant, and through our baptism we are commissioned, as was Ezekiel, to take up a ministry involving suffering service. Whether we are laypersons or clergypersons, how does our Christian life and ministry measure up?

Prayer: *Lord, if there is faithful suffering for me to do, show me where and how. Stand by me, for I am often weak and fearful. Amen.*

Thursday, September 12   Read Mark 8:32-33.

The same destructive force which Jesus exorcised from the Gerasene demoniac (Mark 5:1-13) is rebuked in Peter. There is the same cosmic scope and danger as when, under a darkened sky, the howling wind and raging sea threatened to swamp the disciples' boat (Mark 4:35-41). Jesus knew he had again encountered Satan because it was a temptation to thwart his ministry by perversion of the divine power that was his (Matt. 4:1-11).

How insidious evil can be! One might have expected it among the deranged or disabled, among tax collectors or prostitutes, in the rantings and ravings of a demagogue. Certainly one would not expect it in the reasoned cadences of one's best friend, who, after all, only has "your best interests at heart."

Could that evil still be tempting Jesus' disciples today? Doesn't it speak its treachery by an inner voice cautioning us against "risks" and "rash actions" for the sake of Christ? Doesn't it infect our will making us want earthly security, praise, and promotions. Doesn't it pervert our highest goals and noblest intentions so that consciously or unconsciously our self-interest is served? Doesn't it hide in our best plans so that when they are implemented, they leave injustice and wounded people in their wake? Doesn't it come from our friends who counsel us, "Take care of yourself!" How does one overcome a case of spiritual AIDS (Acquired Immune Deficiency Syndrome)?

Prayer: *Savior God, humble me; make me more aware of my sin and your saving power. As the psalmist prayed, so I pray, "Create in me a clean heart, O God, and renew a right spirit within me."* * *Amen.*

---

*Ps. 51:10, KJV.

267

Friday, September 13   Read Mark 8:34-37.

Pictured is a procession of condemned criminals with rope restraints around their necks, marching off to Jerusalem where they will be crucified. Now it is clear. To be a disciple means not only walking with Jesus, but dying with him, too. It is a paradox of Christian faith that we'll find our lives as we lose them for Christ and his kingdom.

Jesus' dramatic language does not permit us to think of inconveniences we encounter or our picayune trials as cross-bearing. Cross-bearing is a voluntary act, a personal choice, done for the sake of Christ and the kingdom of God, not merely to please friends or to comply with cultural norms or niceties.

Toyohiko Kagawa was a Japanese Christian missionary. During World War II, he had risked his life to nurse and bind up wounds of American pilots shot down over Tokyo. Following the example and teachings of Jesus, he loved his enemies. He also worked with tuberculosis victims until he, himself, caught the disease.

One evening, while speaking at Princeton, his voice was broken and unclear. Kagawa gave his talk and sat down. Two young students, obviously disappointed, commented to each other: "He really didn't say much, did he?" "No, and what he did say was hard to understand."

Overhearing them, an older woman spun around and said, "Young men, when a person is nailed to a cross, he doesn't have to say anything at all!"

Prayer: *Dear suffering Son of man, make my discipleship more than words; make it committed action for you and your kingdom. Give me the courage to deny myself, take up my cross, and follow you. Amen.*

Saturday, September 14   Read James 2:1-5, 8-10.

Does a church gain anything if it shows partiality? If it does, is it not in danger of losing its soul? (See Mark 8:34-37.)

The pastor notices the distinguished visitor in the worship service: The honorable John Doe, state senator, a man of considerable means. If he joined the church, he could make a pace-setting pledge for the annual finance drive. He could also bring leadership skills, business contacts, and status to the congregation. After church, the pastor introduces him to all the "right people" who heartily welcome him.

During the same worship service, a young couple and their children are also visitors. They're new in town. He's a machine operator in a factory. She stays home with the children, but wants to find part-time work to help make ends meet. Nobody notices them that day, though they feel conspicuous because he lacks a suit coat and her dress isn't finely tailored. They decide this church is too rich for their blood; they never return. Ironically, the Honorable Doe doesn't either—at least not until shortly before the next election.

James says to show no partiality on the basis of cultural or class distinctions. The church as an outpost of the kingdom of God is to be the true classless society.

Some church-growth advocates teach that greater growth occurs when new members are recruited from the same socio-economic class as the majority of church members. The principle seems to work. But what do we do with James 2:1-5, 8-10?

Prayer: *Dear God, receive me into your kingdom and let me see through your eyes the inestimable value of every human being. Amen.*

ORDER TODAY!

Then you will be sure to get your copy of the 1986 *Disciplines*—the in-depth meditations that can give fresh meaning to your daily devotional life.

Remember—only a specified number are printed, so it is wise to reserve your copy now.

You may also want to order copies for friends or relatives.

THE UPPER ROOM DISCIPLINES 1986
only $3.95 each; 10 or more, $3.25 each (UR507)
(plus shipping and handling)

SHIPPING AND HANDLING. *On prepaid orders only,* add $1.00 plus 50¢ for each additional $10.00 ordered, or part thereof. On charge orders we will add the actual amount of shipping costs plus $1.00 handling charge to your account.

EXAMPLE: (Prepaid Orders Only)

Total Order	Shipping and Handling Charges
$ 1.00 to $ 9.99	= ADD $1.00 (minimum)
$10.00 to $19.99	= ADD $1.50
$20.00 to $29.99	= ADD $2.00
$30.00 to $39.99	= ADD $2.50, etc.

Order from: The Upper Room
1908 Grand Avenue
P.O. Box 189
Nashville, Tennessee 37202

or

Ask for
The Upper Room
Disciplines
at your local Christian bookstore

Sunday, September 15   Read James 2:14-17.

We hardly need to be reminded. Faith and works are complementary; they must go together. Paul and James are not in conflict. We are saved *by* faith through Jesus Christ. We are saved *for* deeds of love and justice. Faith roots into the soil of God's love with the consequence that the plant bears the fruit of God's love.

Talk is cheap, but discipleship is not. There is a price to be paid. When people are in need we are to help. It is as simple as that. We don't ask about their denominational affiliation nor their national allegiance nor their reputation in the community.

Much of what passes for Christian spirituality today is faith without works of charity. Service and simplicity are just as much spiritual disciplines as are prayer and meditation. Discipleship is not just walking alone in the garden with Jesus. It can be just as spiritual an act to march for nuclear disarmament as it is to go to church. If it is genuine, faith will boldly express itself in social service, social witness, and social action. And even when that is done in love, a price will be paid.

Mother Teresa was awarded the Nobel Prize for her humanitarian work. The irony is that they gave it to her for doing what all of us are called to do. She is doing what Jesus would do if he had her opportunity. Are we doing what Jesus would do if he had our opportunities?

Suggestion for meditation: *Quiet and center yourself. Let Jesus show you where in your life you need to take some faithful, loving action. Ask for his help and listen for his reply.*

WHERE SHALL WISDOM BE FOUND?

September 16-22, 1985   **Dorothy J. Mosher†**
Monday, September 16   Read Job 28:13-17.

"But where shall wisdom be found? And where is the place of understanding?" (Job 28:12) This week we will explore some of the places where wisdom can be found.

The Old Testament writer asked, "Where shall wisdom be found?" Then he proceeded to list a whole category of places where wisdom was *not* found. "It is not found in the land of the living. The deep says, 'It is not in me,' and the sea says, 'It is not with me.' It cannot be gotten for gold, and silver cannot be weighed as its price."

Only God understands about wisdom and knows its place.

The search for wisdom is a search for God. But we do not perform this task alone. God is searching for us, even as we look for God. The task is a lonely one because our society does not reward those who search for things of the spirit. We can devote a lifetime to finding God and wisdom.

In the search for God, we discover our own inner wisdom. This knowledge is found in the search, but also in learning to live with ourselves and to accept ourselves. As we begin to know our inner wisdom, we can reach out to others.

Prayer: *In our search for you, O Eternal One, may we discover your wisdom and also that wisdom you have placed within us that can direct our lives for good. Amen.*

---

†Free-lance writer, Englewood, New Jersey.

Tuesday, September 17   Read Psalm 27:4-6.

Wisdom is found in the search for God.

The psalmist is searching for God and for wisdom and beseeches God for one thing: "One thing have I asked of the Lord, that will I seek after." The one thing turns out to be three things: "That I may dwell in the house of the Lord all the days of my life, to behold the beauty of the Lord, and to inquire in his temple."

Christians need to be involved in a community which puts God at the center of its life and whose actions and thinkings are governed by God. For many people this community may be a covenant group or a house church, but it is some form of the church, which wrestles with problems of faith and guidance.

Our inner selves are nourished by the beauty of the world around us. There is so much loveliness if we are attuned to it. Our souls resonate to the morning sunrise. We are touched by the chattering of birds at the feeder. As stewards of God's creation, we need to appreciate this beauty and also to act responsibly in our care of that creation.

God reaches out to us constantly, but we often succumb to feelings of superiority which lead us into evil paths. These feelings impede God's presence in our lives. We need to keep our minds keen and be open to God's truth. God will guard us, but we need to take responsibility for our actions.

In our search for God we ask again with the psalmist to be able to "dwell in the house of the Lord all the days of [our lives], to behold the beauty of the Lord, and to inquire in his temple."

Prayer: *We seek you, God. May we find you in community, in beauty, and in right living. Amen.*

272

Wednesday, September 18   Read Job 28:20-28.

Wisdom is found in skill.

Have you ever watched a glassblower at work? First
heats the glass to tremendously high temperatures to mak
molten. Then at just the proper moment, he takes it from
heat and begins to shape it. The skill involved in such
operation is amazing.

People in the Bible admired skill such as the glassblowe
The potter who knew how much pressure to apply to a pot ;
the goldsmith who worked with precious ore were conside
wise. Their skill called for keen observation and nin
fingers. Wise people also observed life closely and reflec
on their observations.

Paulo Freire uses the same kind of technique in L
America to help peasants become more involved in t
struggle for social justice. The peasants listen to the Bible
then reflect in a group on what they have learned. From t
practical wisdom come the answers to the problems of vil
life. Village people using this technique learn to work
gether for a better life for the entire village.

As Paulo Freire and the Old Testament writer remind
we need to take time to reflect on the events of our busy li
We need time to still the noisy voices. We need skil
building a rich life with God at the center.

Prayer: *Teach us to reflect as we pray, and to pray as we reflec*
God, that we may become wise in the knowledge of your will. A

Thursday, September 19   Read Mark 9:30-32.

Wisdom breaks through fear.

In our reading today, Peter, James, and John have just experienced the Transfiguration upon the mountain. This event was quickly followed by the attempted healing of the boy with epilepsy by the disciples who remained behind in the valley.

During these days of Jesus' ministry, the disciples watched Jesus in perfect command of each situation. They marveled at his power, but they had little time to reflect. Events were moving much too quickly.

Jesus tried to prepare them for the trials to come as they approached Jerusalem. Jesus was an excellent teacher, but in order for a thought to be communicated, the hearer must not only hear but absorb the thought behind the teaching. The communication between Jesus and the disciples on the way to Jerusalem just didn't get through.

Fear clutched at the disciples' hearts, shutting out all the words. Jesus talked about death and suffering. The disciples didn't want to hear that. They wanted to believe that Jesus was going to be king.

Jesus' words, however, were not completely lost. Later on, after Jesus' resurrection and the Pentecost experience, the connections the disciples missed before began to make sense. They began to understand what their fear had kept from them. And with the fear gone, they became the fearless leaders of the early church.

Prayer: *Break through our barriers of fear, Eternal One. May we listen to your voice and become unafraid. Amen.*

Friday, September 20   Read Mark 9:36-37.

Wisdom is shown through simplicity.

Simplicity helps us achieve wisdom. We live in a consumer-oriented society. We are urged on all sides to buy, buy, buy *things*. We are told that *things* will make us happy. But the more we possess the more enslaved we become. We must clean, store, guard, take out insurance on all those things we own. No wonder we feel rushed and pressured all the time!

Simplicity saves us from this tyranny to things. It allows us to lose our anxiety, since we know that God is to be valued more than things. Simplicity allows us to share with others. When the burden of owning is lifted from our shoulders, we are free to share.

In reaching out to share, we find our lives filled with joy and excitement. Our world expands with new friends. We recover our childlikeness. Children share easily. We can recapture that innocence.

We can learn the wisdom of simplicity by following Jesus and allowing our possessions to take their proper place. Thus we choose "the good portion" (Luke 10:42) for which Jesus commended Mary.

Devotional exercise: *Think of ways you can simplify your life in order to rid yourself of the tyranny wrought by possessions.*

Saturday, September 21   Read James 3:15-18.

Wisdom sets us free from self-centeredness.

Just as the tides ebb and flow with the moon's pull, our lives cannot be full and rich unless we involve ourselves in serving others. If we approach life with ourselves as the focal point, we are constantly out of touch with those around us. If we expect others to see our point of view all the time, we are doomed to disappointment. We simply cannot live as if we were the center of the universe. At best this attitude causes unhappiness; at worst it becomes demonic. The "sin which clings so closely" that the writer of Hebrews wrote about is the sin of operating as though we were the center of the universe.

That is one side of the picture, but James points to another side. When we step out of the spotlight and relinquish the center to God, all kinds of beautiful things begin to happen in our lives. We continue to look toward God and to conquer our self-centeredness; we live with greater confidence. We "sow the seeds which will bear fruit in holiness (James 3:18, TJB). We reach out to others, not from a position of superiority, but as servants wanting to help. The wisdom of God sets us free to become the persons God wants us to be.

Prayer: *Set us free, Teacher of Peace, from our self-seeking. Empower us to sow the seeds which will bear rich harvests in peaceful relationships with your children. Amen.*

Sunday, September 22   Read James 3:13-18.

Wisdom is common sense.

A church executive commented at worship one day that in all his travels to countless church meetings over the years and in many countries, he had come to appreciate the faith and wisdom of "common people"—those who had little or no formal education.

He told of visiting a Latin American country in order to attend a consultation. He had directions for his journey, but they were not too explicit. He arrived at the town, hoping someone would meet him at the train. No one appeared. He retrieved his luggage and asked in the station office about the place he was to go. No one knew where it was.

He wandered through the dusty streets of the town, finally entering a church. There he asked for directions again. Only a shake of the head greeted him.

He was getting anxious. Finally he saw another church and hurried in out of the hot sun.

A woman bent on her knees scrubbed the floor of the narthex. She smiled at him. He gasped in his anxiety, "I'm lost!"

She shook her head. "No one is lost here," she said, referring to the church with a tilt of her head.

A "common person," but one capable of deep theological comment.

Prayer: *Help us, Guide of the Meek, to find wisdom and courage from the example of people whose understanding and common sense comes from their abiding faith in your love. Amen.*

GOD'S PURPOSES CANNOT BE THWARTED

September 23-29, 1985   **KilSang Yoon†**
Monday, September 23   Read Job 42:1-6.

The biblical understanding of humankind's place in the
created order is expressed in Genesis 1:26-31. The affirmation that man and woman were created in God's image allows
us to use creativity and reasoning power.

But as we have developed, discovered, and invented much,
we have created a troublesome dilemma. On the one hand we
have developed powerful weapons; on the other hand we have
brought ourselves to the brink of self-annihilation. Two global
wars, police action, and ongoing regional struggles have
produced political unrest, have created overwhelming unbal-
anced budgets at the expense of social care, and have polar-
ized us into the "haves" and the "have-nots," both as individuals and as nations. We are haunted by the realization that our
creativity may be the source of our destruction in a single
catastrophic moment.

At this critical point we must reaffirm our role as caretakers
of the world. God's intentional gift of creativity is meant to
bring wholeness to the people of the world.

At the end of Job's search for answers, he confessed to
God, "I know that you can do all things; No purpose of yours
can be thwarted."*

Realizing our finite nature, we, like Job, must rediscover
the providence of God.

Prayer: *Dear God, creator of all, you are the beginning and end of*
all things. Help us to be one with you and with your purposes.
Amen.

---

†Minister, Canfield United Methodist Church, Canfield, Ohio.
*Job 42:2. *The Anchor Bible*, vol. J5 (*Job*), by Marvin H. Pope (New York:
Doubleday & Company, Inc., 1973), p. 347.

278

Tuesday, September 24   Read James 4:13-17.

> I talked about things I did not understand, about marvels too
> great for me to know (Job 42:3, TEV).

People today seem to value the ability to reason more than
the ability to feel. Rational thinking has brought the technological and scientific breakthroughs of our age. While our
culture emphasizes reasoning, we have neglected the capacity
to sense the irrational, the unreasonable, and the mysterious.

In the Book of Job, the innocent sufferer and his friends
struggle with the concept of individual retribution, an idea
commonly accepted in their time. They try to frame God's
being and doing within their own human reasoning.

Job tries to affirm his innocence while his friends argue
that his sin is the cause of his suffering. In the face of such
extreme, unjustifiable suffering, Job cries out for vindication
and seeks a reasonable answer as to why he suffers.

With Job we, too, feel anger, hurt, grief, and resentment
when we confront the unbearable conditions of suffering and
injustice. We strive through reason for the amelioration of
apparent injustice. We summon God to be both defender of
our cause and deplorer of the wrongs done to us.

We fret in our frustration. In the face of unfair, irrational,
and unreasonable reality, we struggle to extend the limit of
our reasoning power.

In the self-revealing presence of the Almighty, Job was able
to shake off his own frame of reasonable and rational reference. He was able to comprehend his own finiteness. He
confessed, "And I talked about things I did not understand,
about marvels too great for me to know."

Prayer: *Dear Lord, help me to be aware of your majesty in the
perplexing situations of daily life. Amen.*

Wednesday, September 25   Read Job 42:1-6.

> My ears had heard of you
> but now my eyes have seen you (NIV).

The reality of God cannot be taught; we can learn of God only through our own personal encounters and experiences. Job's understanding of God was part of his heart, of his total being, through his own painful, catastrophic experiences and his personal crises. He confessed that God was not just an entity he had heard about; rather, God had become real in Job's life through those experiences.

If Job had avoided wrestling with his earthshaking ordeal, he might not have been able to encounter the One who was the source of his life—his sustainer, his deliverer. Through those extreme, nearly unbearable conditions, Job clung to his belief in God; he had been taught that God was the deliverer. Job kept faith in the God of Abraham, Isaac, and Jacob, and placed his trust and reliance in the God of Moses, as God became involved in his predicament.

In some way, individuals and communities in every generation need a unique encounter with the living God. Through such faith experiences we find the true purpose of life. Such an experience of God in our life occurs when we dare to face the reality of life beyond the coventional ways of thinking and behaving.

Job persistently and squarely confronted his ordeal. He struggled for vindication. By going beyond the conventions of his time, Job came to a personal experience of God.

Prayer: *In and through our daily tribulations, O God, help us to be strong and to find the meaning and purpose of our life in you. Amen.*

Thursday, September 26   Read Exodus 3:1-16;
                                              Psalm 27:7-14.

In the biblical account, God is understood as "I am who I am" (TEV). The Creator is "the Lord, the God of [your] ancestors, the God of Abraham, Isaac and Jacob" (TEV). But the God of all majesty, power, and transcendence is also immanent, intimate, and personal. The self-sufficient, self-existing God takes risks to come into the realm of human affairs as sustainer, deliverer, judge, guide, and comforter. Yet such a God does not allow humans to scale down the mystery to the measure of human reason. Rather, God challenges humankind to obey their Creator. In such an obedient relationship to God, humankind finds the purpose and the meaning of life and authentic freedom from bondage.

In the midst of adverse conditions in life's conflicts, confusion, and uncertainty, the psalmist prayed for God's help and sought God's presence. Even in the worst condition of desertion and rejection, God's presence, support, and acceptance require our effort to find and to obey God's will.

In the time of conflict and confusion, we need to experience authentic encounters with God. In the presence of God we find what we are, who we are, and whose we are. God's presence, support, and acceptance is the source of wisdom, strength, and courage to find our self-identity and to obey God's will.

God's self-manifestation is not always available to us. But the psalmist admonished us to be patient and to persevere: "Wait for the Lord; be strong, and let your heart take courage; yea, wait for the Lord!"

Prayer: *Lord, strengthen us to go with you through the darkest night of our life—whenever we face it. Amen.*

Friday, September 27 Read James 14:13-17.

Time and again, people gifted with creativity run into tensions between two extreme poles: one, faith in their capability to plan and achieve; two, understanding that they are subject to circumstances beyond themselves. It is when we acknowledge the poles between the infinite and the finite, the possible and the actual, the ideal and the practical, that we have a balanced, wholesome perspective on life.

Recently the emphasis has been on human potential, creating some illusive hope in human capability alone. Some are helped by such catch phrases as "the power of positive thinking," "you can be what you think you can be," "Work! work!" "I'm OK, you're OK!" All have touched some aspect of the truth. However, when these ideals are applied to our personal and communal life without embracing the opposing pole in our life, the shallow catchphrases are no longer true nor ethical.

Today's scripture reminds us of the need to have balance in our life. Planning? Yes, it is good; but it is conditional because we do not know about tomorrow. We are capable. We have great potential. We are created in God's likeness. Yet we are finite and limited. Do we have grace and gifts? Yes, but let us be thankful to the One who gave them; they are for the good of others. We can do only what we are able to do; we are not God. Rather, we must learn to check our plans with the cosmic order of God's will. If our wants are not in accord with that order, we must learn to put our personal wishes aside. If we assume we can do all things, we have set ourselves up to play God. It is neither right nor good to do so.

Prayer: *"O God, give us serenity to accept what cannot be changed, courage to change what should be changed, and wisdom to distinguish the one from the other."* * Amen.

---

*Reinhold Niebuhr.

Saturday, September 28   Read James 5:7-11.

When we encounter the self-revealing God, we experience certain changes in our way of thinking, our values, our attitudes. In such encounters, we also find ourselves aware of an enhanced purpose and meaning of life. Such changes definitely imply certain improved personal relationships—with oneself, with nature, with others, and with God. There are many characteristics that make for good relationships. *Patience* is one.

The scripture for the day offers us the admonition to "be patient." There are reasons for us to be so. As limited and finite beings, we are dependent upon nature's timing, God's mercy, and the idiosyncrasies of others. In order to live in harmony, we need the virtue of patience—endurance, perseverance—especially in the face of adverse conditions.

Patience may be developed by persistent self-discipline—to bring ourselves into oneness with the cosmic order which encompasses and transcends all other mores of any given time and place.

Like all virtues, even patience must not be misused as a means of imposing unjust conditions upon others. Patience cannot be considered as a passive, individualistic virtue which some have used as a means to subordinate others in unjust, oppressive, and exploitative conditions.

The virtue of patience must be shared by all. In any society—and in interethnic, interreligious, and international relations—patience enhances the common good as persons seek mutual understanding under the encompassing reign of God.

Prayer: *Strengthen us, O Lord, to be patient with ourselves, with others, and with your timing. Encourage us to be patient in doing persistently what is right and good to all. Amen.*

Sunday, September 29   Read Mark 9:38-50.

In the presence of the self-revealing God we find ourselves inspired. With such a holy experience, we can easily fall into a spiritual pitfall: "I am holier than you" or "I possess all the wisdom and secrets of God." With such an attitude we can think and act as though we were the only ones who know God. Therefore, we can mistakenly try to control, manipulate, and abuse our "spiritual power" for self-gratification.

Today's scripture shows us that such an incident occurred among the Twelve. Seeing someone who was not a member of their inner circle do an effective ministry in Jesus' name, the disciples forbade it. However, God's power in the name of Jesus was being manifested in works done by others outside the formal membership of the Twelve. The disciples could not understand that others could also be used by the same Spirit to do God's works. Jesus made it clear that what a person is doing is more important than his or her affiliation.

The disciples should have recognized that the same God was revealed and known to others as was revealed and known to them. In different times and places, God's self-revelation comes to people. The ways people respond to God's revelation are variously different. Therefore, for us to impose our own expression of the faith on others is a form of sinning—being a stumbling block.

We hear Jesus say to his disciples, "Be at peace with one another." What we seek is not conformity and uniformity but unity in diversity, where differences can stand while the substance of the faith can be identified, shared, and preserved.

Prayer: *Holy God, make yourself truly known to us, that we may know what you want us to do and in so doing bring glory to you. You alone are God, and we seek you above all else. Amen.*

RELATIONSHIPS, HUMAN AND DIVINE

September 30–October 6, 1985   **Barbara Hargrove†**
Monday, September 30   Read Genesis 2:18-23.

I am currently spending a leave in a mountain cabin, high in the Rockies. As winter nears, I am left more and more alone. My dog and I tramp through the snow, following the tracks of a raccoon or a rabbit. Birds call to us as we go through the woods, and once in awhile we may catch sight of a timid deer. There is a peace here, a quiet, that is a most welcome change from the noise and pace of the city, and I revel in the beauty of the mountains and mountain creatures.

And yet I was very glad when my nearest neighbor returned from a short trip. For in spite of all the peace and beauty, I have come to realize that they are wise words indeed that our reading today attributes to God. It is true: it is not good for us humans to live alone. And all the beasts of the field and the birds of the air cannot take the place of human relationships. We name all the creatures as if we owned them. But to own something is to create a particular relationship with it, one that can never have the mutuality that comes from recognizing one another as equals.

And so our story tells us that only when the man was given another whom he could claim to be flesh of his flesh, bone of his bone, only then could he hope for the fullness of response. Only then could life be good.

Prayer: *God, help us to recognize our kinship with other people, to love them as our own flesh. Amen.*

---

†Professor of the Sociology of Religion, The Iliff School of Theology, Denver, Colorado.

Tuesday, October 1   Read Genesis 2:21-24.

There is an anomaly in the creation story in the second chapter of Genesis. On the one hand, Adam sees Eve as like himself, as "bone of my bones and flesh of my flesh." On the other hand, Eve is not a clone of Adam. Though she is of the very stuff he is, she is also different, a person in her own right. And so we find in this story that celebrates, among other things, the difference between the sexes, a very important lesson indeed. Built into the very order of the universe, this reading suggests, is the value of being closely related to people unlike oneself and affirming the difference.

We so often want to make our friends or loved ones over in our own image, or to seek out acquaintances who only echo our own ideas. In doing so, we are not truly seeking relationships but simply extending ourselves into others, making them passive recipients of our nature. That is not, our lesson indicates, the way it was intended to be. When God sought to provide a co-worker fit to stand at Adam's side, it was not another man but a woman, one whose very difference could be the cause of a joyful expansion of Adam's world.

Why is it that we in the churches continually seek to find people just like us or to make the ones who are different over in our own image? How much larger and more interesting our worlds would be if we could celebrate their differentness, and for this very reason leave the comfort of our familiar surroundings and cling to them in joy, in wonder, and in love!

Prayer: *O God, teach us how to love and affirm one another in likeness and in difference. Amen.*

Wednesday, October 2   Read Mark 10:2-8.

The way Jesus used the Creation story from the second chapter of Genesis attests to its primary meaning. This is not just an objective history of creation; rather, it is a statement that the complementarity of human relationships was built into our nature from the beginning. In coming together to affirm their oneness, a man and a woman exercise their physical dissimilarities, and in doing so affirm one another's otherness as well. But it does not end here, for humans are the products and producers of culture. So it is said a man must leave his father and mother and go to his wife. The home he grew up in was not the same as hers. The home they found will have some of the characteristics of the one he left and some of the one in which she was raised. But it will be richer for having the inheritance of both. It will be a celebration of those family cultural differences as well as the similarities. If we are fortunate enough to be near grandparents, we have the experience of three homes, to all of which we belong in deep and loving ways, and yet which are different from one another.

And so it is in the family of humankind. When we can leave behind old forms and yet celebrate them as we join with others of different backgrounds, we are behaving in a way that is, according to both Old and New Testaments, a part of our very God-given nature.

Prayer: *O God, who has called us into the human family, help us to extend our boundaries beyond the familiar forms of our own culture, to affirm our brothers and sisters around the world. Amen.*

Thursday, October 3   Read Mark 10:13-16.

As there are differences between the sexes and among the lifestyles of different families, so there are differences among the generations. The unity is also evident: who else do we feel as much a part of us as our own children? Yet one of the lessons of parenthood is that each child is an individual in his or her own right, far from a mere extension of our own personalities. Sometimes learning that can be very painful, but few parents would say that it is not an occasion for growth. As we see our children moving out into worlds that are not our own, we sometimes fear, often despair. Yet through our children we learn to be a part of those new worlds, and again we grow.

We may be dragged kicking and screaming into the world of the future, but children face it with the openness and hope that it requires. We learn from them what it means to be open to the world around us, to love, to wonder. All too often we think only of what we teach children, and not what they teach us. Yet Jesus says it is they who know how to come to the kingdom. Dare we risk joining them rather than leaving them out of our religious quest?

What would it mean to our local congregations if we were to deliberately seek to come to God like little children? What would that say about our forms of worship, our priorities? Where would we then put the children in our programs and our organization? How would we treat one another? Would we dare be so open, so ready to accept one another and the world?

Prayer: *O loving God of the young, teach us to be young in heart. Help us come to you, and to one another, without fear and without dissimulation, as children come to one they love. Amen.*

Friday, October 4   Read Hebrews 1:1-4; 2:9-11.

In these passages the writer of Hebrews brings us into one of the primary mysteries of the Christian faith. First, we find the assertion of the transcendent nature of God, upholding the universe, and the claim that Jesus as God's son shares in that transcendent power. Then almost immediately, we find the claim that this same Jesus was for a time made lower than the angels, that is, a human being.

Here again we see that paradoxical situation of likeness and dissimilarity that is celebrated in the Genesis story of the creation of man and woman, two beings alike and yet different. Can we not say, then, of the divine-human encounter that it is only as we recognize the transcendent in human form that we can claim any sort of relationship with God? "For he who sanctifies and those who are sanctified have all one origin."

Yet the relationship does not stop there. The claim is not only that Jesus has been one of us, but also that out of that oneness he has offered a way for us to become a part of his world, the realm of transcendence. Here we find the ultimate in the creative power of relationships, that having found a basis for a relationship with God, we can so expand our own world and ourselves as to become a part of the divine order.

Prayer: *O God, transcendent and yet immanent in human life, help us to know you as a part of our very being, and yet infinitely beyond us, leading us into ever-enlarging circles of love and joy. Let our lives portray the vastness of the horizon that you have opened to us; and may we open ourselves to others as you have opened yourself to us. Amen.*

Saturday, October 5 Read Mark 10:9-12.

How often in the Bible is the relation of humankind to God compared with that of a man and woman to one another! In both cases there is the assumption of an attraction that leads to a lasting commitment. And in each case there is a sense of terrible loss when that commitment is broken.

The prophets continually warned Israel of the dangers of breaking their covenant with God, as if it were a marriage relationship, and of going out whoring after other gods. Taken in that context, it is hardly surprising that Jesus would have had harsh words to say about divorce. Anyone who breaks off such a relationship of commitment as marriage without regret fails to recognize how we are diminished in breaking relationships. But to take such a passage as a law may well diminish what it says. Insofar as we give ourselves to one another, to withdraw the gift and offer it to another is a kind of violation, and we need to admit that. Yet where the kind of growth in union is not occurring, where the relationship is not an occasion for joyful enlargement of our world, we must attest that the brokenness is already there. We still need allowance for the loss of commitment that is part of our human condition.

This is true not only in marriage but in all our relationships with one another. Commitments are very difficult to maintain in this society, and yet social scientists attest to a certain hunger for commitment among us. We *need* to give ourselves to one another in permanent ways.

Prayer: *O God, teach us how, in a world that bids us each to seek our own good separately, to learn that we find it only by holding together. Amen.*

Sunday, October 6　　　　　　　　Read Psalm 128.

So often people seem to want such different things out of life and nations seem so far apart in their ideal of the good life that conflict seems inevitable. And yet, when we strip all else aside, the picture in this psalm is one that seems universal. Here is, in its essence, the vision of the biblical *shalom*. To eat of the fruit of our own hands, surrounded by a loving family, to see our children's children—what more could one ask? Is not all our scrambling after money and status and the right place to live really the pursuit of this simple vision of love and peace? In a time of potential nuclear destruction, dare we hold out this kind of hope for humankind? Dare we not?

Hope is hard to come by, but it is what we live by. That hope is bound up in our relationships to one another, in one-on-one situations, in families, in neighborhoods, nations, and the world—and with God. Perhaps our problem is that we forget that God must come first. What does our psalm tell us? "Blessed is every one who fears the Lord, who walks in [God's] ways!" Then all the other things seem to follow.

It is here we find the culmination of all relationships. It is only when we are so related to God that we are lifted to God's universal plane that we are able to live with our fellow human beings in the kind of peace that can assure shalom. We are only free from threat when we are no threat to others; we are no threat to them when we recognize our oneness in God.

Prayer: *Dear God, lead us into true shalom. May your peace extend to all peoples everywhere. Amen.*

To Accept Our Limitations

October 7-13, 1985   **William G. Smartt†**
Monday, October 7   Read Genesis 3:8-13.

Western culture tends to believe that there are few human
limitations—that all things being equal, any individual can
accomplish given goals of fame and fortune. Without becoming fatalistic or even pessimistic, however, it seems that God
has placed limitations on human creatures. As God told
Adam and Eve not to eat of the tree in the center of the garden,
so does God place restrictions on our lives. Such restrictions
do not necessarily mean that a particular idea or desire is a
bad one. Rather, it might by most standards be very noble.
But we should remember that God's ways are not our ways,
even though we pretend as though we know what God desires.

I am convinced that every now and then God purposely
limits our involvements to draw us closer to our Creator or to
help us recognize our own physical limitations. No matter
how often we may try to accomplish *our* agendas, and no
matter how alluring they may seem, God stops us from
fulfilling some personal dreams and ambitions. This at first is
a hard pill to swallow, but once it is learned and understood,
we become happier and learn that some of our goals are
unhealthy and need to be abandoned. Then we can begin to
discover that the mercies of God are always new. Then we will
have the opportunity to rely more heavily on God's mercy,
grace, and power to perform miracles in and through us.

Prayer: *O merciful Lord, make us humble enough to listen and to
obey the limitations you place on us so that our lives will be rich and
full. Amen.*

---

†Pastor, The United Methodist Parish in Bushwick, Brooklyn, New York.

Tuesday, October 8   Read Genesis 3:14-19.

Unfortunately many North American Christians are confused about the nature of the Christian life and the one limitation we have so little control over—death. After watching an evening of television, or reading popular magazines, one can easily get the notion that our ultimate purpose is to charm the opposite sex, stay slim, be a good jogger or look like one, abstain from meat or at least too much meat, and have a supply of various vitamins and minerals, and of course to be middle class. We have a desire to look the picture of perfect health and a dream to live forever. Somehow if these two goals are accomplished, so many believe, God and the church become obsolete and irrelevant.

Christians, however, should remember that the physical life from a New Testament standpoint was not of great significance. For the Gospels and the letters of the apostles point to a time when the practice of Christianity meant persecution and/or the belief that the Lord's return was imminent: "If the owner of a house knew the time when the thief would come, you can be sure that he would stay awake and not let the thief break into his house. So then, you also must always be ready, because the Son of Man will come at an hour when you are not expecting him" (Matt. 24:43-44, TEV).

What will it take for us to remember that the physical life has definite limitations: "Teach us how short our life is, so that we may become wise"? (Ps. 90:12, TEV)

Prayer: *Help us, O Lord, to appreciate the spiritual life—which has no limitations—a life that draws us close to you. Amen.*

Wednesday, October 9   Read Psalm 90:1-12.

Not long ago a good friend of mine died. When I received the news of his death, I was angry—partly at myself for not having done more for the deceased friend, and partly at God for allowing him to die. He was a Christian minister, so I had no qualms about his spiritual life; it was just that I would miss him. Feeling angry toward God at the death of a loved one is a natural occurrence. How the anger is channeled is the crucial question for the Christian.

Behind the anger is the envy directed at God because of God's infiniteness and our finitude: "A thousand years to you are like one day; they are like yesterday, already gone, like a short hour in the night" (TEV). Even though anger toward God might be justified, Christians are urged to pray to God for deliverance: "Give us now as much happiness as the sadness you gave us during all our years of misery" (Ps. 90:15, TEV).

But in the midst of such suffering is the reminder that God is present to comfort and provide companionship: "If you return, I will take you back, and you will be my servant again" (Jer. 15:19, TEV).

Death of loved ones is never easy to accept. When it occurs, it is as if we are being asked, What is life; what's it all about?

The psalmist presents a realistic view of human limitations and a faithful understanding of a God of love and power. Once we accept our physical limitations, our lives can be enjoyable and fulfilling.

Prayer: *O Lord, the creator of all, forgive us when we forget the finiteness of our minds and bodies. Help us to respond to your continued gracious invitation to live as redeemed people. Amen.*

Thursday, October 10   Read Mark 10:17-30.

This story of the rich man is a familiar one. Its significance should not be overlooked or taken for granted. Like many religious persons, this man evidently lived a good moral life; but eternal-life requirements are beyond "being good." It was difficult for him to part with his wealth to follow Jesus, but Jesus no doubt continued to love him.

Christian discipleship means a willingness to sacrifice everything to follow Jesus. "If anyone wants to come with me, . . . he must forget himself, carry his cross, and follow me. For whoever wants to save his own life will lose it; but whoever loses his life for me and for the gospel will save it" (Mark 8:34-35, TEV).

What Jesus expects is complete dependence upon him. Being good is not the end of the Christian's life; it is the beginning. It is not enough to ask, How good am I? for righteousness can also be the facade for evil intentions. Our motives should be noble and honest: "Examine me, O God, and know my mind; test me, and discover my thoughts. Find out if there is any evil in me and guide me in the everlasting way" (Ps. 139:23-24, TEV).

Being a disciple and seeking personal salvation are alternate steps along the same pathway. They are interwoven. To debate which should come first is to miss the real point: They are provided by God's grace through the sacraments of the church as an important reminder that certain goals can never be earned—only accepted in faith. The rich man's desire to obtain eternal life and the disciples' response, "Then who can be saved?" point to our limitations and the miraculous power of God to change our hearts and minds and make us obedient disciples.

Prayer: *O Lord, take our impure motives and baptize them afresh in your spirit. Give us purpose, power, and fulfillment. Amen.*

Friday, October 11   Read Hebrews 4:1-3.

One day last week, I noticed a leaf suspended between two parallel bars. Looking closer, I could faintly see a spider web tenuously holding this fallen object of nature. That leaf reminded me of the many Christians who have been reborn, redeemed, and sanctified. Because of the ill winds of apathy, uncertainty, and discontentment of one sort or another, many Christians have literally been left blowing in the wind while hanging on by the bearest threads of faithfulness and fidelity to the Lord. If this picture describes you, you are not alone; it also describes the Christians to whom the Letter to the Hebrews was written.

Instead of being teachers of the gospel, these people were mere students. They forgot their role as well as the place of Jesus in their faith. The writer of Hebrews makes the analogy that even though they are adults, they must be fed milk, the food of children, because they cannot swallow the solid food of the gospel.

Perhaps they were initially Jews and well grounded in Judaism. But the writer of Hebrews reminds them that there are sharp differences between the two religious faiths. Jesus reigns in superiority over all the prophets of Judaism. This point seems unnecessary, but even today many of us fail to understand what Jesus meant when he said he had come to fulfil the law and the prophets (see Matt. 5:17-20). Part of our maturing in the faith has to do with moving from a legalistic understanding of our faith to a vision of the kingdom of God, where Jesus' love is the reigning principle.

Prayer: *O God, even in the midst of doubt and inadequate knowledge of our faith, help us to remain faithful to what we believe and understand. Amen.*

Saturday, October 12   Read Hebrews 4:1-3.

The Christians spoken to in the Letter to the Hebrews are reminded of their access to a resting place only if they have been faithful: "We who believe, then, do receive that rest which God promised" (TEV). Only those who labored the six days are entitled to rest on the Sabbath! Scripture says, "By the seventh day God finished what he had been doing and stopped working" (Gen. 2:2, TEV). To believe is to work, to keep faithful, and to remain kingdom bound. To be unemployed for God is to be faithless, rebellious, and disobedient.

The church today has the benefit of 2000 years of history: printed and completed Old and New Testaments, biblical scholarship, organized congregations and denominations. Still millions are not saved, and evil is rampant. Much of this is because many of us have not taken our own ministry seriously. In some congregations there is a kind of apathy and a lack of morale. Nothing kills an organization quicker than a loss of spirit, commitment, and determination. Without these qualities, giant corporations totter, athletic teams lose games, and family relationships crumble.

What is so distressing about the Letter to the Hebrews is the supposition that those being addressed are not questioning the primary bases of the faith like the divinity of Jesus, his mighty miracles, salvation through his name, eternal life, forgiveness of sins. There is no debate over these issues! Their primary problem seemed to be simply loss of interest and commitment to the *way* of Christ. Perhaps personality clashes or false teachings brought turmoil and confusion to them as to any group—including the church.

Prayer: *O Lord, in our attempt to serve thee, may we put aside ill winds of misunderstanding and concentrate upon thy Son for all that we need. Amen.*

Sunday, October 13   Read Psalm 90:1-8;
                                            Hebrews 4:9-13.

To read these poetic words of Psalm 90 is to be touched by a spiritual perspective often missing in the church. The psalmist not only realizes humanity's short tenure on earth but accepts it. Such a realization should encourage many to be saved—as well as to prepare a will.

We are stewards of much of God's creation. How we treat ourselves, our natural resources, and our material possessions is an important indication of Christian commitment and generosity. It also tells the degree to which we take responsibility and control for our lives. More and more ministers are urging congregations to consciously make a deeper commitment to the Lord and to let that relationship shape one's membership vows to the church which include financial gifts and pledges.

There are some who literally want to live forever, who are never satisfied with personal achievements and recognition. Behind the desire to accumulate so many material things may be the unwillingness to accept finitude and the "rest" alluded to in Hebrews 4. We seem to want so much: success, popularity, recognition, and wealth. Perhaps we spend too much time trying to achieve unpossessed dreams and pay too little attention to what we have in the Lord—an eternal rest.

Suggestion for prayer: *Thank God in solitude and silence for desiring to save you. Thank God for the struggles that make us vulnerable and dependent upon our Creator and for God's grace, mercy, and goodness in your life.*

Pray for more patience and faith to remove mountains of doubts. Pray for strength to persevere and be found faithful.

SUFFERING AND SERVANTHOOD

October 14-20, 1985   **Robert Reddig†**
Monday, October 14   Read Isaiah 53:7-9.

With a simple, poignant image, that of a passive and vulnerable animal, the poet-prophet of Isaiah tells how the Suffering Servant shall be brought as a lamb to the slaughter and shall be dumb as a sheep before shearers. It is an image of vulnerability and of seeming helplessness. This victimization is to be the occasion for mortal salvation, and yet the proud and sinful heart wonders if lambs really understand the way the world works. It's a pity when they die, but they don't take reasonable precautions. Sheep are mute in tragedy, and that seems dumb to our practical reflection.

Something in human nature resents and resists fulfillment by sacrifice of innocence. We do not even want to be in need of salvation or rescue. We are determined to make it off the field under our own power. Often just beneath our guilt for needing rescue is unexpressed anger at the rescuer for being able to meet our needs, for dashing our pride in self-sufficiency. We'd rather not need a lamb. In fact, we'd rather *be* a lamb than *need* a lamb, for the lamb indicts and convicts us with its innocence. The chronicle of God's covenants with the people of God and their recurrent failure to merit those covenants is rich with the theme "We'd rather do it ourselves!"

Nevertheless, God's final offering is a Lamb.

Prayer: *Dear God, help us to accept the reality of our need and the offering of your grace through Christ. Amen.*

---

†Psychotherapist, Nashville, Tennessee.

Tuesday, October 15   Read Isaiah 53:10-12.

Of things which threaten our emotional security, meaningless pain is rarely absorbed and tolerated. Suffering without meaning sets our very being adrift. The suffering portrayed and foretold by Isaiah is a suffering undeserved—but not unplanned. It is a suffering with meaning for all.

In human relationships, particularly those which are violently imperfect, meaning is often belatedly added to suffering, and often the suffering is intensified rather than resolved. The wife abused by her husband, and unwilling to accept the reality of being unloved, professes that the beating was deserved: "I asked for it." The victim sacrifices dignity and self-esteem to preserve the illusion of being loved: "Even a loving husband would feel like beating me." The child, when victimized by his mother, comes to say, "I was bad," and thereby keeps a mother-image intact.

While it is not easy to accept pain and suffering, to entertain the prospect of meaninglessness stirs the deepest dread. We too quickly invent reasons for suffering when we might expand our faith through the ordeal of doubt.

The suffering of Christ foretold in Isaiah was an exceptional event. It remains the anchor of our salvation, not a model by which we can attain our own salvation. Unfortunately, much of human suffering is purposeless, and not every terrible loss is sacrifice. For the Christian, Christ's suffering was a single, expiating event. Our suffering is rarely a consequence of our belief in Christ's suffering. More often it is a consequence of our disbelief in the true sacrifice.

Prayer: *Dear God, let not our suffering lead us to disavow that of our Lord. Amen.*

Wednesday, October 16   Read Psalm 35:17-28.

Ancient Greek theatrical productions often presented situations in which mortals were in terrible and seemingly insurmountable crises. But unlike modern drama, which tends to portray unresolved pain and anxiety as the permanent condition of human existence, Greek theater had a marvelous resolution of problems. Greek gods were lowered with ropes, baskets, or mechanical devices onto the stage for the precise and timely rescue of mortals in distress. The logic or probability of plot was sacrificed so that everything could turn out right. Later, the Latin term *deus ex machina* or "god from the machine," was used to describe any resolution of dramatic plot with an unlikely coincidence, preposterous rescue, or strained invention. Rescue remains a staple of plot for countless TV shows in which the character, car, or career must be sustained, however preposterously, for a season. Rescue is our expectation in cartoons, for we willingly surrender meaning for entertainment.

Unfortunately, the expectation of rescue infects our faith as well, and all too often we say, "Yes, let meaning slide. Make it come out right for me." In the psalmist's pleas for rescue we experience our own heartfelt longing for relief in distress. The psalmist makes a special case—his righteousness—and suggests a *quid pro quo*. For rescue he will publicly praise the Lord. We do special pleading and promising when overwhelmed with disaster. But how do we interpret rescue? How do we interpret silence and more suffering? For Christians, the Cross interprets life and death. It is salvation, not a lucky break. Jesus gave one thief meaning before he and both thieves died. There were no machines, only God's love.

Prayer: *Dear God, help us to know thy enduring and sustaining love in all circumstances. Amen.*

Thursday, October 17   Read Hebrews 4:14-16.

As a boy struggling to understand North Dakota farming and my father's politics at the same time I would occasionally be present when he would draft a letter to our congressman in Washington. Back then the issues were price supports for wheat ("We don't need 'em") and acreage allotments ("We don't want 'em"). My father always seemed to withhold a measure of trust when he wrote his congressman, and he usually couched his requests in language which implied retribution at the polls if things didn't improve. When things invariably didn't improve, I suspect my father voted as he always did, for with North Dakota farming there are too many variables to assign blame. But we always got a letter back from Washington, and my father always tested the signature with a wet thumb. It always smeared and gave us evidence of our congressman's personal interest in our circumstances. It was years later that I saw a signature machine, signing letters in an otherwise vacant congressional office.

It is a perfect representative which the writer of Hebrews proclaims. Jesus, as priest, as intermediary, as the bridge from death to life perfectly meets our needs because he is "one who in every respect has been tempted as we are, yet without sin." It is difficult to imagine two more marvelous attributes in a representative: an absolute intimacy with our guilty need and a strength to sustain innocence.

Our confidence is justified not simply by the majesty of Christ, but by the course of his life among us. His authority is his perfect sacrifice for our sins. His signature is perfect love.

Prayer: *Dear God, we confess our infirmities before thee and boldly claim thy love through Jesus. Amen.*

Friday, October 18   Read Mark 10:35-37.

This brief passage in the Gospel of Mark presents the disciples James and John as being reassuringly human in their ambition. But it is not just a request for a favor that catches our attention. There is the clear implication that Jesus has an obligation to meet. "Teacher, we want you to do for us whatever we ask of you." It is as if his fame were in some way initiated by their devoted discipleship. "Grant us to sit, one at your right hand and one at your left, in your glory." The disciples ask not just to be remembered, but to be conspic-uously honored. James and John, along with the other disci-ples, had just heard Jesus summarize the suffering he was about to experience: "They will mock him, and spit upon him, and scourge him, and kill him" (Mark 10:34). James and John do not ask for any part of this, but rather for the glory.

There is an important distinction between a disciple and a fan. Being close, being favored with a kiss, an autograph, a handshake, or a sequined glove is the harvest for a fan. Some fans expect that the tribute will be reflected back upon them like an adoring echo. Discipleship is different. It is shared devotion to something greater than privilege. Discipleship demands an understanding of the entire journey, not just appreciation for a magnificent destination.

In matters of daily life and of Christian faith we are more inclined to be fans than disciples. We believe we have tickets. We applaud Jesus from our seats, and we love the association. We know the performance but not the passion. We know James and John.

Prayer: *Dear God, lead us not into privilege but into true disci-pleship with Jesus. Amen.*

Saturday, October 19   Read Mark 10:38-41.

When James and John ask for seats of honor at the right and left hand of Jesus, they are gently rebuked. Jesus reminds them, as he had in other times, other ways, that their reach was beyond their grasp. "You do not know what you are asking." The disciples' eager enlistment in an enterprise they cannot fully fathom brings to mind the enthusiasm of military enlistees who aspire to a uniform and guaranteed career training, with no notion of the dark business of war. Jesus knows the sorrow he is about to face and seeks to turn his disciples toward an understanding of the sorrow which, despite their unknowing, they, too, will face. "The cup that I drink you will drink; and with the baptism with which I am baptized, you will be baptized." The disciples, we presume, heard honor in Jesus' prediction.

There is something exhilarating about signing up. We sign up for things with reward in mind, as if the reward simply follows the first gesture of commitment. We join health clubs and assume that health begins. We enroll in Spanish classes and think immediately of travels in Spain. We send in our registration fee and think of how a marathon T-shirt will look with tan slacks. We marry and anticipate anniversaries. We have children and think of Christmas Eve secrets. We join churches and savor the kiss of peace. To his disciples and to us, Jesus lifts a cup and offers a baptism. As symbol and sacrament they are as rich as life itself, with full meanings of bitterness, fire, cleansing, purging, salvation, and sacrifice. Jesus offers us the prize, but not without the path.

Prayer: *Dear God, help us to know that for which we ask. Help us to accept the full measure of your promise through Christ. Amen.*

Sunday, October 20   Read Isaiah 53:4-5.

As Jesus speaks to his disciples, he brings servanthood full circle. The prophecy in Isaiah signaled a suffering servant, one to bear our sorrows, suffer our griefs, claim our guilt, and one to effect our healing. Jesus now invites his disciples into servanthood, and it was not what they (or we) were looking for.

Jesus had much to say about rank and privilege, nearly all of it paradoxical and seemingly contrary to the human longing for power, honor, and authority. The privilege he offered them was that of service; the rank he offered was that of servant, even slave. But he did not model or require apologetic passivity. He urged a strong and knowing labor—washing feet, caring for the needs of the least among humanity, slaving for justice, and suffering in acts of love.

Good service in a restaurant has quiet and reassuring authority. The focused skill of a physician is at its best a service of the heart. The servanthood of parenting is sacrificial and long-suffering. Again, Jesus does not present a model for slavery, false modesty, or faintheartedness. Jesus asks that we be slaves to the task, bold in love, bold in service. The disciples, we presume, as we look to our own hearts, felt demoted, as if taken off the stage of history and asked to be ushers for someone else's salvation. God asks not that we bow and scrape, but that we find our honor in fidelity of love, fidelity of service. To do less, to demand more, is insufferable.

Prayer: *Dear God, draw us, through the experience of thy love in Christ, to the honor of service. Amen.*

REJOICE, FOR THE LORD RESTORES!

October 21-27, 1985   **Mark S. Womack†**
Monday, October 21   Read Jer. 31:7-9; Matt. 7:7-8.

The church may be seen as the great leveler. The distinctions of rank that sometimes characterize secular society (and which are not necessarily inappropriate in that setting) are not part of the Christian community.

The wealthy and the paupers, the educated and the illiterate, the liberal and the conservative, the robust and the weak, the mystical and the practical, and those in between, may worship God side by side, as brothers and sisters in Christ.

To be sure, individuals within the church have differing roles, but this is a matter of structure, not an evaluation of people's worth. Persons' needs differ, also, and no two individuals are at the same spot in their quests for Christian wholeness. Still, there is no prerequisite for approaching God other than the desire to know God.

It is interesting for me to worship in a large congregation when Holy Communion is celebrated. To observe the diversity of communicants as they approach the altar or return to their pews is a moving and dramatic portrayal of the pluralism that we are called upon to embrace.

God's redeeming grace knows no boundaries of rank or station!

Prayer: *Thank you, God, that my only qualification to seek your salvation is to acknowledge my need of you. Amen.*

†United Methodist local pastor, Clifton Hills United Methodist Church, Chattanooga, Tennessee.

Tuesday, October 22   Read Psalm 126:1-3.

Emotions play an influential role in our day-to-day experiences. The emotions we feel and sometimes express are part of our innermost selves. They determine our morale and our outlook on life. They may be exhilarating, celebrative, or joyful; and, conversely, hostile, grouchy, or resentful.

We are the chief architects of our emotions. We can control how we react to what we feel, and even change how we feel. For instance, we may feel depressed, but if we choose to smile and reach out to others, our feelings can become more positive. We may influence how others feel by the way we respond to them, and we ourselves may be influenced by others.

The psalmist compares some people to dreamers. The lessons for us are clear.

First, dreams can accompany feelings of joy, praise, and elation for those into whom the redeeming and restoring spirit of God has entered. Second, the Lord can restore the fortunes of a nation and can likewise redeem individuals. God can buy back lives marred by sin and restore them to the abundant life that we can experience through Jesus (see John 10:10).

> Come, thou Fount of every blessing,
> Tune my heart to sing thy grace;
> Streams of mercy, never ceasing,
> Call for songs of loudest praise.
> Teach me some melodious sonnet,
> Sung by flaming tongues above;
> Praise the mount! I'm fixed upon it,
> Mount of thy redeeming love!*

Prayer: *For the restoration you bring, O God, I rejoice. I pray also that I may be an instrument of your restoration in others. Amen.*

*Robert Robinson, "Come, Thou Fount of Every Blessing," the United Methodist *Book of Hymns*, no. 93.

Wednesday, October 23   Read Gen. 12:1-9;
                                          Ps. 126:4-6.

The "watercourses in the Negeb" may be considered to be symbolic of the resources for good (restoration, from the vitality of flowing water) in situations the details of which may be uncertain or unknown. Abram moved out in faith on God's command: "Go from your country and your kindred and your father's house to the land that I will show you. . . . And Abram journeyed on, still going toward the Negeb."

This pilgrimage of Abram turned out to be successful, and he and Sarah became the parents of the nation called "God's chosen people." Still, their journey was not without hardship. Going where God told them to required courage, persistence, and discipline.

Life has its seasons of sadness and is not without discouragement, bewilderment, and sometimes despair. The uncertainty of the future is a mystery which continually overshadows us. Yet we can overcome, because there is more reason for hope and optimism than for apprehension and fear. As Paul said, "We are more than conquerors through him who loved us" (Rom. 8:37). A conqueror may certainly celebrate the victory.

In the closing lines of "Thanatopsis," William Cullen Bryant said we are to live "sustained and soothed by an unfaltering trust." This "unfaltering trust" is a faithful acceptance of the ultimate goodness and reality of God, a willingness to follow where God shall lead, with an attitude of confident expectation.

Prayer: *Loving God, accept my gratitude that you can bring me through my unknown Negebs. Give me the perception to know and the courage to do your will. Amen.*

Thursday, October 24   Read Hebrews 5:1-4.

The doctrine of the priesthood of all believers was thought of as an outgrowth of Martin Luther's activities. Certainly it was supported by Luther's concern for the sanctity of the church as he understood it. But long before Luther's time, the Bible gave ample support to the view that every person is, to some extent, a priest.

"If anyone wants to come with me, he must forget himself, carry his cross, and follow me," said Jesus (Matt. 16:24, TEV). "Bear one another's burdens, and so fulfil the law of Christ," wrote Paul (Gal. 6:2). These admonitions are addressed to each follower of Jesus, the Christ.

In our Christian discipleship or ministry, whether we are clergy or lay, we must be sensitive to the needs of others. We must also be aware of our weaknesses and our own need for spiritual renewal.

Reflect on the words of a hymn by Washington Gladden:

> O Master, let me walk with thee In lowly paths of service free;
> Tell me thy secret; help me bear The strain of toil, the fret of care. . . .
> Teach me thy patience; still with thee In closer, dearer company,
> In work that keeps faith sweet and strong,
>   In trust that triumphs over wrong;
> In hope that sends a shining ray Far down the future's broadening way;
> In peace that only thou canst give, With thee, O Master, let me live.*

Prayer: *Lord God, help me to do what I can and should to make your church what you want it to be. Amen.*

---

*"O Master, Let Me Walk with Thee," the United Methodist *Book of Hymns*, no. 170.

Friday, October 25   Read Hebrews 5:5-6.

The doctrine of the Incarnation is, to say the least, enigmatic, but Christians can faithfully accept the reality of Jesus in his unique divine-human duality.

His humanness is seen in his birth, infancy and childhood, in his weariness and thirst at Jacob's well, his occasional frustration and annoyance at his disciples, his sorrow at Lazarus' death, his anguish and despair on the cross. These are feelings that we, too, experience, and that enable us better to identify with Jesus.

As a boy and young man, surely Jesus was prepared and summoned for his earthly ministry. His ministry began at his baptism in the Jordan River and with God's announcement, "Thou art my beloved Son; with thee I am well pleased" (Mark 1:11). His example still calls us to ministry.

> O young and fearless Prophet of ancient Galilee:
> Thy life is still a summons to serve humanity,
> To make our thoughts and actions less prone to please
> the crowd,
> To stand with humble courage for truth with hearts
> uncowed. . . .
> O young and fearless Prophet, we need thy presence here,
> Amid our pride and glory to see thy face appear;
> Once more to hear thy challenge above our noisy day,
> Again to lead us forward along God's holy way.*

Prayer: *That we may understand and yield as you beckon to us, O God, just as Jesus answered your call, is our humble and resolute prayer. Amen.*

---

*S. Ralph Harlow, "O Young and Fearless Prophet," the United Methodist *Book of Hymns*, no. 173.

Saturday, October 26   Read Mark 10:46-49.

Is something missing?

Without God in our lives, we are incomplete, ill-equipped to meet the challenges which confront us. We may be despondent as was Isaiah, who said, "Woe is me! For I am lost," (Isa. 6:5), or tormented like the Gerasene but not knowing why (see Luke 8:26-33). We may be terrified as were the disciples in the boat during the storm, when they called, "Master, Master, we are perishing!" (Luke 8:24)

God can indeed supply the missing ingredient. Our submission to God can bridge the chasm of perplexity and discontent. Then we can walk a firm road, not to worldly peace but to the peace of God, the peace which "passes all understanding" (Phil. 4:7).

We can call upon the Lord, and we shall be answered, for anyone who comes to Christ will not be cast out (John 6:37). The plea of Bartimaeus was heard and heeded. We, too, can call on God and be heard, but God calls us also to be disciples. What shall our answer be?

> God calling yet! Shall I not hear?
> Earth's pleasures shall I still hold dear?
> Shall life's swift passing years all fly,
> And still my soul in slumber lie? . . .
> God calling yet! I cannot stay;
> My heart I yield without delay;
> Vain world, farewell, from thee I part;
> The voice of God hath reached my heart.*

Prayer: *Lord God, help me through life's rough spots, and help me, too, to minister so that others may likewise be helped. Amen.*

---

*Gerhard Tersteegen, "God Calling Yet! Shall I Not Hear," the United Methodist *Book of Hymns*, no. 105.

Sunday, October 27   Read Mark 10:46, 50-52.

Bartimaeus had a physical problem which he believed Jesus could heal. Expecting Jesus to pass by, Bartimaeus had been sitting by the roadside.

Bartimaeus sought the Lord while he could be found, called on Christ while he was near. Bartimaeus' springing up after having been seated illustrates that we may need to make changes in our outlook, that we must be willing to reach out and appropriate God's salvation.

Bartimaeus was healed of his natural blindness because of his faith. Having been healed, he followed Jesus "on the way." Through our faith we also can be made whole, can have our insights sharpened, and can bear the fruit of the Spirit. But, like Bartimaeus, we, too, need to be followers on the way.

Following "on the way" means following as a supporter and not merely as an admirer. We are to be not only hearing but doing the word. We are not told how Bartimaeus followed, and that may be best. There is no one way to follow Christ; each of us must take on the yoke of Christian service in our own individual way.

In any event, we who are reborn in God can, through faith, experience the victory that overcomes (see 1 John 5:4).

Rejoice, for Christ brings healing and restoration!

> [Christ] speaks, and listening to his voice,
> New life the dead receive;
> The mournful, broken hearts rejoice;
> The humble poor, believe.*

Prayer: *How thankful I am, O God, that through you everything becomes new. Amen.*

---

*Charles Wesley, "O for a Thousand Tongues to Sing," the United Methodist *Book of Hymns*, no. 1.

GOD'S INVITATION TO RELATIONSHIP

October 28–November 3, 1985   **Loretta Girzaitis†**
Monday, October 28   Read Deuteronomy 6:1-3.

This week's readings focus on the Lord God and the covenants God has made. The covenants emphasize God's greatness, goodness, power, and love. They also underscore God's desire to be loved by us.

In interaction with Abraham, God makes a unilateral, unconditional promise, an obligation which God assumed in relationship to Abraham. This was possible because Abraham had already proven himself (see Gen. 22:15-19).

God renewed this covenant with Abraham's children and grandchildren, and the Israelites were led out of bondage centuries later because "God heard their groaning, and God remembered his covenant with Abraham, with Isaac, and with Jacob" (Exod. 2:24).

The covenant that God made with Moses on Sinai was different. It was a conditional one and required a response from the chosen race. The people would continue to possess the land if they observed the Law which was being given to them on Sinai. If the people lived according to the Law, the Lord would bless their land and protect them. If the people rejected the Law, God would leave them to their own devices, and these would trap them in slavery. This week we will reflect on this invitation and try to understand its freedom.

Prayer: *Lord God, king of the universe, help us to see that submission to you brings us freedom. Help us to recognize that your blessing is more important than gold medals, first places, and the plaudits of the crowds. Grant us this kind of wisdom, O God! Amen.*

---

†Director of Adult Education, Archdiocese of St. Paul and Minneapolis, St. Paul, Minnesota.

Tuesday, October 29   Read Deuteronomy 6:4-5.

These two verses became a prayer which Jews still pray daily, the *Shema*. The Israelites had come from Egypt where the worship of the sun, moon, and other forms in nature was common. They were soon to enter a land where Baal, El, and their consorts were honored. God wanted this people's total allegiance and made it quite clear that if they ever worshipped other gods, disaster would follow.

In addition, they were told how to love God: with heart, and soul, and might. Loving God with their hearts meant turning all their feelings—envy, anger, hatred, etc.—toward good. Loving God with their souls meant giving up their lives if need be to live their faith. Loving God with their strength meant using all of their resources for God's glory.

Victor Frankl, the Jewish psychiatrist, was arrested by the Nazis in World War II and stripped of everything, even his clothes. He inherited the rags of an inmate who had been sent to the gas chamber. In a pocket he found a page torn from a Jewish prayer book. It contained the *Shema*.

Frankl later wrote that this coincidence became a challenge to him to live and to love as God commanded. He discovered meaning in life and later shared his insights in his famous book on logotherapy.

Prayer: *Lord God, king of the universe, the one and only God, I accept your invitation to love. Help me to turn all my inclinations toward good. Give me courage to act on what I believe, and show me how to place all my strengths and power at your disposal. Amen.*

Wednesday, October 30   Read Mark 12:28-31.

Jesus knew the Torah well. He had studied it for years. When he appeared in the synagogue to read on the Sabbath day, he read from Isaiah. He knew exactly how to proclaim his mission.

Whenever Jesus taught, he quoted scripture and explained its implications. Pharisees, Sadducees, men, and women listened to his interpretations. It was rarely a surprise to him when he was questioned.

So when a teacher of the Law asked, "Which is the greatest commandment?" Jesus did not hesitate. He repeated the *Shema,* adding the phrase, "with all your mind." Jesus then emphasized that there was another great commandment: "Love your neighbor as you love yourself."

Jesus' parables highlighted love of neighbor frequently. The forgiving father loved the prodigal son. The Samaritan loved the wounded man. The master loved the watchful servants. Mary and Martha loved their brother Lazarus.

Love of God and love of neighbor go hand in hand. When a person is willing to serve the Lord God, then loving one's neighbor must follow. If it does not, we make a mockery of the love of God.

Every person has been created in God's image and likeness and so carries characteristics and qualities that make her or him like God. It is in recognizing these Godlike qualities in one another that God becomes visible and knowable on earth.

Prayer: *Lord God, king of the universe, I rejoice that you have given us hearts with which to love. Enlarge our hearts so we may love you and others more each day. Amen.*

Thursday, October 31   Read Mark 12:28-31.

As we reread Jesus' injunction to love our neighbors as we love ourselves, we need to examine it from another perspective. Jesus sets a special standard for the love of neighbor: as great as love of self.

Not too many of us feel comfortable with such a requirement. We find it difficult to accept God's total, unconditional love for us. We cannot admit that we are made in God's likeness. We consider it pride to list our good qualities, abilities, successes.

Yet if we do not acknowledge the strengths and beauties within us, the Lord will not be glorified. Mary proclaimed loudly and joyfully, "My soul magnifies the Lord, and my spirit rejoices in God my Savior . . . for he who is mighty has done great things for me, and holy is his name" (Luke 1:46-49). We should make a similar affirmation.

Love of self means caring for and developing mind, spirit, and body. It means deepening one's relationship with God. It means recognizing the purpose for existence, finding meaning in life. It also means acknowledging limitations and dealing with them.

When each of us can accept self as a unique individual whom God created and loves very much, then there is no need to compare self with others, to compete, or to put others down. Acceptance of self as God's creation is true love of self.

And this becomes the standard for loving neighbors: I love others for who they are and not for what they can give me. I don't try to change them. Their compassion, understanding, patience, goodness, and love mirror God to me.

Prayer: *Lord God, king of the universe, thank you for your wisdom in requiring us to love others as we love ourselves. Help us truly to accept ourselves. Amen.*

Friday, November 1   Read Psalm 119:33-48.

Some religious traditions commemorate the sainthood of God's people in a special way today, recalling those who followed God's decrees and who found delight in God's commands.

Corrie Ten Boom was such a person. She overcame the pain and despair of concentration camps.

Martin Luther King, Jr., defied convention and government to live out the precepts of the Lord. So did the theologian Theresa of Avila and Francis of Assisi. Their freedom lay in accepting God's unfailing love.

Some, like Paul of Tarsus and Augustine of Hippo, experienced spiritual earthquakes which gave them totally new perspectives on God and themselves. Each was a disciple, one constantly learning from the Lord.

Each of us knows individuals who run the race and seek the prize which the Lord has prepared for them. We, too, can acknowledge that we are saints, not men and women who have reached the destination, but individuals who are searching, yearning, responding as God guides us toward a loving relationship.

As we strive for a healthy relationship with God, we examine our priorities and juggle the price tags that we have placed on each of our values. We acknowledge that God's invitation to intimacy is the final reward, and we know that we need only to accept it. The importances of yesteryear seem drab and lusterless. So we strip ourselves of the baggage that burdens us and seek the Lord's companionship forever.

Prayer: *Lord God, king of the universe, I am deeply grateful for your invitation to be your friend for all eternity. Your love enfolds and encourages me. Amen.*

Saturday, November 2   Read Leviticus 1:1-2.

The Book of Leviticus details the meaning of sacrifice, how sacrifice is to be offered, and itemizes the requirements for priesthood.

Burnt offerings symbolized devotion to God, while meal offerings demonstrated the Israelites' dependence upon God. Peace offerings expressed gratitude for daily blessings. These three forms were called the "sweet savor" offerings and were voluntary expressions of worship and commitment to God.

There were also mandatory sacrifices to restore the sinner to fellowship with God. The sin offering was for sins committed unintentionally. The trespass offering ensured payment for injury or property loss.

The sin offering was only for sins that were not premeditated. One who sinned deliberately was cut off from among the people (Num. 15:30-31) and excluded from religious privileges for some time.

Sacrifices could be offered only by Levites, who were anointed and set apart for their sacrificial work. The high priest was the most important person in the religious community. Once a year, the high priest offered the sacrifice of atonement in the Holy of Holies. He spilled fresh blood on the altar to pay the penalty for the nation's sins. Then he laid his hands upon the head of a young goat and confessed the sins of the nation over it. This scapegoat was then sent into the wilderness to die, carrying the people's sin.

Prayer: *Lord God, king of the universe, help me to understand the ugliness of sin and the need for reparation. You have been sacrifice and scapegoat for me. I thank you for it. Amen.*

Sunday, November 3   Read Hebrews 7:23-28.

Because Jesus was "bruised for our iniquities" (Isa. 53:5) he became our scapegoat. Because his atoning sacrifice was perfect and since he lives forever, Christ is able to save completely those who come to God through him. The sacrifice is final because Christ who is blameless offered himself to cure the people's guilt.

We can compare the high priest of Leviticus 16 and the high priest described in Hebrews 4, 7, 9 to better understand the perfection and power of Jesus Christ, the ultimate high priest. In the old order, the high priest (Aaron or one of his descendants) entered the Holy of Holies once each year to offer the blood of a bull or goat for the sins of the nation of Israel. The high priest had to purify himself first by sacrifice in order to offer the sacrifice for the nation.

In the new order, Jesus Christ was the high priest who entered heaven itself. He made atonement by sacrificing his own blood to save those who come to God through him and lives forever to plead for them.

Whatever sacrifices are now performed are done so in order to acknowledge God's place in our life. We no longer sacrifice animals. Instead, we offer self in a continual sacrifice of praise and thanksgiving because we believe that Christ has saved us from our sins.

Prayer: *Lord God, king of the universe, I accept Jesus as my Savior to intercede for me constantly. I open myself to the Holy Spirit; purify me and make me enthusiastic in your love. Praise is my daily sacrifice to you. Amen.*

GIVING OURSELVES TO GOD

November 4-10, 1985   **Bruce R. Ough†**
Monday, November 4   Read Psalm 146;
Mark 12:38-44.

Giving one's total being to God is the central issue of the spiritual pilgrimage. God's call to faithfulness is a call to open our lives ever more fully to God's will and presence. There is no greater struggle in our effort to walk with God. Even Jesus approached the conclusion of his earthly journey wrestling at Gethsemane with giving his total being to God.

The very desire to give ourselves fully to God is a gift from God, an expression of God's unconditional love for each of us. We intellectually and doctrinally embrace the concept. But, for the most part we do not want to be saints; we just do not want to be sinners. That is, we are willing to give a small portion of our lives to God, but we resist giving ourselves totally.

Like the Pharisees and rich men of Jesus' time, we give what we can spare of our lives. The widow did not have much money to give God. Yet, she gave all that she had to live on. In giving the very resources that could keep her alive, the widow, in effect, offered her total being to God. Jesus made a special point of this with his disciples. And Jesus invites us to give all that we have—our total being—to God.

Suggestion for prayer: *Reflect on what it means to give yourself totally to something or someone. To what extent do you give yourself to God? Pray for the desire to give yourself to God completely.*

---

†Director, Oakwood Spiritual Life Center, Syracuse, Indiana.

Tuesday, November 5   Read 1 Kings 17:8-16.

Giving one's total being to God is a continuous process—a journey. Like most journeys it begins with our curiosity to move beyond where we are. In our effort to see Jesus more clearly, or to be more open to God's will, we acknowledge and begin the journey.

This is a journey with more seasons of movement than seasons of arrival. For at the very moment we arrive at a new destination, God invites us to take yet another step in the journey.

Even as the widow at Zarephath was going to bring Elijah a drink of water, she was asked to respond even more fully to God. Elijah asked her to bring him some bread as well. As if that were not enough, the widow was then asked to use her last handful of flour to prepare the bread. God was inviting the widow to walk ever more closely with her God—to enter ever more fully into the journey of faith.

The widow initially protested each invitation. Yet she was blessed by an endless source of nourishment as she displayed faithful obedience. We can learn a great deal from the widow of Zarephath about giving ourselves fully to God.

The journey has a very distinct rhythm. There are seasons of acceptance when we actively embrace God's call and seasons of resistance when we actively move away from God. Those on the journey know the dark periods of doubt, disorientation, and suffering as well as the bright moments of awakening, faithfulness, and blessing.

These seasons of resistance and acceptance are the pivotal points in the process of giving ourselves to God. They are the times when God is inviting us to take yet another step in the journey.

Prayer: *Almighty God, continually draw me to yourself, even when I resist. Amen.*

Wednesday, November 6   Read Hebrews 9:24-28.

Giving one's total being to God is a response to God's gift of unconditional and boundless love. Jesus was God's ultimate gift to each of us. God offered the Christ to the world to take away our sins and to open a way for us to offer ourselves to God.

God's gift of Jesus Christ was a one-time offering. Christ was not offered many times, like the blood sacrifices of the Jewish high priest. Love is unconditional only if it is offered once and for all with no reservations, no strings, and no loopholes to seduce us into believing one can earn or purchase that love.

God does not want to manipulate or obligate us to return his love. God's unconditional love breaks the bonds of manipulation, oppression, and obligation. God always judges in favor of the oppressed and lifts those who have fallen and seeks out the sinner precisely because it is the broken and despised who have known love only with strings attached.

Have you ever been given a gift that had stated or implied strings attached? If so, you have probably felt used or manipulated or obligated to return the favor. When we receive a gift that is given unconditionally, simply because we are loved, our response is quite different. The gift of love can be returned unconditionally, freely, totally. Can you imagine how difficult it would be to give one's total being to God if God had not set the stage by first loving us?

Opening our lives ever more fully to God's will and presence does involve choice at many junctures in our journey. But it is not something we can initiate. God first loved us and chose us and opened the way.

Prayer: *Loving God, clothe me in yourself and enable me to offer myself to you and others after the pattern of Jesus. Amen.*

Thursday, November 7   Read Mark 12:38-44.

Giving one's total being to God requires faithful seeking. Faithfulness is more than an external display of "faith behaviors" and spiritual disciplines. It is also, perhaps more so, the strong desire to stand inwardly before God. It is in our hungering and thirsting for God that we offer ourselves to God most fully.

When I was first introduced to the spiritual disciplines, I was overjoyed. I had finally discovered some ways to hold myself open and available to God. Before long I was practicing the disciplines religiously. Soon I was taking great pride in how faithfully and how often I prayed, retreated, and studied the scripture. One day I was sharing my achievement with a small group of colleagues. I was about to experience my first lesson in spiritual accountability.

A dear and trusted friend lovingly explained to me there was a difference between the disciplines and faithfulness. He pointed out that in my seeking mastery of the disciplines I had turned from seeking God. I had begun to rely solely on my actions rather than depend on God's leading. The disciplines are only a means for channeling our seeking after God; they are not a substitute for God.

The poor widow at the temple treasury was a great woman of faith. She practiced the spiritual disciplines of charity, service, and humility. Her stewardship was inpeccable. Yet what caught Jesus' eye was her utter trust and dependence upon God to sustain her. Her two copper coins proved to be the means by which she expressed her desire and longing for God. It was the seeking, with utter recklessness and abandon, that was her true offering.

Prayer: *O God, grant me grace and strength to faithfully seek you all the days of my life. Amen.*

Friday, November 8   Read 1 Kings 17:8-16.

Giving one's total being to God requires the path of obedience. Obedience is indispensable for those who seek God. Obedience quickens our sensitivity to God and makes more real our sense of God's presence. Every act of obedience increases our capacity to give ourselves even more fully to God.

We all have practical experience in being obedient. We obey persons and institutions, even symbols, that have been endowed with authority or power. We have all sought obedience from other persons. And we have all resisted or rebeled against others' attempts to demand our obedience.

Obedience is generally viewed as restrictive, interfering with our individual rights and privileges. We sometimes believe obedience denys freedom and enslaves us. Thus, when we speak of being obedient to God, it feels limiting rather than liberating. But these are cultural and political understandings of obedience. The biblical understanding is quite different.

Obedience to God is always connected to God's promise to humankind. Obedience is the way to know God. By submitting to God's will, that will is revealed. Through obedience the blessings of God's promises are made known. The psalmist affirms that God's promises are always kept—and that is why we should obey and trust in the Lord God.

The widow in Zarephath reacts much as you and I do to God's commandments. She viewed her calls to obedience as restrictive, even life-threatening. But every act of obedience by the widow increased her capacity to give herself more fully to God. It is on this path of obedience that God's promise of abundant life is both revealed and fulfilled.

Prayer: *God of power and promise, help me to begin now to obey you in every way I can. Amen.*

Saturday, November 9   Read Hebrews 9:24-28.

Giving one's total being to God leads to the way of the cross. Those who proceed on the spiritual journey without suffering will bear no fruit. Those who endeavor to hold themselves totally open and available to God will ultimately be called to share in Christ's Passion—called to deny self, even unto death, so that others might have new and abundant life. It is in sharing the cross of Christ that offering ourselves to God becomes complete.

How do you handle your suffering? Or the suffering of those around you? Your initial response is probably like mine. I tend to look for the positive aspects or the potential benefits that could result from the suffering. Or I wax philosophical about how into every life a little pain must come. Such is human nature; we strive to deny our suffering.

This was not the case with Jesus' suffering on the cross. After the struggle in the garden to do God's will, Jesus embraced his suffering. Hebrews tell us he offered himself to suffer for us. Jesus took an active stance. There was no denial, no passivity, no philosophical whining. There was pain and death so that there could be resurrection.

Denying self, suffering for others, is an act of abandonment to God's will and purposes. For like Christ's "one time" suffering and death on the cross, the risk is tremendous. There are no guarantees that the suffering will produce positive results. Those we step aside for may not follow in Jesus' way.

God does not ask us to share the cross of Christ just for the sake of suffering. God asks us to share in Christ's Passion so that we can be agents of transformation and heralds of resurrection.

Prayer: *Lord Jesus Christ, make me strong to do your work and will, even unto death. Amen.*

Sunday, November 10   Read 1 Kings 17:8-16;
                                           Ps. 146; Heb. 9:24-28;
                                           Mark 12:38-44.

Giving one's total being to God leads to a life of service and servanthood. The servant places his or her very life in the hands of the master. The servant desires not to live for self, but for others.

Jesus shows us what it means to be a servant of God. He placed his life in the hands of God, and he offered his life in service to others. He became the least of all so that he might serve. On the cross he performed a perfect act of love. The power of his witness was in his vulnerability, his simple and transparent love for God and humankind.

For Jesus there was no distinction between giving his total being to God and offering himself in service to others. Christian servanthood must contain both dimensions of offering one's self. Jesus assumed the role of servant with his disciples to make this very point. And he prayed that his disciples would faithfully follow in his footsteps.

The poor widow at the temple treasury and the widow in Zarephath followed in the footsteps of servanthood. That is, they placed their lives in the hands of God. In offering the very last of their resources—two copper coins and a handful of flour, respectively—they risked all and became utterly vulnerable. In placing themselves totally in the hands of God, they trusted God to provide what they needed. It is only out of such complete vulnerability and trust in God that we can venture forth to serve others.

Suggestion for prayer: *Reflect on what opportunities you have to offer yourself to others in service. How do you experience God's call to servanthood? Pray for grace and strength to faithfully follow in the footsteps of servanthood.*

KINGDOM WORDS

November 11-17, 1985   **Duane A. Ewers†**
Monday, November 11   Read Daniel 7:9-14.

Judgment

It is tempting not to read these words from Daniel. The images do not fit our modern age. Visions of a throne, a white-robed occupant, wheels of fire, and a dead beast are not usually part of our daily thinking.

But let us not brush Daniel aside too quickly. The images may not be the problem. As a matter of fact, similar images are used throughout the Bible. The real problem may be with the theme—judgment. Judgment is not a favorite topic in our day either. Yet it is a part of God's kingdom, whether we want it to be or not. Judgment takes place whenever individuals, institutions, or nations go against God's will.

Daniel envisions one who would be "given dominion and glory and kingdom, that all peoples, nations, and languages should serve him." As Christians, we believe that Jesus, the Christ, fulfills that vision. It is precisely that Jesus who serves as a mirror for us. When we view our lifestyles, some of our loves, and our lack of commitment over against the glimpse of God's kingdom we see in Jesus, we are judged.

Prayer: *O God, nudge us to look at who we are and those for whom we care in light of Jesus, the Christ, in whose name we pray. Amen.*

---

†Assistant General Secretary, Section on Christian Eduction, Board of Discipleship, The United Methodist Church, Nashville, Tennessee.

Tuesday, November 12   Read Psalm 145:8-9.

Grace

What are some words or images you might use to describe God? We already know one that Daniel would use: *judge*. But most of us would not stop there. The psalmist will not let us stop there! Descriptive words about God tumble from the psalmist's pen:

> *gracious*
> *compassionate*
> *forebearing*
> *constant*
> *good*
> *tender care*

It would be difficult to develop a more powerful description of God. Reflect on each of the psalmist's words for a few moments. Turn them over in your mind and let them sink into your spirit. Add descriptive words from your own experience.

These are words of grace. It is good to be reminded that God's grace is always acting upon our lives. God beckons to us as we are. We do not have to earn God's love. All we need to do is to accept God's embrace—daily. It is even judgment's purpose to catch our attention, to remind us of what we are missing when we live too much for ourselves, and to turn us toward the intimacy, tenderness, and acceptance of God's grace.

"[God's] greatness is unsearchable" (Ps. 145:3). It is, isn't it? Think on that for a few moments. Celebrate it!

Prayer: *O God, we turn to you because of the promise that when we fail, you are a God of grace, compassion, and tender care. Amen.*

Wednesday, November 13   Read Psalm 145:10-13.

Praise

One of the great movements of faith is praise. When we lift our voices in praise to God, we are not dealing with personal issues or hurts. When we give praise, we are not reaching out to take something for ourselves. When we praise God, the focus is on God for who God is and for what God has done:

> All thy saints shall bless thee! They shall speak of the glory of thy kingdom, and tell of thy power.

In our kind of world, it is easy to see only the tragedy and the brokenness. In a world of war, hunger, injustice, disease, and death, it would be easy to let tears blind us. Praise tends to bring our fractured lives into focus around the living God who stands beside us among all the hurt. Praise tends to awaken us to the good, the beautiful, and the gracious that is in the world amid all the discordant sounds. Praise tends to awaken us to awe and wonder when so much around us tries to deaden our spirits.

The psalmist reminds us that praise is the only proper response of creature to Creator; praise is the only response to judgment; praise is the only response to God's graciousness.

Suggestion for prayer: *In a moment of reflection, recall some of the words you would use to describe God. Think of what God has done and what God promises to do. Reread Psalm 145:10-13. In prayer or through a favorite hymn, give praise to God. If, because of a difficult circumstance or because of some of the tragedy in our world, you find you are unable to praise, then ask God to help you praise aright.*

Thursday, November 14　　　　Read Psalm 145:14-17.

Justice

The psalmist's message is clear: God has a special concern for the poor and the powerless. "The Lord upholds all who are falling, and raises up all who are bowed down." The same note is sounded by Isaiah, by the ministry of Jesus, and by James. God hears the cries and the groans of those who have been pushed to the margins of our society. That should be a word of hope.

But that message of God's special concern for the poor and the hurting might make some of us a bit anxious. Many of us are anything but poor and powerless. We might even be contributing to the hurt of others. If God cares for them in a special way, where do we fit in? The word from the psalmist is that in God's kingdom there is room for all. "The eyes of all look to thee, and thou givest them their food in due season."

It is simply that God has a special concern for those who seem to have been left out or left behind. It is a matter of justice. It becomes clear in the ministry of Jesus that God is best served when the poor and the powerless catch our attention and receive our energies. Indeed, time and again, the saints of the kingdom speak of becoming more aware of God and of experiencing the living Christ as they moved nearer to those who had been pushed to the margins of their society.

Suggestion for prayer: *In God's presence, name and pray for persons in your community for whom God might have special concern—and be prepared to serve them.*

Friday, November 15   Read Psalm 145:18-21.

Faithfulness

"The Lord is near to all who call upon him." That is a nice thought, but is it true? Some persons might have a difficult time believing what the psalmist affirms. There are some experiences in life that might be so tragic that one feels alone in the universe. There might be hurts so persistent that one feels isolated. Even the psalmist once cried, "My God, my God, why hast thou forsaken me?" (Ps. 22:1) Jesus obviously experienced that sense of abandonment when he cried the same words from the cross.

Is God faithful or fickle? Is God near at all times or just when the going is good? Or could it be that in the midst of tragic experiences the channels of communication are clogged up from our end?

The witness of the psalmist is that God is faithful. God is unchanging. God is not whimsical. Our task is to turn to God with singleness of heart. Don't give up! Be persistent! A little fear is even appropriate. Fear is related to wisdom. It grows out of an understanding that we are creatures who can sometimes lose sight of the faithful God.

Prayer: *O God, who stands behind and among all of our experiences in life, it is easy to praise you when things go well and we sense your gracious, tender care. It is more difficult to turn to you when life tumbles in around us. In those moments especially, remind us that you are always near to those who call upon you. Amen.*

Saturday, November 16   Read Hebrews 10:11-18.

Perfection

Perfection is not a word many of us would use to describe our pilgrimage as a disciple. Indeed, we live in a world that demands less than the best! Yet perfection is an important dimension of life in God's kingdom. Once we experience new life in Christ there is that challenge to become Christlike.

To be sure, striving toward perfection (sanctification) has often been a source of pride for some Christians. Growth in faith or an increase in servanthood has often been viewed as the results of one's own efforts. At other times, the call to perfection has had such strong moralistic overtones that it seemed far removed from God's graciousness in accepting us as we are.

The writer of Hebrews tries to avoid both problems by reminding us that the source of all assurance resides in Christ. "By a single offering he has perfected for all time those who are sanctified." The necessary and important task of growth in our Christian lives is not the result of our work or extra effort. It is the work of Christ, the great High Priest, who puts the laws within our hearts.

It might be helpful to spend time in prayer and reflection to think on this perfecting work of Christ. Since we do not have to worry about making ourselves perfect before God, we are free to use our minds to struggle with the issues of the day. We are free to use our strength to love and to serve.

Prayer: *O God, thank you for what Christ has done in drawing us closer to perfection. Amen.*

Sunday, November 17   Read Mark 13:24-33.

Watchfulness

Predictions of the end-time abound. They have been with us for over nineteen centuries. The fact that none of the predictions, including Mark's, have ever been fulfilled does not seem to deter people from making ever new warnings of an imminent end.

But failed predictions may not be our greatest concern. An even greater danger may be found among disciples who do not expect anything more from God's kingdom.

Mark's real message is not in the prediction of the end-time. The real message is the call to faithful watching for a fuller expression of God's kingdom as we go about our day-to-day living. "Take heed, watch; for you do not know when the time will come."

It can be as easy to get caught up in a busy world as it is to get caught up with worrying about the end-time. In either case we are not present with family and friends, with persons who hurt, or with those who hunger in mind, body, and spirit. Mark's call to watch is a call to live as faithful disciples in the present time. Indeed, it is faithful living now that prepares us for the fullness of God's kingdom that shall surely come.

Prayer: *O God, help us to live and love as if the world will last for a million years, but to watch and be faithful as if your kingdom might come in its fulfillment in the next few moments. In the name of the living Christ. Amen.*

THE VISION OF FAITH

November 18-24, 1985   **Shelley M. Douglass†**
Monday, November 18   Read Luke 18:35-43.

"Jesus, Son of David, have mercy on me!" We have all said these words. What does it mean to pray for the mercy of God?

The blind man beside the road near Jericho prayed for sight. His blindness prevented him from seeing the world as God made it, the faces of his loved ones, the beauty of nature. Jesus recognized his faith and granted his prayer. Immediately the blind man could see. He rejoiced and praised God, and followed Jesus.

We, too, are blind to the glory of God's creation. We allow our sight to be dimmed by cultural diseases. We cannot see brothers and sisters in those who are poor—or, sometimes, in those who are rich. We do not see God's children; we see enemies. We do not see God's creation; we see resources to be exploited.

When we pray for Christ's mercy, we are asking that our blindness be taken away—that we be enabled to see with the eyes of faith. When our prayer is granted, we find ourselves disoriented. Like a blind person seeing for the first time, we are not sure what we are seeing or how to respond. Will we rejoice in the world of God's creation and follow Jesus, or will we close our eyes and return to our selfish blindness?

Prayer: *Lord, take away my blindness. Give me the courage to see with the eyes of faith. Amen.*

---

†Free-lance writer; member of Ground Zero Center for Nonviolent Action (a community committed to learning to live nonviolently from a faith perspective), Silverdale, Washington.

Tuesday, November 19   Read Luke 19:1-10.

Zacchaeus was a collaborator with the Roman occupation of Israel. He was a traitor and a thief. He worshipped material gain above his God and his people. Zacchaeus was ostracized and scorned by everyone who saw him through the eyes of his culture.

Jesus, however, saw him through the eyes of faith: someone in trouble, someone lost, a child of God. He was able to recognize Zacchaeus, to call him by name and accept him as a brother. In doing this, Jesus restored Zacchaeus' sight as well. A man who had worshipped money and had "sold out" his God and his country to attain wealth suddenly saw with the eyes of faith.

Many of us have had that experience of sudden insight: a fleeting glimpse of love in an enemy's face, a feeling of compassion for someone we have hated. But Zacchaeus acted on faith's vision. He gave half of his goods to the poor and restored fourfold what he had stolen.

Zacchaeus saw with the eyes of faith, rejoiced, and followed Jesus in a very practical way; he acted on his faithful vision. He began to share out of love for his sisters and brothers.

It must have been very frightening for a hated person to relinquish wealth and power, but Zacchaeus found joy in doing it because he could remain close to Jesus only by following him.

Prayer: *Jesus, our brother, have mercy on our weakness. Help us to act on our visions of your kingdom. Be with us in our fear. Give us the courage to do your will. Amen.*

Wednesday, November 20   Read 2 Maccabees 7:1,
20-31.

Here, in an account that could be a contemporary report
from many countries today, we read of the cost of holding to
the vision of faith. In verses 22-23, the valiant mother sets
forth faith's vision: God created the world and its people. God
loves us and will give us life; we owe our allegiance to God
and to none other.

Opposed to this vision are two temptations, each difficult
to refuse because it is, in itself, a good thing. It is good to love
our children and care for them. It is good to have enough of
the world's goods to live on. But it is not good to put either
before service to God.

The mother in our story knows that it is better to watch
one's children perish than to ask them to deny their consciences. The son knows that it is better to be imprisoned or
even executed than to gain wealth and lose one's soul. How
many of us would respond with such clarity?

Those of us who live in wealthy countries know about our
sisters and brothers in poorer places. We help from our
surplus. But the vision of faith challenges us to change the
systemic evil that creates the need, though we know that in
doing so we risk our material welfare and our families'
comforts. How many of us dare to live by that vision when
faith calls us?

Prayer: *God, you love us even more than our own mothers.
Strengthen us as we face temptation. Help us to do your will in spite
of threats. Be with us in our fear, for we need your presence. Amen.*

Thursday, November 21   Read Luke 19:41-44.

What does it mean to live without the vision of faith? Jesus weeps over Jerusalem because he understands that her people have abandoned the vision God offered. He knows that the "things that make for peace" are visible only to eyes cleared by faith. He knows that the logical result of closing our eyes to faith's vision is death and destruction.

Let us not deceive ourselves. Jesus is not predicting that God will destroy the world as punishment. God is making in Jesus a new covenant of suffering love, a covenant that elaborates Noah's rainbow sign. God will love us and forgive us no matter what we do. The spirit of God will always be present to help the faithful bring good from evil.

But evil will unquestionably come if we continue to avoid God's way. It will be our own evil, inflicted upon us by ourselves. It will be the fruit of our own actions. Sowing the wind, we will reap the whirlwind. God will suffer with us in sorrow, as Jesus suffered over the city of Jerusalem.

Jesus' life was spent in calling people to repent and believe the good news of God's love and care for us. If we do believe this news, we will do what Jesus said: love our enemies, do good to those who hate us, sell what we have and give to the poor. In doing this we will help create a just and peaceful society. If we do not do this, the outcome is clear: world war, nuclear war, death and destruction. The choice is ours to make.

Prayer: *Thank you, God, for Jesus' life and call. We ask the grace to see and hear and do your will. Help us to repent; help us to make your ways our ways. Amen.*

337

Friday, November 22   Read Luke 19:45-48;
                                       1 Maccabees 4:36-37, 52-59.

Our lives are temples to God. We know that very often we sully them by devotion to false idols. A false idol is anything that takes God's place of preeminence in our hearts and minds. In the reading from Luke the false idol is our desire for money.

In the time of the Maccabees, Jewish freedom fighters liberated their Temple in Jerusalem, swept it clean of abominations, and adorned it again for the true worship. They established a yearly feast—Hanukkah—to commemorate the victory of the Maccabees over Antiochus of Syria, their rededication of the restored Temple, and God's faithfulness to them. In the story from Luke we find Jesus cleansing the Temple, first by driving out the merchants who profited from the pilgrims. Then for a few days in the Temple he teaches the word of God.

Jesus saw and corrected the sin of the Temple merchants, but he did more. He directed attention to love and cleansing the inner temple of their lives so as to become acceptable children of God once more. We, too, are offered this opportunity to repent and cleanse our lives.

Prayer: *Lord, take the beam from my eyes and help me to see clearly what takes my worship away from you. Is it my family? My political party? My home? My possessions? Help me to order my life so that you are my first priority. In Jesus' name. Amen.*

Saturday, November 23   Read Luke 20:27-40.

Jesus had a direct way of going to the point of a matter and refusing to be sidetracked. In this reading his questioners try to prove the illogic of a belief in eternal life by holding it up to ridicule. Jesus, however, refuses to be sidetracked and responds to the real issue: the nature of God and of humankind. "[God] is not God of the dead, but of the living; for all live to him." In God none of us is lost. All that we are lives on.

What does it mean to see with eyes cleared by this knowledge? Someone once said to me, "The worst that 'they' can do is to kill you. All the other things—the loss of work, jailing, even torture—are just threats to do that. If we no longer fear death, 'they' have no power over us."

The ultimate idolatry that blinds our eyes is the worship of our own lives. We do not take steps to live as Christ lived because we know that those steps lead to the death that Christ died. But if, in fact, we all live in God; if, in fact, Christ rose from the dead, none of that matters. The more alive we become to Love, who is God, the fuller our life, even if we die. The more we deny God, who is love, out of concern for our own lives, the less alive we are.

Prayer: *Merciful God, help us to find our life in serving you. Make us willing to give our lives in following you. Amen.*

Sunday, November 24   Read John 18:33-37.

What is the nature of Jesus' kingdom? Jesus says that it is not of this world, yet he has spent his ministry announcing that it is at hand. Preaching this kingdom is about to cost him his life, yet it is not one to be defended by fighting. What is this kingdom?

The kingdom of God is to come—and it is present. It is present

• when we begin to see with the eyes of faith

• when we who are blind see

• when we who are sinners repent

• when we cowards give our lives for God's word

• when we are rebuked and learn to change our ways

• when we share our goods with the poor and learn to love our enemies

Jesus brought the kingdom to the present when he died on the cross, loving his enemies and giving his life for them. The kingdom of God is one in which we defend the truth by giving our lives, while loving those who take them.

Mahatma Gandhi, Martin Luther King, Jr., and Dorothy Day all helped to usher in God's kingdom by taking hatred and returning love in its place. This is the central truth of God's kingdom, the thing that makes for peace: hatred ends where love begins. This weapon can conquer any enemy, defend any cause. The kingdom of God is built by love and sacrifice. We, too, say that Jesus is king. Do we believe it?

Prayer: *Come, Lord, bring your kingdom. You are our life; help us to love as you do. Bring us peace. Amen.*

A Servant of the Servants

November 25–December 1, 1985   **Alston A. Morgan**†
Monday, November 25   Read Jeremiah 33:14-16.

Although Jeremiah has been called the weeping prophet, another name also applies—a servant of the servants. Jeremiah longed to see his people free of bondage and restored to their homeland.

Jeremiah had a vision of the kingdom of God, which eventually would encompass Christ's bride, the church. Jeremiah understood God never intended for a human to sit on an earthly throne, for the ultimate throne was reserved for Jesus Christ. From Genesis to Revelation, God's word points to a theocracy.

It was a dark period for Jeremiah. And, while centuries separated Jeremiah and the apostle Paul, they both understood the secret of a transformed life (see Rom. 12:2). They both understood that God's children are to be servants. Jeremiah understood that God's people are to be transformed by the renewing of the mind. He knew that all humankind was alienated from the life of God through ignorance (see Eph. 4:17-25). Jeremiah was understanding and sympathetic, but he was bold in predicting Judah's destruction at the hands of the Babylonians because of their continued sin, especially the sin of idolatry.

Prayer: *We praise you, God, that we have a record of your dealings with your people. Help us to learn that obedience to you is our hope, for sin will always separate us from you. Amen.*

---

†Associate Professor, Oral Roberts University; ordained Southern Baptist minister, Tulsa, Oklahoma.

Tuesday, November 26   Read Psalm 25:1-10.

The Psalms are like a picture window looking on Christ as the servant of all servants. Our present reading takes on even richer meaning in the context of the preceding three psalms.

Psalm 22 is the first road sign to Christ. It is here we first read the words that Jesus said from the cross about his feeling of being forsaken by God. Jesus cried out at feeling left alone on the cross. But the psalm also adds, "But thou art holy, O thou that inhabitest the praises of Israel (Ps. 22:3, KJV). This is what it means to be a servant of the servants.

The next psalm, Psalm 23, is one of the most common passages of scripture in the whole Bible. Psalm 22 taught about the Good Shepherd, and Psalm 23 is the story of the Great Shepherd. A servant has one role or job. It is to meet the needs of other people. The psalmist wrote, "I shall not want"—nothing I need shall be lacking.

Finally, in Psalm 24 God is shown as the servant of servants, the "Chief Shepherd." In this psalm, God is sovereign, yet also the great servant, the one who comes into our lives to minister to us completely.

The psalmist prays in Psalm 25 to learn the ways of God as the greatest of servants: "Lead me in thy truth, and teach me: for thou art the God of my salvation" (KJV).

Prayer: *O God, we pray as the psalmist did, asking you to teach us. Make us servants, willing as Jesus was to lay down our lives in order to show others the extent of your love. Amen.*

Wednesday, November 27   Read 1 Thess. 3:9-10.

Paul always wanted to minister to people, to be their servant. One way he did that was by teaching.

The Thessalonians took Paul's teaching to heart. Timothy's report to Paul was positive, and Paul was glad. Like a professor whose cup of joy runs over when the students pass, Paul rejoices that his teaching has not been in vain.

The servant serves out of love. But Paul is not with his people, and thus he is not serving them according to his calling. The Thessalonians are his "glory and joy" (1 Thess. 2:20), and Paul desires to see them, to teach them personally. The major emphasis of this epistle is on life right now, in preparation for the second coming of Christ. Apparently, the Thessalonians had been somewhat confused about teachings on Christ's return. Paul wrote to help them understand.

It is easier to talk face-to-face than it is to handle problems by letters, but Paul wanted to handle the problems immediately. And Silas and Timothy's report of faith among the Thessalonians greatly encouraged Paul. So it should be with us when we see "our" converts mature in God's word.

Prayer: *Lord, when we are absent in body from those we love, let us feel the same love as if we were in their presence. Amen.*

Thursday, November 28 Read 1 Thess. 3:6-13.

As a journalist, I've learned a few sayings. One of them, author long since forgotten, says, "Those who toot their own horns may not get them tooted, but the ones who toot their own horns too much may run their battery down." First Thessalonians (ch. 3) tells how Paul rejoiced over Timothy's report. Timothy comments on the Thessalonians' continued spiritual progress even in the midst of persecution.

Paul's sense of servanthood is seen in his concern for the Thessalonians, that their faith may be increased so they will not be moved out of their place by their afflictions.

Timothy reports, in verses 6-10, that the Thessalonians had faith, love, and affection toward Paul. As their servant, Paul prays for God's direction, that their love will both "increase" (inward growth) and "abound" (outward expansion) day by day.

Paul apparently looked upon the Thessalonian Christians as orphans. He had fled Thessalonica, but he stayed with the believers there in both spirit and heart. This passage shows the true heart of Paul as a pastor, a servant.

Prayer: *Lord God, let us walk about as a habit of life worthy of God, who called us into the kingdom. Let our conversion be reflected in our discipleship. Amen.*

Friday, November 29   Read 1 Thess. 3:9-13.

God uses love to strengthen our inner purposes and desires. As a result, hearts filled with God's love are strengthened to the point that sin, or an unseparated life, is unattractive.

God expects believers to be blameless, to live a life separated from the ways of the world. God demands holiness.

We don't often hear the terms *holiness* or *a separated life*. But the same meaning is implied in a contemporary term, *spiritual pediatrics*. Just as a baby must learn to walk and talk, so must Christians learn a new walk and talk after being born again. This is called a Christian lifestyle. Perhaps we have few true servants in the body of Christ because we have never learned there is only one Master.

Christians grow through the leadership of God's Holy Spirit, who fills them the moment they accept Jesus as Savior. We come to understand what it means to be a servant of the servants as we mature spiritually. Christ's church is not a building with a name on it; Christ's church is us. God lives in us through the Holy Spirit.

Prayer: *Dear God, help us to draw closer to you so that sin no longer fits in with who we are. Make us a holy people. Amen.*

Saturday, November 30   Read Luke 21:29-31.

The fig is a most interesting fruit. What we think of as the fruit of the fig is really a protective shell. At its tip is a very small opening through which the fig wasp enters to pollinate the flower inside the shell. This is an analogy of how people see the church. Many believe the four walls of the building are the church, but in reality the church is the people inside the shell of the building.

The parable of the fig tree follows Jesus' remarks about the signs preceding his advent and is just ahead of his warnings against becoming too worldly. The warnings have received little attention through the years. These suggest four categories of people, described by their relation to Christ.

• Those who neither call Christ Lord nor do the things which he says. To these people, Jesus says, "Ye must be born again" (John 3:7, KJV).

• Those who call him Lord, but do not the things which he says. We hear Jesus' words, "Many will say to me in that day, Lord, Lord . . . . then will I profess unto them, I never knew you: depart from me" (Matt. 7:22-23, KJV).

• Those who do not call him Lord, but do the things which he says for selfish gain. Jesus' words echo, "He that is not with me is against me" (Matt. 12:30, KJV).

• Those who both call him Lord and do the things he says. "To all who received him, to those who believed in his name, he gave the right to become children of God" (John 1:12, NIV).

Prayer: *Lord God, let us examine ourselves honestly to see where we stand in relation to Christ's call. Amen.*

Sunday, December 1   Read Luke 21:25-36.

The great promise of Jesus' return to earth (Luke 21:27) is a part of today's reading. During the day Jesus preached in the temple, and at night he taught on the Mount of Olives. He spoke of the signs of his return.

A servant prepares, drawing water for a hot bath, turning down the bed covers at night. A servant has many tasks. This passage is a scene of Jesus' servanthood. He is seen as the servant of our great Creator. Jesus is getting things ready for God.

What is in this name, Jesus, for us who live in the twentieth century? We've heard about Jesus, yet few of us really know him. Paul's letter to the Romans (12:1*f*) reminds us that we are to be completely transformed as our very minds are renewed. We are to give up our lives in being a servant of the servants of those who are God's people.

Paul declared in his letter to the Colossians (1:15-20) that Christ had an unqualified supremacy, that Christ is the image of the invisible God, the firstborn over all creation. Christ is the head of the church and "in all things [has] the preeminence," yet he is also a servant (KJV). This is the paradox. We who are God's own sons and daughters, "more than conquerors," are also to be servants, to give up our power and prestige in order to show God's love. This is what it means to follow Jesus Christ.

Prayer: *Dear God, most of the time we'd really rather not give up our power and prestige to be servants. Give us the mind of Christ and let the attitude which was in him be in us, that we may willingly serve. Amen.*

THE TRUE PROPHET

December 2-8, 1985   **Sister Mary Lou Kownacki†**
Monday, December 2   Read Malachi 3:1-4;
Philippians 1:3-11;
Psalm 126; Luke 3:1-6.

I have often wished we could give a litmus test to those who claim to "prepare the way of the Lord." After all, Jerry Falwell and Thomas Merton, Dorothy Day and Phyllis Schlafly preach very different messages. Is it possible to determine which human voice echoes the heart and mind of God?

Jesus volunteered an answer when he said, "By their fruits you will know them" (Luke 6:44). And this week's readings bring those "fruits" into sharper relief.

Read all four passages with these questions in mind: What is God's message in each passage? To whom does the prophet speak? What personality characteristics emerge relative to each prophet?

These scripture passages provide rich details from which a composite picture of *prophet* begins to develop. This week's readings give us some clues about how a messenger of God—and each of us is a messenger of God—should live.

Suggestion for meditation: *Reflect on this ancient Hasidic story:*
One of the Just Men came to Sodom, determined to save its inhabitants from sin and punishment. He walked the streets tirelessly and preached against violence and hate, falsehood and indifference. Before long, interest in him and his message faded, and the sinning continued. Finally a child asked him why he kept on preaching when his efforts changed no one. He answered, "If I still shout today, if I still scream, it is only to prevent others from ultimately changing me."

---

†O.S.B., Erie, Pennsylvania.

348

Tuesday, December 3   Read Luke 3:1-6.

The message of the true prophet is radical. It zeroes in on the root of human misery and does not flinch at the cure. Before the full glory of God can be revealed, we must repent. "Turn back from your sins," the prophet proclaims (AP).

But what does it mean to repent? From what sins?

Today's scripture reading offers some critical insights. The passage opens by immersing us in history: the Roman Empire reigns, keeping the peoples of the world subject by military power; the political situation in Palestine is corrupt; the religious institution has bent the knee to Caesar.

Into this scene of death and decay, John bursts forth, a bloom from a barren desert. "Turn away from your sins if you want God's mercy to overflow," the prophet proclaims, and Isaiah provides a poetic vision of what repentance will entail.

All the rough spots, all the violence will be smoothed; all the winding paths that mark human relationships—the lying, deceit, hatred—must be straightened out. If you can imagine the land without valleys, hills, and mountains, you can begin to build a world without inequality: no rich or poor, no prejudice, no oppression. In this setting, repentance has social ramifications. Before "humankind will see God's salvation" in all its glory, the political and religious institutions of the world must undergo profound transformation.

This is not a popular message, but it should be on the lips of anyone who claims to "prepare the way of the Lord" (Isa. 40:3).

Suggestion for meditation: *Contemplate one troubled spot in your personal life and one troubled spot in the world that is in need of God's salvation. How can you prepare a way for the Lord in each situation?*

Wednesday, December 4   Read Malachi 3:1-4.

In today's reading, Malachi tells us that God will send a messenger who will confront the religious institution and purify the priests, who are not faithful to the covenant and whose sacrifices are not acceptable.

A scanning of the Gospels presents a Jesus who tried to put the house of God in order. He was not polite. He called the Pharisees and Sadducees—the religious leaders of the time— hypocritical and self-righteous. He condemned their exclusiveness as harsh and their rigorous interpretation of the law as intolerable.

The final blow came when Jesus entered the Temple and overthrew the money changers. Jesus' action was a sign of great love and hope—he expected those with moral authority to model the covenant and to sacrifice the "right kind of offerings to God."

Faithfulness to the covenant, Jesus reminded them, means to care for the needy and helpless, to put trust in God alone, and to build a society marked by justice and integrity. In the tradition of Isaiah, he insisted that the only offerings acceptable to God were to "help those who are oppressed, give orphans their rights, and defend widows" (Isa. 1:17, TEV).

It was not a message the rel2gous authorities wanted to hear. After the demonstration in the Temple, the chief priests and the teachers of the law sought to have Jesus killed.

So it goes for true prophets. All of them suffer for the telling of a message they did not seek and often did not fully understand. But they would not, could not be silent.

Suggestion for meditation: *Spend a few minutes reflecting on these two questions: What message do you think God wants spoken to today's religious leaders? What kind of offerings do you bring to God?*

Thursday, December 5   Read Philippians 1:3-7.

A true prophet possesses deep, inner peace.

The conclusion of an ancient story describes such a person. Tibet was being invaded and overrun by foreign soldiers. Special objects of their atrocities were the monks. If they were alerted in time, the monks fled to the mountains. In one instance a monk remained in the monastery. The enemy commander was informed of this. He became enraged and marched to the monastery and kicked in the gate. There in the courtyard stood the monk. The commander glowered at him, "Do you know who I am? I am he who can run you through with a sword without batting an eyelash." The monk replied, "And do you know who I am? I am he who can let you run me through with a sword without batting an eyelash."

In today's scripture passage, such great joy and gratefulness pervade that it is easy to miss the harsh reality—Paul is writing the letter from jail. Paul, like the monk in the story, has become a person of deep, inner strength, so centered in God that nothing can frighten or disturb him.

Sometimes the world's problems seem so crucial that we pay mere lip service to nurturing the inner person and place all our hope in frenetic action. Yet Paul is proof that it is only people who take time to listen to the silence and act from that inner stillness who will make a significant difference.

Devotional exercise: *Memorize these words of St. Theresa of Avila: "Be not perplexed, Be not afraid, Everything passes, God does not change. Patience wins all things. He who has God lacks nothing: God alone suffices."* *

---

*Complete Writings of Saint Theresa of Jesus. As quoted in Walter Nigg, *Great Saints,* trans. William Stirling (Hinsdale, Ill.: Henry Regnery Company, 1948), p. 135.

Friday, December 6   Read Philippians 1:8-11.

A true prophet grows in love.

This is Paul's prayer, "I pray that your love will keep on growing more and more" (TEV). And love has a lot to do with patience.

Faced with human suffering, grave injustices, widespread poverty, nuclear horror, and all the rest, our temptation is to flee or to fight. But the testing ground is patient service. We become true lovers if we remain steadfast in the face of all difficulties, be they personal affronts or nuclear threats.

Let us be clear. Patience is not passive waiting; it is not powerless; it is not dependence. The paradox is that true patience implies great impatience.

I heard Daniel Berrigan say, "I have known people who have died of impatience. My friend Rabbi Heschel was one. He entered so fully into the Civil Rights struggle, was so torn with the Vietnam War tragedy that his heart could bear it no longer. It is better to die that way than to get used to the way things are."*

The more serious we are about growing in love, the more uncomfortable we will be. We will not be able to rest until the hungry are fed, the prisoners freed, the sorrowing comforted, and every tear of sadness is wiped from the land.

We cannot, we must not, seek out martyrdom. But I am convinced that a messenger of God has no excuse whatsoever for not dying of impatience.

Prayer: *During the day repeat this petition: "God, grant me an urgent patience; God grant me a wild patience; God grant me a revolutionary patience."*

---

*Notes from Kirkridge retreat with Daniel Berrigan, November, 1982.

352

Saturday, December 7 Read Philippians 1:3-11.

A messenger of God is a person of prayer.

One way to tell a person of prayer is to observe them while they are undergoing great trial. In this reading Paul is locked in a jail cell and can pray "with joy." Remarkable. I contrast this with my own quasi prison experience, an overnight stay in the Washington, D.C., jail a few years ago for praying at the White House for an end to the nuclear arms race.

My journal reads: "I never expected the waiting to bother me like it did. It shocked me that I couldn't be at ease with the present moment. . . . It was as if the grey prison walls began to seep through my pores and settle inside me. All my words and actions for peace seemed futile, senseless, and empty. I couldn't pray or concentrate, merely struggle to maintain an exterior calm."

That experience sobered me. Since then I have made a concerted effort at two disciplines to get into the habit of praying constantly.

The first is to memorize scripture passages and to spend thirty minutes a day slowly repeating one. I want to become someone whose heart and mind are always filled with beautiful and inspiring words.

Second, I have begun to experiment with repeating a mantra. For my mantra I use *maranatha*, "Come, Lord Jesus." Back in my unconscious, I think this is my prayer: "Maranatha—I want Jesus to come, I want to become Jesus."

There is a danger in measuring the depth of our prayer by how tranquil and centered we are during crisis. The best criterion for determining whether we actually pray or only kid ourselves is this: Is my life changing; am I becoming more compassionate?

Devotional exercise: *Choose and repeat a mantra during the day.*

Sunday, December 8   Read Psalm 126.

A true prophet is a person of hope.

It is a rare kind of hope. Not the kind that believes if we get enough good legislation passed, discrimination, poverty, or war will be eliminated, and things will get better.

True hope is usually present in those who go through the dark night of despair and come out on the other side. I touched this hope when I interviewed Sheila Cassidy, the British physician who shocked the world ten years ago by describing how she was arrested and tortured by Chile's secret police for treating a bullet wound of an Allende sympathizer. Like the throng in today's psalm, Sheila Cassidy wept while sowing the seeds and now sings a quiet song of joy. She has emerged from the valley of darkness with purity of heart and a sense of God's presence.

Life is not all sadness and suffering. There are moments, however brief, when the oppressed are freed, the hungry fed, and tears wiped from the land. Think of June 12, 1982, when close to a million people walked together for peace in New York City without any incident of violence; remember the euphoric, though short-lived, triumph of SOLIDARITY in Poland; try to recall the day of victory for the poor in Nicaragua when Somoza was overthrown.

But, you may argue, tomorrow the new government begins to get corrupt or in time the "little people" are crushed again. Of course. Yet for that one second in time everyone had a taste of new beginnings, new possibilities, new life.

It is this promise that the prophet passes on to the next generation.

Suggestion for meditation: *Today take time to listen to a hymn or popular song that speaks of hope, of a new earth.*

REJOICE IN THE LORD ALWAYS

December 9-15, 1985   **Lois N. Erickson†**
Monday, December 9   Read Isaiah 12:5-6.

Because God is in our midst, we "rejoice in the Lord always" (Phil. 4:4).

When we read the first chapters of the Book of Isaiah, we might think of Isaiah as "the prophet of woes." He tells how the Lord chastises a sinful people.

Similarly we could label Zephaniah "the prophet of calamity." He urges the people of Judah to "Come together and hold assembly, O shameless nation, before you are driven away like the drifting chaff . . . " (Zeph. 2:1-2).

After warning the people regarding the consequences of their evil deeds, both Isaiah and Zephaniah announce a message of hope. They declare that in a coming day the people will shout and sing for joy because the Lord will be in their midst.

This hopeful message is strong in chapter 12, Isaiah's superb psalm of praise to the Lord. The prophet stresses God's saving power.

What a contrast exists between our day and the day of Isaiah and Zephaniah! Because the Messiah came as promised and because his Holy Spirit remains with us, we raise our voices in joyful praise.

Especially in times of personal stress, we feel the comforting presence of our Lord and we respond to Paul's exhortation, "Rejoice. . . . The Lord is at hand" (Phil. 4:4-5).

Prayer: *We praise you, Lord Jesus, because you fulfilled the prophecy. You came and you will come again. Amen.*

---

†Free-lance writer, Eugene, Oregon.

Tuesday, December 10   Read Isaiah 12:2;
                                                             Psalm 118:12-16.

Because God is our strength and our song, we rejoice in the Lord always.

In a beautiful hymn of thanksgiving, a king, returning after victorious battle, declares, "The Lord is my strength and my song; he has become my salvation." Numerous enemies had surrounded his army; but when the king called for help, God scattered the forces of evil.

The prophet Isaiah also announced God's salvation to the people of his day. At that time the Assyrians had captured inhabitants of the tribes of Naphtali, Reuben, Gad, and the half-tribe of Manasseh and had deported them to Assyria. There they were tempted to worship false gods.

Yet Isaiah proclaims, "The Lord God is my strength and my song, and he has become my salvation." He urges the people to "sing praises to the Lord, for he has done gloriously" (Isa. 12:5).

We, too, are beset by forces of evil, by temptations of all kinds. Strong desires hold us captive. We run after false gods of money, success, a bigger house, a newer car. I am so busy preparing steak for my own dinner, I find no time to take a bowl of soup to a sick neighbor.

By ourselves we are too weak to win against these temptations. With God as our strength we can surmount selfish desire and concern ourselves with justice for the oppressed, alleviation of world hunger, equal opportunities, peace.

Prayer: *We praise you, God, for your saving strength that flows into us when we are weak. Amen.*

Wednesday, December 11
Read Isaiah 12:3-4.
John 4:6-15.

Because God gives us living water, we rejoice in the Lord always.

Small white daisies grow around the base of Jacob's well in Samaria. Ancient olive trees stand nearby. Perhaps these trees were young when Jesus met the Samaritan woman at the well and promised living water. Although the olive trees have grown old, Jesus' promise is as new today as it was when he told the woman, "Everyone who drinks of this water will thirst again, but whoever drinks of the water that I shall give him will never thirst; the water that I shall give him will become in him a well of water springing up to eternal life."

Jesus not only gives us the water of salvation, he assures us that eternal life from God is like a spring of water, a source that never runs dry, an artesian well that overflows, an unending supply.

For God's gift of salvation we continue to rejoice each day.

The ancients expected a savior king who would deliver them from their enemies' oppression as King David had done.

Jesus said, "My kingship is not of this world" (John 18:36). Instead of an earthly kingdom, he gives us the spiritual water of eternal life. Illness, tragedy, fear, loneliness—these enemies may attack us—but God's promise of salvation brings us hope and everlasting joy.

Prayer: *We praise you, God, for giving us the living water of salvation. Every time we see pure, flowing water, help us to remember that it is a symbol of your promise—eternal life. Amen.*

Thursday, December 12   Read Philippians 4:4-6.

Because we can trust and not be afraid, we rejoice in the Lord always.

In western Oregon dark clouds can obscure the blue sky in a matter of minutes. Strong winds might toss and capsize a small boat on a lake. Ocean boating can be even more dangerous. Life preservers are a necessity.

Matthew tells how a great storm arose on the sea. The disciples were terrified. They awoke Jesus and pleaded, "Save, Lord; we are perishing." Jesus asked them, "Why are you afraid, O men of little faith?" (Matt. 8:25-26)

On many occasions Jesus advised the people to put away their fears. "Do not fear, only believe" (Mark 5:36). "Fear not, little flock" (Luke 12:32).

How do we know that we can trust God? We know because from the beginning God made promises and God has always been faithful. One promise God made was for a kingdom that would never end. Jesus fulfilled that promise. Because Jesus came to earth and because he promised to come again, we know that God's kingdom will never end.

Through the miracle of stilling the storm, Jesus showed that God has power over all destructive forces. We should never go out on the sea of life without Jesus, our Savior. We can trust him as we face any evil. Sudden temptations and dangers may arise, but we can call for help. "Save, Lord, we are perishing" (see Matt. 8:23-27).

Prayer: *We praise you, God, for fulfilling your promises. Help us remember that we can trust you and never be afraid. Amen.*

Friday, December 13   Read Zephaniah 3:14-16.

Because God has taken away judgments, we rejoice in the Lord always.

If I were a guilty thief standing before a judge, I'm confident I would plead for his mercy. Justice is what I would deserve. Justice at that time would mean punishment for my crime and a need for me to make restitution. Yet in my human weakness, I would beg for mercy.

As we stand before our Creator, knowing full well that we have sinned, we look for mercy, not justice.

"Lord, have mercy. Lord, have mercy," we repeat anxiously in our prayers. We want God, through Christ, to forgive our sin. We want grace—that unearned, unmerited gift of love.

When we read Zephaniah, we find the prophet assuring us that we can rejoice and exult with all our hearts because "the Lord has taken away the judgments against you."

What a relief! What a joy! We are free again. We can go on our way completely free, completely forgiven, not because we have made restitution, not because we deserve to escape God's judgment. We are free because of grace. Through Jesus Christ, our merciful God has given the abundant gift of love.

"But God, who is rich in mercy, out of the great love with which he loved us, even when we were dead through our trespasses, made us alive together with Christ (by grace you have been saved)" (Eph. 2:4-5).

Prayer: *We praise you, God, for taking away judgments and for giving us your steadfast love and your saving grace. Amen.*

Saturday, December 14 Read Zephaniah 3:17-20;
Psalm 126.

Because God renews us in love, we rejoice in the Lord always.

"Sow in tears, reap in joy" is the theme of Psalm 126. Babylonian captivity brought affliction and suffering to the people of Judah. Then Cyrus, the Persian king who had captured Babylon, decreed that the people of Judah could go back to Jerusalem. With great joy the people returned home to their sacred city.

Now, however, they faced new tragedy in the form of locusts and drought. They prayed for renewed life like the life that comes from the winter rains in the arid Negeb wilderness.

When joy is mentioned in the Bible, it is almost always named in contrast to sorrow and suffering. God's love renews us and takes away our sadness. John 16:21-22, for example, observes that a woman labors in anguish to bring forth a child. The result is joy when her child is born into the world.

Human happiness is not the same as Christian joy. We hope for health, security, and good friends, but these are not the root of Christian joy. God is the source of true joy.

A friend told me that he suffered for years from stressful migraine headaches and depression. Today she radiates with an outpouring of Christian concern for a Cambodian refugee family. God renews her in love and gives her true joy through service to others.

Prayer: *We praise you, God, for your daily renewal and for your song of joy that sings within us and overflows in Christian concern. Amen.*

Sunday, December 15   Read Philippians 4:7-9.

Because God is a God of peace, we rejoice in the Lord always.

I recently returned from a trip to Bangladesh, where the people speak Bengali. When I used the one word that I knew in their language, smiles and expressions of friendship were my reward. The word was *salem*—peace.

Peace serves as a greeting in many languages. *"Shalom,"* Israelis say to you in the narrow streets of Old Jerusalem. *"Salem,"* shepherds salute you in Kashmir's Himalayan Mountains.

Peace. What a heartwarming word! It brings to mind acceptance, reconciliation, tranquility, harmony, quietness, agreement, friendliness, rest, and love.

In Old Testament times peace meant complete security, prosperity, and absence of war. When the prophet Deborah was judge of Israel, a battle against the Canaanite army ended in victory for the Israelites. One passage of only eight words states, "And the land had rest for forty years" (Judg. 5:31). The land had rest after years of war and loss through the enemy's plundering. Peace at last!

In New Testament times peace denoted an inner tranquility of the Christian. Jesus revealed God's grace and assured his followers of God's care. Today Christ continues to lead us into calm trust so that we can cope with all of life's experiences.

Prayer: *We praise you, God, for overcoming our fears and for giving us the peace that passes understanding. We thank you for blessing us with your presence, your strength, your grace, your joy, your living water of salvation. We praise you for renewing us daily in your love. Amen.*

O COME, O COME, EMMANUEL!

December 16-22, 1985   **James W. Holsinger, Jr.**†
Monday, December 16   Read Micah 5:2-3.

O little town of Bethlehem

This famous prophecy has been only slightly rephrased in the Gospel of Matthew as the answer to Herod's inquiry about the Messiah's birthplace:

> "In Bethlehem of Judea; for so it is written by the prophet: 'And you, O Bethlehem, in the land of Judah, are by no means least among the rulers of Judah; for from you shall come a ruler who will govern my people Israel' " (Matt. 2:5-6).

Irrespective of Matthew's view of this passage, Micah obviously was not thinking specifically of Jesus, who was not to be born for several centuries. However, this passage does fit the circumstances of Jesus' birth, particularly in terms of the significance of his birthplace. Not only was Jesus born in the small, insignificant village of Bethlehem but the great King David was born there also.

The double name "Bethlehem of Judea" is used to specify the Bethlehem in the region of Ephrathah rather than the Bethlehem in the territory of Zebulun. However insignificant this poor village may have been, Micah clearly states that a person greater than the great king David will be born in it. Out of the little town of Bethlehem will come greatness; out of the obscurity of Ephrathah will come fame; out of the simplicity of Judah will come high destiny.

Prayer: *O God, help us as we prepare for Christmas to look for you in the little town of Bethlehem. Amen.*

---

†Medical Center Director, Hunter Holmes McGuire Veterans Administration Medication Center, Richmond, Virginia.

Tuesday, December 17 Read Micah 5:4-5*a*.

The hopes and fears of all the years are met in thee tonight

As the early Christian church looked back on the life, ministry, death, and resurrection of Jesus, it saw in the words of the prophet Micah a picture of Jesus the Christ. For it was in Bethlehem that the hopes and fears of all the years were found the night that Jesus was born.

The royal psalms use the motif of the shepherd—a motif used throughout the Near East—to portray the ideal king. Particularly in Israel with its persistent pastoral culture, the term *shepherd* maintained its connotations of protection, guidance, and provision for the needs of the people. The church saw Jesus as the good shepherd who feeds the flock.

Micah continues by stating that the coming ruler will rule, not by his own power, but by the power and strength which comes from Yahweh. The coming king's reign will be an expression of, not a replacement for, Yahweh's kingship. The greatness of the coming ruler will be unlimited; therefore, his people will dwell in security and stability. His sovereignty will fulfill the hopes of his people as set forth in the psalms that celebrate the destiny of the people of God. In Bethlehem was born a worldwide Savior who brought into being a universal kingdom. In Isaiah's words, he was the ideal king:

His name will be called
"Wonderful Counselor, Mighty God,
Everlasting Father, Prince of Peace" (Isa. 9:6*b*).

It is no wonder that over the centuries Micah's prophecy has held such rich meaning for Christians.

Prayer: *O God, each of us hopes and fears. Help each one of us to know that in you we can discover the Savior. Amen.*

Wednesday, December 18 Read Psalm 80:1-7.

Yet in thy dark streets shineth the everlasting light

Psalm 80 is a community lament interspersed with a congregational refrain. The national sorrow that brings about the psalm is a military defeat. To Israel, God appears bent on the destruction of the chosen nation. The shepherd motif found in Micah 5 is repeated in the opening invocation. The psalmist moves rapidly from the shepherd metaphor to that of the king, the splendid one. God is seen as the symbol of power that could save either the flock or the congregation, whether God was seen in the fields or in the temple with the cherubim.

The congregational refrain "Restore us, O God; let thy face shine, that we may be saved!" expresses the mood of the people in this psalm of lamentation. God's might will save Israel. The refrain likewise is based on the faith which instinctively knows that humanity's existence is to be found in the hand of God. The refrain petitions God to be concerned not only with a person's external welfare but also with the condition of the soul as well. Both of these ideas express the renewal of the covenant, and both of them are possible only if God turns once again to the people so that interaction may again occur. This encounter is the focal point of Psalm 80. The incarnation of Jesus is the ultimate such encounter. Indeed, it was to this end that this psalm has been included in the lectionary during Advent.

Prayer: *O Sovereign Eternal One, let your face shine upon your people this day just as the everlasting light shone upon Bethlehem so many years ago. Amen.*

Thursday, December 19   Read Hebrews 10:5-10.

So God imparts to human hearts the blessings of his heaven

The author of Hebrews uses Psalm 40:6-8 to demonstrate that with the life, death, and resurrection of Jesus the old system of sacrifice was abolished. Since Jesus made the one perfect sacrifice, no other sacrifices were necessary. The author of Hebrews contrasts the one sacrifice of Jesus with the continual sacrifices of the old law. By consummating Jesus' sacrifice once and for all, God has opened for us the way to our Creator.

Psalm 40 also speaks of those who see their lives as being totally committed to God. As a consequence in this passage from Hebrews, Christ is shown as fulfilling the whole meaning of sacrifice as the Hebrews understood it. Because Jesus' entire life was lived in dedication to God's work, sacrifice is abolished. It is abolished not because it was never needed but because it is no longer needed for the job at hand.

Sacrifice had a valid role in preparing people for God, but with the advent of the Christ, obedience becomes the acceptable sacrifice. Jesus was the perfect sacrifice because he perfectly did the will of God. By obeying to the bitter end, Jesus demonstrated that God's love is with each of us to the end as well. Thus we are reminded that God is with us in Jesus, who properly claims the name of Emmanuel, God With Us.

Prayer: *O God, it is through the perfect obedience of your Son, our Savior, that you impart to human hearts the blessings of your heaven. Amen.*

Friday, December 20   Read Luke 1:39-45.

How silently, how silently, the wondrous gift is given

Is this lyrical passage Elizabeth extols the blessedness of Mary. Through the faith of this young woman, all have received salvation. Mary represents perfect trust and obedience. By saying yes to God, Mary accepted the role of being wholly dedicated and committed to God's purposes. Having been called, her life became an example of simple faith. Mary, as well as the rest of Jesus' family, failed to understand fully his mission; but Mary is found at the cross, where Jesus commends her to his friend John for safekeeping.

Mary's life demonstrates the paradox of blessedness. Mary was blessed by being the mother of the Son of God; but that very glory would break her heart, for she would one day see her son hanging on a cross. Mary exemplifies the simple fact that being chosen by God can mean both a crown and a cross. God chooses a person not for comfort and selfish joy but for a great task that will take all that the individual can bring to it! Mary was chosen by God for a purpose. She exemplified the great paradox of blessedness in that the greatest joy in the world—to be the mother of the Lord—carried with it the heaviest burden—to see her son hanging on a cross.

Prayer: *O God, you gave your Son to the world in silence in a small insignificant town. Help us today to recognize the wondrous nature of your gift. Amen.*

Saturday, December 21   Read Luke 1:46-55.

For Christ is born of Mary

This well-known biblical hymn is called the Magnificat; its title comes from the opening Latin word in the poem.

The first part of the hymn expresses Mary's personal thanksgiving for the opportunity of being the mother of Jesus. She first speaks of her thanksgiving and joy at what God is doing through her. God has chosen her to bear Jesus without regard for her position in the world, her lack of a meritorious claim, or her humble origins. She is indeed the lowly handmaiden of God, but through her God will bring salvation to the world.

The Magnificat is a revolutionary document. William Barclay speaks of the three revolutions which are expressed in these verses: a moral revolution, a social revolution, and an economic revolution. The death of pride, a death which is the hallmark of Christianity, initiates the moral revolution. Comparing our lives to that of Jesus tears the last vestiges of pride from us.

The social revolution comes with the knowledge that Christ died for all humankind. This knowledge wipes away all radical and cultural barriers, making it impossible to view anyone as inferior in the face of Christ's sacrifice for all.

The economic revolution is expressed by a Christian society in which no one dares have too much when there are those who do not have enough.*

Prayer: *O God, help us this day to be revolutionaries for you, demonstrating by our lives that your Son, the Christ, has been born of Mary. Amen.*

---

*See Barclay's *The Gospel of Luke* (Philadelphia: The Westminster Press, 1956), p. 9-10.

Sunday, December 22   Read Micah 5:2; Psalm 80:3;
                            Hebrews 10:7; Luke 1:48.

O holy Child of Bethlehem, descend to us we pray

As we prepare for Christmas, the celebration of the coming of Emmanuel—God With Us—we find ourselves in the same plight as the people of Israel. They longed for a king who would lead them back to greatness as a nation. But after he had come, the Jews of Jesus' day failed to recognize Jesus as the Messiah. As Christmas draws near, we, too, must search our hearts to determine if we have failed to recognize the One who has come, or if we still long for another.

Christmas is an appropriate time to reflect on whom and what we are searching for in the Christ. Is it the revolutionary, who will change the world in his image? Is it one who will come with his angels to overthrow the powers of our world? Is it a great religious leader who will lead the people of God? It is possible that we have such fixed ideas of what the Christ must be that we, too, have failed to recognize Emmanuel when he has come again into our world—into our hearts and minds as God With Us.

The prophet Micah found Emmanuel in the small, insignificant village of Bethlehem. Luke tells the story of Emmanuel's birth to a young, insignificant woman. The Psalms relate that God's face will shine upon the people in order that they may be saved. The Letter to the Hebrews reminds us that the Christ came to do God's will. As Advent leads us to search for Emmanuel, we will find God With Us where we least expect.

Prayer: *"O holy child of Bethlehem, descend to us, we pray. Cast out our sin, and enter in; be born in us today."* * Amen.

*Phillips Brooks, "O Little Town of Bethlehem," The United Methodist Book of Hymns, *no. 381.*

COME, THOU LONG-EXPECTED JESUS

December 23-29, 1985   **James Clair Jarvis†**
Monday, December 23   Read 2 Corinthians 5:16-21.

Charles Wesley set the tone of the Advent season when he wrote, "Come, thou long-expected Jesus, Born to set thy people free; From our fears and sins release us; Let us find our rest in thee." The day of his coming is at hand; let us welcome him anew as Lord and Savior, friend and benefactor.

JESUS CAME AS RECONCILER. Never directly called the Reconciler, our Lord willingly played this role as an important facet of his ministry.

The need for reconciliation smolders throughout the Bible where broken human relationships are seen in every generation. Such broken relationships alienate persons from God, creating barriers of separation.

The Amsterdam Assembly (1948) agreed that the purpose of God is to reconcile all persons to himself and to one another in Jesus Christ. Those who understood Christ best were convinced that reconciliation would come to those who applied his teachings in human relationships.

Jesus came as one who reconciles God and persons, who in turn are reconciled to each other. He established a new level of love between Creator and creature. He showed how hostility can give way to love, and how love can break down barriers and heal separations.

Thanks be to God! The Reconciler has come.

Prayer: *O Christ of Christmas, may we be instruments of your will through which alienation from God and broken human relationships can be healed. We are grateful that you came as reconciler and friend. Amen.*

---

†Minister (retired), West Virginia Annual Conference, The United Methodist Church, Charleston, West Virginia.

Tuesday, December 24   Read Psalm 111;
                                            Isaiah 9:2-7.

JESUS CAME AS REVEALER. He was never directly spoken of as the Revealer, yet revelation was a significant part of the mission assigned Jesus Christ when he came into the world. On the eve of his birth, let us hail the Christ as the great revelation of God.

The prophet Isaiah visualized that great revelation as a light capable of dispelling darkness and bringing new joy to disheartened people. The coming of Christ set in motion an endless chain of events revealing the true nature of God.

Psalm 111 records the author's attempt to give his understanding of God. He sees the Almighty as praiseworthy because God is gracious and merciful, faithful and just, and completely trustworthy in the fulfillment of his covenant.

It is the duty of a revealer to make known the will of God; throughout his ministry that purpose was paramount in the life of Jesus. He was convinced that God had a special purpose for his life; he believed his understanding of God was greater than all others; and he offered to share that understanding with all who would hear and believe.

Jesus unveiled the true nature of God. In a clear and simple fashion he spoke of God's love which encompasses all, illustrating this truth through his own life and ministry.

The good news is never withheld from those who are willing to receive it. Let us again welcome Christ the Revealer into a world where he is so desperately needed.

Thanks be to God! The Revealer has come.

Prayer: *O Christ, Son of God and Lord of life, let your light shine among us; let your truth prevail throughout the world; and continue your revelation of the God who created us, and whose love unfolds us all. Amen.*

Wednesday, December 25 (Christmas)
Read Luke 2:1-20;
Luke 4:16-22.

The opening words of the Easter hymn, "Welcome, Happy Morning" are appropriate for Christmas Day. The day of our Lord's birth was a happy morning, and across the earth the faithful welcome him again and acknowledge him as Lord and Savior.

JESUS CAME AS DELIVERER. As with the words *reconciler* and *revealer, deliverer* was never directly applied to Jesus Christ. Kindred words were used to speak of his mission in the world; by implication he was indeed the Deliverer.

The Christmas event shows God at work in history, providing a means of deliverance. Throughout the scriptures the inability of human beings to save themselves is much in evidence; deliverance was promised by the God of all creation; the fulfillment of that promise came on Christmas Day.

Jesus thought of himself as the Deliverer sent from God to set the people free from sin and death. In an early visit to his home synagogue, upon invitation he read the morning lesson from Isaiah 61 where examples of human need are listed. When the reading was completed, Jesus spoke of himself as the fulfillment of the scripture and the Deliverer through whom these human needs could be met. It was an unpopular position to take, but the three years of his ministry were sufficient to attain the purpose of his coming into the world.

Thanks be to God! The Deliverer has come.

Prayer: *O Christ of Christmas, thank you for your willingness to come into an unfriendly world. Thank you for the light you brought to dispel darkness and for setting us free from sin and death. Stay with us and be our deliverer, O chosen one of God. Amen.*

Thursday, December 26　　　　　Read Luke 2:41-52.

Mental and physical exhaustion frequently follows the Christmas celebration. It seems paradoxical that the acts of preparation overshadow the event to be observed. Some people show their weariness by immediately dismantling all the exterior symbols of the season, packing them away in boxes, returning them to storage, and settling down to life as usual.

Such is never possible for those who have made a serious effort to recapture the magic and mystery of Christmas. The spirit of Christmas is rekindled, and the covenant with Christ renewed.

Christ came as reconciler, revealer, and deliverer, but his coming also made possible the church. Building on the concept of the church as an assembly of believers in Christ, Paul declared that Christ is present when such assemblies are held. He spoke of the church as the body of Christ (see Eph. 1:22-23). Furthermore, the believing community is an important part of that body, for we are one in Christ (see Rom. 12:5).

The family incident recorded in Luke 2:41-52 is more than an expression of anxiety on the part of the parents; almost parenthetically, yet very clearly, the writer declares that there is room for growth in Christian discipleship. Jesus set the example. A biographical line reads, "Jesus increased in wisdom and in stature, and in favor with God and man."

Followers of Christ must grow in the faith. A renewal of our commitment to Christ and the church is a desirable goal for the celebration of Christmas.

Prayer: *O Christ of Christmas, strengthen us in our faith. May your spirit continue among us long after the symbols of the season are laid aside and we have returned to business as usual. Forgive us if we do otherwise. Amen.*

Friday, December 27　　　　Read 2 Corinthians 5:16-21.

Earlier this week reference was made to the involvement of Christian disciples in a ministry of reconciliation. Paul places our relationship to Christ in a clear and proper perspective. There is a road of faith we must travel before we qualify as ministers of reconciliation.

The road leads to the amazing discovery of a new life in Jesus Christ. If Christmas has added new illumination to this discovery, we have correctly celebrated the day. A successful pilgrimage to Bethlehem means life can never be the same. Prophecy has been fulfilled; a new life in Christ has been reaffirmed; the darkness of life has been dispelled by the light made known through Christ; new hope has come; commitments to Christ has been renewed. Our appointment as ambassadors for Christ is delivered anew at Christmastime.

According to Paul, the new life in Christ begins when a person concludes that life has been unfruitful, and a new lifestyle is necessary for inner peace and a sense of well-being. The new life is God's gift through Jesus Christ. Separated from the old, and reconciled with God, there is a new beginning when Christ is recognized as Savior and friend. Past transgressions are forgiven, and a whole new life is opened to us.

Cleansed and forgiven, we enlist in discipleship, are appointed as ambassadors for Christ, and our Christian pilgrimage begins. Along the way we engage in a ministry of reconciliation.

Such is the gift of God for the people of God.

Prayer: *Lord Jesus, Savior and friend, thank you for setting us free from the past and opening a new life to us. Help us to be your faithful ambassadors serving as instruments of peace and goodwill. Amen.*

Saturday, December 28   Read Colossians 3:12-17.

The "nothing-to-do-after-Christmas" syndrome has appeared again throughout the land. The days of preparation have been accomplished, the annual celebration of Christmas is behind us, and the dark days of winter are at hand. Among winter options are: hibernate—sit back and do nothing; take a trip—but the end of the year economics may make that difficult; still another option is to use the days for a spiritual journey.

Christmas can be the beginning point for such a journey if the day has been properly observed. New insight into discipleship and new commitments to Christ can result from this annual pilgrimage. When the days of celebration are over, the realization that we are the chosen people of God should linger.

In the Letter to the Colossians, Paul spoke of the different lifestyle appropriate for those who are "God's chosen ones." There is an all-consuming change which comes into the life of those whom Christ has chosen. The end of a calendar year and the beginning of a new spiritual journey is suitable time to review the behavior pattern of those who have recently been with Christ.

After listing undesirable "earthly" things, Paul speaks of the qualities which make the Christian disciple a different person: "compassion, kindness, lowliness, meekness, and patience, . . . forgiving each other. . . . And above all these put on love. . . . And let the peace of Christ rule in your hearts. . . . And be thankful."

Prayer: *Lord of light and truth, we acknowledge that your way is best. Help us to practice the faith and to implement the gospel in our life each day. Amen.*

Sunday, December 29   Read John 13:34-35;
                                        John 15:8-17.

Christina G. Rossetti expressed the truth of Christmas in writing, "Love came down at Christmas, Love all lovely, Love divine; Love was born at Christmas; Star and angels gave the sign." The recognition of divine love manifest in the Christ Child is the ultimate test of our Christmas celebrations.

The Christmas event requires more than an annual observance; it demands the application of love in all human relationships.

Late in his ministry, Jesus phrased this in undeniable terms when he said, "A new commandment I give to you, that you love one another; even as I have loved you, that you also love one another. By this all . . . will know that you are my disciples, if you have love for one another." True discipleship is recognized by the quality of love expressed in the community of faith.

The birth of Christ was an expression of divine love. God's redemptive love was made known, and a saving grace became available for all who would accept it. Barriers of separation were broken down, and believers became chosen people.

In chapter 15, the fourth Gospel describes the remarkable transition from servant to friend. Through obedience to Christ's will, one is assured of a fruitful life.

Paul's greeting to the Roman Christians was, "Grace to you and peace from God our Father and the Lord Jesus Christ" (1:7). That is a suitable greeting for those who recognize their oneness in Christ and who are obedient to the new commandment to love one another.

Prayer: *Creator of all, and Father of our Lord Jesus Christ, thank you for the divine love expressed through Christ's coming into the world. Help us pass the ultimate test of a living faith as we journey onward. Amen.*

OUR RESPONSIBILITY IN GOD'S CREATION

December 30-31, 1985   **S. Michael Yasutake†**
Monday, December 30   Read John 1:1-18;
Gen. 1:1–2:4.

The Bible's Creation story is not an explanation of cosmic origins but the history of the salvation of the human race. The creative and saving acts of God make up one integrated historical theme.

Prominent in the Creation theme is the redemptive history of the Hebrew people, who went from slavery in Egypt to freedom in the promised land. In keeping with this tradition, Jesus offered his life to free humankind from the bondage of sin to a free life in God. This is a creative act just as surely as when the universe was created: a re-creation, a process continuing to this day. Our task as Christians is to participate. We have been chosen for this mission.

This sense of election by God is at once a tremendous privilege and a heavy responsibility. We must labor to overcome the inequality, exploitation, and inhumanity that rule over our world. We are called to work toward a free and equal society for all. This is the meaning of our election to responsibility in God's mission, a mission that cannot fail.

Prayer: *Almighty God, our Creator and Lord of history, you have chosen us to do your will on earth as it is done in heaven. Grant that we do not rest in the performance of our mission until it is completed. Amen.*

---

†Casework supervisor, Cathedral Shelter of Chicago, Episcopal Diocese of Chicago, Illinois.

Tuesday, December 31   Read Gen. 1:4*b*-25;
                                            John 1:1-4.

The Creation doctrine mandates far-reaching social responsibility. God as creator is the ultimate owner of all our properties and possessions. We are merely caretakers or stewards. As such, we are responsible to God for what we do with what we have.

This idea of divine ownership lays the foundation for full equality for all. God did not create material goods to end up in the hands of only a few with the masses lacking even the most basic human necessities: health care, education, and adequate food, clothing, and shelter.

Almsgiving, a familiar term to Christians, is not so much an act of mercy as it is a matter of justice. The Constitution of the United States implies this. All people have the right to have their needs met, whether they be born rich or poor, white or colored, educated or uneducated.

Some critics grumble against the poor whom they label "welfare cheats." They fail to apply the same ethical standard to all classes of people. We must not be more critical of the powerless than of the powerful. Cheating goes on everywhere, even in the splendor of a White House among the nation's privileged.

All that we have is God's gift. We did not earn or deserve it. What we have freely received we are to share. Our political, economic, and social systems must reflect this truth about the creation work of God.

Prayer: *Lord, everything in heaven and earth is yours. We only give back what is yours already when we share our gifts with others. Let this truth be ingrained in our hearts, and guide our actions. Amen.*

New Common Lectionary, 1985
(*Disciplines* Edition)

January 6
Epiphany

Isaiah 60:1-6
Psalm 72:1-14
Ephesians 3:1-12
Matthew 2:1-12

January 13

Genesis 1:1-5
Psalm 29
Acts 19:1-7
Mark 1:4-11

January 20

1 Samuel 3:1-10 (or 20)
Psalm 63:1-8
1 Corinthians 6:12-20
John 1:35-42

January 27

Jonah 3:1-5, 10
Psalm 62:5-12
1 Corinthians 7:29-31 (or 35)
Mark 1:14-20

February 3

Deuteronomy 18:15-20
Psalm 111
1 Corinthians 8:1-13
Mark 1:21-28

February 10

Job 7:1-7
Psalm 147:1-11
1 Corinthians 9:16-23
Mark 1:29-39

February 17

2 Kings 2:1-12*a*
Psalm 50:1-6
2 Corinthians 4:3-6
Mark 9:2-9

February 24

Genesis 9:8-17
Psalm 25:1-10
1 Peter 3:18-22
Mark 1:9-15

March 3

Genesis 17:1-10, 15-19
Psalm 105:1-11
Romans 4:16-25
Mark 8:31-38

March 10

Exodus 20:1-17
Psalm 19:7-14
1 Corinthians 1:22-25
John 2:13-22

March 17

2 Chronicles 36:14-23
Psalm 137:1-6
Ephesians 2:4-10
John 3:14-21

March 24

Jeremiah 31:31-34
Psalm 51:10-17
Hebrews 5:7-10
John 12:20-33

March 31
Passion/Palm Sunday

Isaiah 50:4-9*a*
Psalm 118:19-29
Psalm 31:9-16
Mark 11:1-11

April 7
Easter

Isaiah 42:1-9
Isaiah 52:13–53:12
Psalm 22:1-18
Psalm 118:14-24
1 Corinthians 1:18-31
Hebrews 4:14-16; 5:7-9
Acts 10:34-43
Mark 14:12-26
John 19:17-30
John 20:1-18

April 14

Acts 4:32-35
Psalm 133
1 John 1:1–2:2
John 20:19-31

April 21

Acts 3:12-19
Psalm 4
1 John 3:1-7
Luke 24:35-48

April 28

Acts 4:8-12
Psalm 23
1 John 3:18-24
John 10:11-18

May 5

Acts 8:26-40
Psalm 22:25-31
1 John 4:7-12
John 15:1-8

May 12

Acts 10:44-48
Psalm 98
1 John 5:1-6
John 15:9-17

May 19

Acts 1:15-17, 21-26
Psalm 1
1 John 5:9-13
John 17:11*b*-19

May 26
Pentecost

Acts 2:1-21 or
   Ezekiel 37:1-14
Psalm 104:24-34
Romans 8:22-27 or
   Acts 2:1-21
John 15:26-27; 16:4*b*-15

June 2

Isaiah 6:1-8
Psalm 29
Romans 8:12-17
John 3:1-17

June 9

1 Samuel 16:14-23
Psalm 57
2 Corinthians 4:13–5:1
Mark 3:20-35

June 16

2 Samuel 1:1, 17-27
Psalm 46
2 Corinthians 5:6-10, 14-17
Mark 4:26-34

June 23

2 Samuel 5:1-12
Psalm 48
2 Corinthians 5:18–6:2
Mark 4:35-41

June 30

2 Samuel 6:1-15
Psalm 24
2 Corinthians 8:7-15
Mark 5:21-43

July 7

2 Samuel 7:1-17
Psalm 89:20-37
2 Corinthians 12:1-10
Mark 6:1-6

July 14

2 Samuel 7:18-29
Psalm 132:11-18
Ephesians 1:1-10
Mark 6:7-13

July 21

2 Samuel 11:1-15
Psalm 53
Ephesians 2:11-22
Mark 6:30-44

July 28

2 Samuel 12:1-14
Psalm 32
Ephesians 3:14-21
John 6:1-15

August 4

2 Samuel 12:15b-24
Psalm 34:11-22
Ephesians 4:1-6
John 6:24-35

August 11

2 Samuel 18:1, 5, 9-15
Psalm 143:1-8
Ephesians 4:25–5:2
John 6:35, 41-51

August 18

2 Samuel 18:24-33
Psalm 102:1-12
Ephesians 5:15-20
John 6:51-58

August 25

2 Samuel 23:1-7
Psalm 67
Ephesians 5:21-33
John 6:55-69

September 1

1 Kings 2:1-4, 10-13
Psalm 121
Ephesians 6:10-20
Mark 7:1-8, 14-15, 21-23

September 8

Proverbs 2:1-8
Psalm 119:129-136
James 1:17-27
Mark 7:31-37

September 15

Proverbs 22:1-2, 8-9
Psalm 125
James 2:1-5, 8-10, 14-17
Mark 8:27-38

September 22

Job 28:20-28
Psalm 27:1-6
James 3:13-18
Mark 9:30-37

September 29

Job 42:1-6
Psalm 27:7-14
James 4:13-17; 5:7-11
Mark 9:38-50

October 6

Genesis 2:18-24
Psalm 128
Hebrews 1:1-4; 2:9-11
Mark 10:2-16

October 13

Genesis 3:8-19
Psalm 90:1-12
Hebrews 4:1-3; 9-13
Mark 10:17-30

October 20

Isaiah 53:7-12
Psalm 35:17-28
Hebrews 4:14-16
Mark 10:35-45

October 27

Jeremiah 31:7-9
Psalm 126
Hebrews 5:1-6
Mark 10:46-52

November 3

Deuteronomy 6:1-9
Psalm 119:33-48
Hebrews 7:23-28
Mark 12:28-34

November 10

1 Kings 17:8-16
Psalm 146
Hebrews 9:24-28
Mark 12:38-44

November 17

Daniel 7:9-14
Psalm 145:8-13
Hebrews 10:11-18
Mark 13:24-32

November 24

Jeremiah 23:1-6
Psalm 93
Revelation 1:4b-8
John 18:33-37

December 1

Jeremiah 33:14-16
Psalm 25:1-10
1 Thessalonians 3:9-13
Luke 21:25-36

December 8

Malachi 3:1-4
Psalm 126
Philippians 1:3-11
Luke 3:1-6

December 15

Zephaniah 3:14-20
Isaiah 12:2-6
Philippians 4:4-9
Luke 3:7-18

December 22

Micah 5:2-5a
Psalm 80:1-7
Hebrews 10:5-10
Luke 1:39-55

December 29

1 Samuel 2:18-20, 26
Psalm 111
Colossians 3:12-17
Luke 2:41-52

January 5, 1986

Jeremiah 31:7-14
Psalm 147:12-20
Ephesians 1:3-6, 15-18
John 1:1-18